Books by Nicholas Pileggi

Casino

Wiseguy

Blye, Private Eye

W SE GUY

NICHOLAS PILEGGI

with an Introduction by Martin Scorsese

SIMON & SCHUSTER PAPERBACKS

New York   London   Toronto   Sydney   New Delhi

Simon & Schuster Paperbacks
An Imprint of Simon & Schuster, Inc.
1230 Avenue of the Americas
New York, NY 10020

This Simon & Schuster trade paperback edition April 2019

SIMON & SCHUSTER PAPERBACKS and colophon are
registered trademarks of Simon & Schuster, Inc.

For information about special discounts for bulk purchases,
please contact Simon & Schuster Special Sales at
1-866-506-1949 or business@simonandschuster.com

The Simon & Schuster Speakers Bureau can bring authors to your live event. For
more information or to book an event contact the Simon & Schuster Speakers Bureau
at 1-866-248-3049 or visit our website at www.simonspeakers.com.

Manufactured in the United States of America

10   9   8

Library of Congress Cataloging-in-Publication Data is available.

ISBN 978-1-4516-4221-6
ISBN 978-1-9821-2990-3 (pbk)
ISBN 978-1-4516-4278-0 (ebook)

For Nora

Introduction

The first time I read *Wiseguy*, I was astonished. It was everything I'd hoped for and then some.

Some of the greatest actors I ever knew were people from my old neighborhood, the guys who could keep you absolutely riveted when they told you a story—*their* story. Nick Pileggi knew the world of Italian-American culture inside out, and he understood that storytelling was fundamental, from the people who succeeded and "assimilated" to the ones who were stuck in the middle, the ones who tried to be decent but somehow couldn't. Nick knew every side of this bygone world, and he never judged anyone for what they said or did. And he knew that if the story was *really* going to be told, he had to find exactly the right person to tell it.

In Henry Hill, Nick found someone with access to every level of the life, who knew it on a daily, minute-by-minute basis, who was ready and willing to tell his story as an act of survival. Nick had grown bored with, as he puts it, "the egomaniacal ravings of illiterate hoods masquerading as benevolent Godfathers." Henry was an insider and something of an outsider at the same time, and he *wanted*, even *needed* to remember everything down to the smallest detail.

Of course, when I read the book that first time, I found it hard to put it down. I found myself making notes, visualizing movements, cuts, passages of music. I realized: I *had* to make this movie. For me it was an evolution, in a direct line with what I'd tried to do in *Mean Streets*. Only here, there was no central character per se, no equivalent to Charlie—the lifestyle was so big and so compelling that there was no need for a main character, just someone to guide us along. I saw the possibility of making the lifestyle itself the main character.

When I called Nick, I asked him to write the script with me, for what would eventually become *Goodfellas*. I think he was a little surprised, but excited. I wanted to stay as close to the facts as we could. There was a natural rise and fall narrative there, but that wasn't what made it special. It was the places, the restaurants and bars, the food they ate; the clothes, the sense of style; the gestures, the body language, the way of being with one another; the ease with which they committed murder. On the one hand, an immersion in detail that was sensual *and* documentary at the same time; on the other hand, a forward propulsion that moved with their energy and exhilaration, and then with their paranoia and stone-cold fear. We had a great time putting it together. Nick is one of the greatest collaborators anyone could ever hope for—patient, hard-working, detail-oriented, and absolutely concentrated on the work.

I often think back to that first reading of *Wiseguy* and the sense of excitement I felt. Nick and I have been good friends for years now, we've made a second movie together and, fingers crossed, we'll get to make a few more. But I need him to know just how special our collaboration has been to me.

It all started with this book, which you're about to read. If it's your first time, set aside a few hours. Because you won't be able to put it down.

—Martin Scorsese
March 2011

Author's Note

I want to acknowledge the contributions made to this book by U.S. Attorney Raymond Dearie of the Eastern District of New York; Asst. U.S. Attorney Edward McDonald, who headed the Brooklyn Organized Crime Strike Force; and Thomas P. Puccio, his predecessor. I would also like to thank Special Attorneys of the Organized Crime Strike Force Jerry D. Bernstein, Laura Ward, Douglas Behm, Douglas Grover, Michael Guadagno, and Laura Brevetti, as well as Brooklyn homicide prosecutor John Fairbanks and detectives and agents Doug LeVien, Mario Sessa, Thomas Sweeney, Steve Carbone, Joel Cohen, Edmundo Guevera, Arthur Donelan, James Kapp, Daniel Mann, Jack Walsh, Alfie McNeil, Ben Panzarella, Steve DelCorso, and John Wales.

WISE
GUY

Prologue

On Tuesday, May 22, 1980, a man named Henry Hill did what seemed to him the only sensible thing to do: he decided to cease to exist. He was in the Nassau County jail, facing a life sentence in a massive narcotics conspiracy. The federal prosecutors were asking him about his role in the $6 million Lufthansa German Airlines robbery, the largest successful cash robbery in American history. The New York City police were in line behind the feds to ask him about the ten murders that followed the Lufthansa heist. The Justice Department wanted to talk to him about his connection with a murder that also involved Michele Sindona, the convicted Italian financier. The Organized Crime Strike Force wanted to know about the Boston College basketball players he had bribed in a point-shaving scheme. Treasury agents were looking for the crates of automatic weapons and Claymore mines he had had stolen from a Connecticut armory. The Brooklyn district attorney's office wanted information about a body they had found in a refrigeration truck which was frozen so stiff it needed two days to thaw before the medical examiner could perform an autopsy.

When Henry Hill had been arrested only three weeks earlier, it hadn't been big news. There were no front-page stories in the newspapers and no segments on the evening news. His arrest was just another of dozens of the slightly exaggerated multimillion-dollar drug busts that police make annually in their search for paragraphs of praise. But the arrest of Henry Hill was a prize beyond measure. Hill had grown up in the mob. He was only a mechanic, but he knew everything. He knew how it worked. He knew who oiled the machinery. He knew, literally, where the bodies were buried. If he talked, the police knew that Henry Hill could give them the key to dozens of indictments and convictions. And even if he didn't talk, Henry Hill knew that his own friends would kill him just as they had killed nearly everyone who had been involved in the Lufthansa robbery. In jail Henry heard the news: his own protector, Paul Vario, the seventy-year-old mob chief in whose house Henry had been raised from childhood, was through with him; and James "Jimmy the Gent" Burke, Henry's closest friend, his confidant and partner, the man he had been scheming and hustling with since he was thirteen years old, was planning to murder him.

Under the circumstances, Henry made his decision: he became part of the Justice Department's Federal Witness Protection Program. His wife, Karen, and their children, Judy, fifteen, and Ruth, twelve, ceased to exist along with him. They were given new identities. It should be said that it was slightly easier for Henry Hill to cease to exist than it might have been for an average citizen, since the actual evidence of Hill's existence was extraordinarily slim. His home was apparently owned by his mother-in-law. His car was registered in his wife's name. His Social Security cards and driver's licenses—he had several of each—were forged and made out to fictitious names. He had never voted and he had never paid taxes. He had never even flown on an airplane using a ticket made out in his own name. In fact one of the only pieces of documentary evidence that proved without doubt that Henry Hill had lived—besides his birth certificate—was his yellow sheet, the police record of arrests he had begun as a teenage apprentice to the mob.

A year after Henry Hill's arrest I was approached by his attorney, who said that Hill was looking for someone to write his story. At that point I had been writing about organized-crime figures for most of my career as a journalist and had gotten bored with the egomaniacal ravings of illiterate hoods masquerading as benevolent Godfathers. In addition, I had never heard of Henry Hill. In my office are four boxes of index cards upon which I compulsively jot the names and various details of every major and minor organized-crime figure I run across in the press or court dockets. When I looked in it I discovered I had a card on Hill, dated from 1970 and misidentifying him as a member of the Joseph Bonanno crime family. And yet, from the mountain of data the feds had begun to compile about him since his arrest a year earlier and the importance they attached to him as a witness, it was clear that Henry Hill was at least worth meeting.

Since he was in the Federal Witness Program, the meeting had to take place at a location where his safety was guaranteed. I was instructed to meet two federal marshals at the Braniff counter at LaGuardia Airport. When I got there the two men had my ticket in their hands. They asked if I had to go to the bathroom. It struck me as a bizarre question coming from federal agents, but they explained that once they gave me the ticket I could not leave their sight until we boarded the plane. They couldn't take the chance that I might see the destination and tip someone off as to where I was going. As it turned out, the plane we took was not a Braniff plane, and the first place we landed was not the place where Henry Hill was waiting. It took more than one flight that day to finally get to a town where, I learned later, Hill and his federal agent bodyguards had arrived just a couple of hours earlier.

Hill was a surprising man. He didn't look or act like most of the street hoods I had come across. He spoke coherently and fairly grammatically. He smiled occasionally. He knew a great deal about the world in which he had been raised, but he spoke about it with an odd detachment, and he had an outsider's eye for detail. Most of the mobsters who have been interviewed for books and articles over the years have been unable to detach themselves from their experiences long enough to put their lives in some perspective. They so blindly followed the mobster's path that they rarely saw any of the scenery along the way. Henry Hill was all eyes. He was fascinated by the world in which he had grown up, and there was very little about it that he did not remember.

Henry Hill was a hood. He was a hustler. He had schemed and plotted and broken heads. He knew how to bribe and he knew how to con. He was a full-time working racketeer, an articulate hoodlum from organized crime, the kind of rara avis that should please social anthropologists as much as cops. On the street he and his friends referred to each other as wiseguys. It seemed to me that a book about his life might provide an insider's look at a world usually heard about either from the outside or from the *capo di tutti capi,* top.

One

enry Hill was introduced to life in the mob almost by accident. In 1955, when he was eleven years old, he wandered into a drab, paint-flecked cabstand at 391 Pine Street, near Pitkin Avenue, in the Brownsville–East New York section of Brooklyn, looking for a part-time, after-school job. The one-story, storefront cabstand and dispatch office was directly across the street from where he lived with his mother, father, four older sisters, and two brothers, and Henry had been intrigued by the place almost as far back as he could remember. Even before he went to work there Henry had seen the long black Cadillacs and Lincolns glide into the block. He had watched the expressionless faces of the cabstand visitors, and he always remembered their huge, wide coats. Some of the visitors were so large that when they hauled themselves out of their cars, the vehicles rose by inches. He saw glittering rings and jewel-studded belt buckles and thick gold wristbands holding wafer-thin platinum watches.

The men at the cabstand were not like anyone else from the neighborhood. They wore silk suits in the morning and would drape the fenders of their cars with handkerchiefs before leaning back for a talk. He had watched them double-park their cars and never get tickets, even when they parked smack in front of a fire hydrant. In the winter he had seen the city's sanitation trucks plow the snow from the cabstand's parking lot before getting around to cleaning the school yard and hospital grounds. In the summer he could hear the noisy all-night card games, and he knew that no one—not even Mr. Mancuso, who lived down the block and groused about everything—would dare to complain. And the men at the cabstand were rich. They flashed wads of twenty-dollar bills as round as softballs and they sported diamond pinky rings the size of walnuts. The sight of all that wealth, and power, and girth was intoxicating.

At first Henry's parents were delighted that their energetic young son had found a job just across the street. Henry's father, Henry Hill Sr., a hardworking construction company electrician, always felt youngsters should work and learn the value of the money they were forever demanding. He had seven children to support on an electrical worker's salary, so any additional income was welcome. Since he was twelve years old, when he had come to the United States from Ireland shortly after his own father died, Henry Hill Sr. had had to support his mother and three younger brothers. It was work at an early age, he insisted, that taught young people the value of money. American youngsters, unlike the children of his native Ireland, seemed to dawdle about in their adolescence much longer than necessary.

Henry's mother, Carmela Costa Hill, was also delighted that her son had found a job nearby but for different reasons. First, she knew that her son's job would please his father. Second, she hoped that the after-school job might get her feisty young son out of the house long enough to keep him from bickering incessantly with his sisters. Also, with young Henry working, she would have more time to spend with Michael, her youngest son, who had been born with a spinal defect and was confined to either his bed or a wheelchair. Carmela Hill was further pleased—almost ecstatic, really—when she found that the Varios, the family that owned the cabstand, came from the same part of Sicily where she had been born. Carmela Costa had been brought to the United States as a small child, and she had married the tall, handsome, black-haired young Irish lad she had met in the neighborhood at the age of seventeen, but she never lost her ties to the country of her birth. She always maintained a Sicilian kitchen, for instance, making her own pasta and introducing her young husband to anchovy sauce and calamari after throwing out his catsup bottle. She still believed in the religious powers of certain western Sicilian saints, such as Santa Pantaleone, the patron saint of toothaches. And like many members of immigrant groups, she felt that people with ties to her old country somehow had ties with her. The idea of her son's getting his first job with *paesani* was the answer to Carmela's prayers.

It wasn't too long, however, before Henry's parents began to change their minds about their son's after-school job. After the first couple of months they found that what had started out as a part-time job for their son had become a full-time compulsion. Henry junior was always at the cabstand. If his mother had an errand for him to run, he was at the cabstand. He was at the cabstand in the morning before going to school and he was at the cabstand in the afternoon when school let out. His father asked about his homework. "I do it at the cabstand," he said. His mother noticed that he was no longer playing with youngsters his own age. "We play at the cabstand," he said.

"My father was always angry. He was born angry. He was angry that he had to work so hard for next to nothing. Electricians, even union electricians, didn't earn much in those days. He was angry that the three-bedroom house was so noisy, with my four sisters and two brothers and me. He used to scream that all he wanted was peace and quiet, but by then we'd all be like mice and he'd be the only one screaming and yelling and banging dishes against the wall. He was angry that my brother Michael should have been born paralyzed from the waist down. But mostly he was angry about me hanging around the cabstand. 'They're bums!' he used to scream. 'You're gonna get in trouble!' he'd yell. But I'd just pretend I didn't know what he was talking about and say that all I was doing was running errands after school instead of running bets, and I'd swear that I was going to school when I hadn't been near the place in weeks. But he never bought it. He knew what really went on at the cabstand, and every once in a while, usually after he got his load on, I'd have to take a beating. But by then I didn't care. Everybody has to take a beating sometime."

Back in 1955 the Euclid Avenue Taxicab and Limousine Service in the Brownsville–East New York section of Brooklyn was more than just a dispatch center for neighborhood cabs. It was a gathering place for horseplayers, lawyers, bookies, handicappers, ex-jockeys, parole violators, construction workers, union officials, local politicians, truck drivers, policy runners, bail bondsmen, out-of-work waiters, loan sharks, off-duty cops, and even a couple of retired hit men from the old Murder Incorporated days. It was also the unofficial headquarters for Paul Vario, a rising star in one of the city's five organized-crime families and the man who ran most of the rackets in the area at the time. Vario had been in and out of jail all his life. In 1921, at the age of eleven, he had served a seven-month stretch for truancy, and over the years he had been arrested for loan-sharking, burglary, tax evasion, bribery, bookmaking, contempt, and assorted assaults and misdemeanors. As he got older and more powerful, most of the charges brought against him were dismissed, either because witnesses failed to appear or because very generous judges chose to fine rather than jail him. (Brooklyn Supreme Court Judge Dominic Rinaldi, for instance, once fined him $250 on bribery and conspiracy charges that could have sent him away for fifteen years.) Vario tried to maintain a modest amount of decorum in a neighborhood known for mayhem. He abhorred unnecessary violence (the kind he hadn't ordered), mainly because it was bad for business. Bodies deposited haphazardly on the streets always made trouble and annoyed the police, who at that time could generally be relied upon to be reasonably complacent about most mob matters.

Paul Vario was a large man, standing six feet tall and weighing over 240 pounds, and appeared even larger than he was. He had the thick arms and chest of a sumo wrestler and moved in the lumbering manner of a big man who knew that people and events would wait for him. He was impervious to fear, impossible to surprise. If a car backfired or someone called his name, Paul Vario's head would turn, but slowly. He seemed invulnerable. Deliberate. He exuded the sort of lethargy that sometimes accompanies absolute power. It wasn't that Vario couldn't move swiftly if he wanted to. Henry had once seen him grab a sawed-off baseball bat from his car and chase a nimbler man up five flights of stairs to collect a loan-shark debt. But usually Vario was reluctant to exert himself. At twelve Henry began running Paul Vario's errands. Soon he was getting Vario his Chesterfield cigarettes and coffee—black, no cream, no sugar—and delivering his messages. Henry got in and out of Paulie's black Impala two dozen times a day when they made their rounds of meetings throughout the city. While Vario waited behind the wheel Henry would bring supplicants and peers to the car for their conversations.

"On 114th Street in East Harlem, where the old guys were suspicious of their own noses, they used to look at me through their slit eyes whenever Paulie brought me into the clubs. I was a little kid and they acted like I was a cop. Finally, when one of them asked Paulie who I was, he looked back at them like they were nuts. 'Who is he?' Paulie said. 'He's a cousin. He's blood.' From then on even the mummies smiled.

"I was learning things and I was making money. When I'd clean out Paulie's boat I'd not only get paid but I'd also get to spend the rest of the day fishing. All I had to do was keep Paulie and the rest of the guys aboard supplied with cold beer and wine. Paulie had the only boat in Sheepshead Bay without a name. Paulie never had his name on anything. He never even had his name on a doorbell. He never had a telephone. He hated phones. Whenever he was arrested he always gave his mother's Hemlock Street address. He had boats his whole life and he never named one of them. He always told me, 'Never put your name on anything!' I never did.

"I got to know what Paul wanted even before he did. I knew how to be there and how to disappear. It was just inside me. Nobody taught me anything. Nobody ever said, 'Do this,' 'Don't do that.' I just knew. Even at twelve I knew. After a couple of months, I remember, Paul was in the cabstand and some guys from out of the neighborhood came for a talk. I got up to walk away. I didn't have to be told. There were other guys hanging around too, and we all got up to leave. But just then Paulie looks up. He sees that I'm leaving. 'It's okay,' he says, smiling at me, 'you can stay.' The other guys kept walking. I could see that they were afraid to even look around, but I stayed. I stayed for the next twenty-five years."

When Henry started working at the cabstand, Paul Vario ruled over Brownsville–East New York like an urban raja. Vario controlled almost all of the illegal gambling, loan-sharking, labor rackets, and extortion games in the area. As a ranking member of the Lucchese crime family Vario had the responsibility for maintaining order among some of the city's most disorderly men. He assuaged grievances, defused ancient vendettas, and settled disputes between the stubborn and the pigheaded. Using his four brothers as his emissaries and partners, Vario secretly controlled several legitimate businesses in the area, including the cabstand. He owned the Presto Pizzeria, a cavernous restaurant and pizza stand on Pitkin Avenue, around the corner from the cabstand. There Henry first learned to cook; there he learned how to tot up a comptroller's ribbon for the Vario policy bank that used the pizzeria's basement as its accounting room. Vario also owned the Fountainbleu Florist, on Fulton Street, about six blocks from the cabstand. There Henry learned to twist wires onto the flowers of elaborate funeral wreaths ordered for departed members of the city's unions.

Vario's older brother, Lenny, was a construction union official and ex-bootlegger who had the distinction of once having been arrested with Lucky Luciano. Lenny, who was partial to wraparound sunglasses and highly buffed nails, was Paul's liaison to local building contractors and construction company managers, all of whom paid tribute in either cash or no-show jobs to guarantee that their building sites would remain free of both strikes and fires. Paul Vario was the next oldest. Tommy Vario, who was the third oldest in the family, was also a union delegate for construction workers and had a record of several arrests for running illegal gambling operations. Tommy oversaw Vario's bookmaking and loan-sharking operations at dozens of construction sites. The next in order, Vito Vario, also known as "Tuddy," ran the cabstand where Henry first went to work. It was Tuddy Vario who hired Henry the day the youngster walked into the cabstand. Salvatore "Babe" Vario, the youngest of the brothers, ran the floating card and dice games in apartments, school basements, and the backs of garages every night and twice a day on weekends. Babe was also in charge of accommodating, or paying off, the local cops to guarantee peaceful games.

All the Vario brothers were married and lived in the neighborhood, and they all had children, some of them Henry's age. On weekends the Vario brothers and their families usually gathered at their mother's house (their father, a building superintendent, had died when they were young), where raucous afternoons of card games and an ongoing banquet of pasta, veal, and chicken dishes emerged from the senior Mrs. Vario's kitchen. For Henry there was nothing as exciting or as much fun as the noise and games and food on those afternoons. There was an endless procession of Vario friends and relatives who came marching through his life, most of them stuffing folded dollar bills inside his shirt. There were pinball machines in the cellar and pigeons on the roof. There were trays of cannoli, the cream-filled Italian pastries, sent over as gifts, and tubs of lemon ice and gelato.

"From the first day I walked into the cabstand I knew I had found my home—especially after they found out that I was half Sicilian. Looking back, I can see that everything changed when they found out about my mother. I wasn't just another kid from the neighborhood helping out around the stand. I was suddenly in their houses. I was in their refrigerators. I was running errands for the Vario wives and playing with their kids. They gave me anything I wanted.

"Even before going to work at the cabstand I was fascinated by the place. I used to watch them from my window, and I dreamed of being like them. At the age of twelve my ambition was to be a gangster. To be a wiseguy. To me being a wiseguy was better than being president of the United States. It meant power among people who had no power. It meant perks in a working-class neighborhood that had no privileges. To be a wiseguy was to own the world. I dreamed about being a wiseguy the way other kids dreamed about being doctors or movie stars or firemen or ballplayers."

Suddenly, Henry found, he could go anywhere. He no longer had to wait in line at the local Italian bakery for fresh bread on Sunday mornings. The owner would just come from around the counter and tuck the warmest loaves under his arm and wave him home. People no longer parked in the Hill driveway, although his father never had a car. One day neighborhood youngsters even carried his mother's groceries home. As far as Henry could see there was no world like it, certainly no world he could ever have entered.

Tuddy (Vito) Vario, who ran the cabstand, had been looking for a sharp and speedy kid for weeks. Tuddy had lost his left leg in the Korean War, and even though he had adapted to his disability, he still couldn't move about as swiftly as he wished. Tuddy needed someone to help clean out the cabs and limos. He needed someone who could run around to the Presto Pizzeria in a pinch and deliver pies. He needed someone whom he could send to the tiny four-stool bar and grill he owned two blocks away to clean out the register, and he needed someone smart enough to get sandwich orders straight and fast enough to bring the coffee back hot and the beer cold. Other youngsters, including his own son, Vito Junior, had been hopeless. They dawdled. They moped. They lived in a fog. Sometimes one would take an order and disappear. Tuddy needed a sharp kid who knew his way around. A kid who wanted to hustle. A kid who could be trusted.

Henry Hill was ideal. He was quick and he was smart. He ran errands faster than anyone had ever run errands before, and he got the orders right. For a buck apiece he cleaned out the taxicabs and limousines (the limos were used for local funerals, weddings, and delivering high rollers to Vario card and dice games), and then he cleaned them out again for free. Tuddy was so pleased with Henry's seriousness and dispatch that after Henry's first two months at the cabstand he began teaching him how to jockey the cabs and limos around the cabstand's parking lot. It was a glorious moment—Tuddy walking out of the cabstand carrying a phonebook so Henry could see over the dashboard, determined that the twelve-year-old would be driving cars at the end of the day. It actually took four days, but by the end of the week, Henry was tentatively edging the cabs and limousines between the water hose and the gas pumps. After six months Henry Hill was backing limos with inch-clearing accuracy and tire-squealing aplomb around the lot while his schoolmates watched in awe and envy from behind the battered wooden fence. Once Henry spotted his father, who had never learned to drive, spying on him from behind the fence. That night Henry waited for his father to mention his skill in driving, but the senior Hill ate dinner in silence. Henry of course knew better than to bring up the subject. The less said about his job at the cabstand the better.

"I was the luckiest kid in the world. People like my father couldn't understand, but I was part of something. I belonged. I was treated like I was a grown-up. I was living a fantasy. Wiseguys would pull up and toss me their keys and let me park their Caddies. I couldn't see over the steering wheel and I'm parking Caddies."

At twelve Henry Hill was making more money than he could spend. At first he would treat his classmates to galloping horse rides along the bridle paths of the Canarsie marshes. Sometimes he would pay for their day at Steeplechase Amusement Park, topping off the treat with a 260-foot parachute drop. In time, though, Henry grew bored with his schoolmates and tired of his own largesse. He soon learned that there were no heady rides on sweaty horses and no amusement parks he had ever seen that could match the adventures he encountered at the cabstand.

"My father was the kind of guy who worked hard his whole life and was never there for the payday. When I was a kid he used to say he was a 'subway-man,' and it made me want to cry. He helped organize the electrical workers' union, Local Three, and got flowers for his funeral. He worked on skyscrapers in Manhattan and housing projects in Queens, and we could never move out of our crummy three-bedroom house jammed with seven kids, one of them stuck in his bed with a bum spine. We had money to eat, but we never had extras. And every day I saw everyone else, not just the wiseguys, making a buck. My old man's life wasn't going to be my life. No matter how much he yelled at me, no matter how many beatings I took, I wouldn't listen to what he said. I don't think I even heard him. I was too busy learning about paydays. I was learning how to earn.

"And every day I was learning something. Every day I was making a dollar here and a dollar there. I'd listen to schemes and I watched guys score. It was natural. I was in the middle of the cabstand every day. Swag came in and out of that place all day long. There'd be a crate of stolen toasters to be fenced, hot cashmeres right off a truck, cartons of untaxed cigarettes hijacked off some cowboy truckers, who couldn't even complain to the cops. Pretty soon I was delivering policy slips to apartments and houses all over the neighborhood, where the Varios had guys with adding machines counting up the day's take. People used to rent a room in their apartment to the Varios for $150 a week and a free phone. It was a good deal. The wiseguys took only two or three hours in the late afternoon to add up the policy bets on the adding machine tape and circle all the winners. Lots of times the places Paulie and the numbers guys rented belonged to the parents of the kids I went to school with. At first they were surprised to see me coming in with a shopping bag full of slips. They thought I was coming to play with their kids. But pretty soon they knew who I was. They could see I was growing up different.

"After I got my first few bucks and the nerve to go shopping without my mother, I went to Benny Field's on Pitkin Avenue. That's where the wiseguys bought their clothes. I came out wearing a dark blue pinstriped, double-breasted suit with lapels so sharp you could get arrested just for flashing them. I was a kid. I was so proud. When I got home my mother took one look at me and screamed, 'You look just like a gangster!' I felt even better."

At thirteen, Henry had worked a year at the cabstand. He was a handsome youngster with a bright, open face and a dazzling smile. His thick black hair was combed straight back. His dark brown eyes were so sharp and bright that they glittered with excitement. He was slick. He had learned how to duck under his father's angry swats, and he was a master at slipping away from the racetrack security guards, who insisted he was too young to hang around the clubhouse, especially on school days. From a distance he almost looked like a miniature of the men he so admired. He wore an approximation of their clothes, he tried to use their street-corner hand gestures, he ate their kind of scungilli and squid dishes though they made him retch, and he used to sip containers of boiling, bitter black coffee even though it tasted awful and burned his lips so badly he wanted to cry. He was a cardboard wiseguy, a youngster dressed up for the mob. But he was also learning about that world, and there were no adolescent aspiring samurai or teenage Buddhist monks who took their indoctrination and apprenticeship more seriously.

was around the stand from morning till night, and I was learning more and more every day. By the time I was thirteen I was collecting numbers and selling fireworks. I used to get the cabdrivers to buy six-packs of beer for me, and then I'd sell them at a markup to the kids in the school yard. I was acting like a mini-fence for some of the neighborhood's juvenile burglars. I'd front them the money and then sell the radio, portable, or box of sweaters they glommed to one of the guys around the cabstand.

"Before big-money holidays like Easter and Mother's Day, instead of going to school I'd go 'cashing' with Johnny Mazzolla. Johnny, who lived across the street from the cabstand, was a junkie horse-player, and every once in a while he would take me out and we'd go cashing counterfeit twenties he picked up from Beansie the counterfeiter in Ozone Park for ten cents on the dollar. We'd go from store to store, neighborhood to neighborhood, and Johnny would wait in the car and I'd run in and buy something for a buck or two with the fake twenty. Johnny taught me how to soften up the counterfeit bills with cold coffee and cigarette ashes the night before and leave them out to dry. He taught me to pretend I was in a hurry when I went up to the cashier. He also told me never to carry more than one bill on me at a time. That way, if you get caught, you can pretend that somebody passed it off on you. He was right. It worked. I was caught a couple of times, but I could always cry my way out. I was just a kid. I'd start to yell and cry and say I had to tell my mother what happened. That she'd beat me up for losing the money. Then I'd run out of the store fast as I could and we'd be off for another neighborhood. We'd usually get a couple of days in a neighborhood—until the twenties started showing up in the local banks and they'd alert the stores. Then the cashiers would have a fist of the fake bills' serial numbers tacked up right next to the register, and we'd have to change neighborhoods. At the end of a day's cashing we'd have so many two-dollar purchases of doughnuts and cigarettes and razor blades and soap piled up in the back of the car we couldn't see out the rear window.

"At Christmas, Tuddy taught me how to drill holes in the trunks of junk Christmas trees he'd get for nothing, and then I'd stuff the holes with loose branches. I'd stuff so many branches into those holes that even those miserable spindly trees looked full. Then we'd sell them for premium prices, usually at night and mostly around the Euclid Avenue subway stop. It took a day or two before the branches came loose and began to fall apart. The trees would collapse even faster once they were weighed down with decorations.

"We were always scheming. Everything was a scheme. Tuddy got me a job unloading deliveries at a high-class Italian food store just so I could toss the store's most expensive items through the windows of Tuddy's cabs, which he had parked strategically nearby. It wasn't that Tuddy or Lenny or Paul needed the stuff—the imported olive oil, prosciutto, or tuna fish. The Varios had more than enough money to buy the store a hundred times over. It was just that stuff that was stolen always tasted better than anything bought. I remember years later, when I was doing pretty well in the stolen credit-card business, Paulie was always asking me for stolen credit cards whenever he and his wife, Phyllis, were going out for the night. Paulie called stolen cards 'Muldoons,' and he always said that liquor tastes better on a Muldoon. The fact that a guy like Paul Vario, a *capo* in the Lucchese crime family, would even consider going out on a social occasion with his wife and run the risk of getting caught using a stolen card might surprise some people. But if you knew wiseguys you would know right away that the best part of the night for Paulie came from the fact that he was getting over on somebody. It wasn't the music or the floor show or the food—and he loved food—or even that he was going out with Phyllis, who he adored. The real thrill of the night for Paulie, his biggest pleasure, was that he was robbing someone and getting away with it.

"After I was at the cabstand about six months I began helping the Varios with the card and dice games they ran. I would spend the days with Bruno Facciolo assembling the crap game tables, which were just like the ones they have in Vegas. I spent my nights steering the high rollers from various pickup spots in the neighborhood, such as the candy store under the Liberty Avenue el or Al and Evelyn's delicatessen on Pitkin Avenue, to the apartments and storefronts where we were having games that night. A couple of times we had the games in the basement of my own school, Junior High School 149, on Euclid Avenue. Babe Vario bought the school custodian. I kept an eye out for cops, especially the plainclothesmen from the division or headquarters, who used to shake down the games in those days. I didn't have to worry too much about the local cops. They were already on the payroll. It got so that I could always make a plainclothesman. They usually had their shirts outside their pants to cover their guns and handcuffs. They used the same dirty black Plymouths all the tune. We even had their plate numbers. They had a way of walking through a block or driving a car that just said, 'Don't fuck with me, I'm a cop!' I had radar for them. I knew.

"Those games were fabulous. There were usually between thirty and forty guys playing. We had rich garment-center guys. Businessmen. Restaurant owners. Bookmakers. Union guys. Doctors. Dentists. This was long before it was so easy to fly out to Vegas or drive down to Atlantic City for the night. There was also just about

every wiseguy in the city coming to the games. The games themselves were actually run by professionals, but the Varios handled
the money. They kept the books and the cashbox. The guys who
ran the game got a flat fee or a percentage depending on the deal
they cut. The people who ran the games for Paulie were the same
kind of professionals who would run games in casinos or carnivals.
The card games had professional dealers and the crap games had
boxmen and stickmen, just like regular casinos. There were doormen—usually guys from the cabstand—who checked out everyone
who got in the game, and there were loan sharks who worked for
Paulie who picked up some of the action. Every pot was cut five or
six percent for the house, and there was a bartender who kept the
drinks coming.

"I used to make coffee and sandwich runs to Al and Evelyn's delicatessen until I realized I could make a lot more money if I made the
sandwiches myself. It was a lot of work, but I made a few more bucks.
I had only been doing that a couple of weeks when Al and Evelyn
caught me on the street. They took me into the store. They wanted
to talk to me, they said. Business was bad, they said. Since I started
making sandwiches they had lost lots of the card game business. They
had a deal. If I went back to buying the sandwiches from them, they'd
cut me in for five cents on every card game dollar I spent. It sounded
great, but I didn't jump at the opportunity. I wanted to savor it. I was
being treated like an adult. 'Awright,' Al says, with Evelyn frowning at
him, 'seven cents on the dollar!' 'Good,' I said, but I was feeling great.
It was my first kickback and I was still only thirteen.

"It was a glorious time. Wiseguys were all over the place. It was
1956, just before Apalachin, before the wiseguys began having all
the trouble and Crazy Joey Gallo decided to take on his boss, Joe
Profaci, in an all-out war. It was when I met the world. It was
when I first met Jimmy Burke. He used to come to the card games.
He couldn't have been more than twenty-four or twenty-five at the
time, but he was already a legend. He'd walk in the door and ev-

erybody who worked in the joint would go wild. He'd give the door-man a hundred just for opening the door. He shoved hundreds in the pockets of the guys who ran the games. The bartender got a hundred just for keeping the ice cubes cold. I mean, the guy was a sport. He started out giving me five bucks every time I got him a sandwich or a beer. Two beers, two five-dollar bills. Win or lose, the guy had money on the table and people got their tips. After a while, when he got to know me a little bit and he got to know that I was with Paul and the Varios, he started to give me twenty-dollar tips when I brought him his sandwich. He was sawbucking me to death. Twenty here. Twenty there. He wasn't like anyone else I had ever met. The Varios and most of the Italian guys were all pretty cheap. They'd go for a buck once in a while, but they resented it. They hated losing the green. Jimmy was from another world. He was a one-man parade. He was also one of the city's biggest hijack-ers. He loved to steal. I mean, he enjoyed it. He loved to unload the hijacked trucks himself until the sweat was pouring down his face. He must have knocked over hundreds of trucks a year, most of them coming and going from the airports. Most hijackers take the truck driver's license as a warning. The driver knows that you know where he lives, and if he cooperates too much with the cops or the insurance company he's in trouble. Jimmy got his nickname 'Jimmy the Gent' because he used to take the driver's license, just like ev-erybody else, except Jimmy used to stuff a fifty-dollar bill into the guy's wallet before taking off. I can't tell you how many friends he made out at the airport because of that. People loved him. Drivers used to tip off his people about rich loads. At one point things got so bad the cops had to assign a whole army to try to stop him, but it didn't work. It turned out that Jimmy made the cops his partners. Jimmy could corrupt a saint. He said bribing cops was like feeding elephants at the zoo. 'All you need is peanuts.'

"Jimmy was the kind of guy who cheered for the crooks in movies. He named his two sons Frank James Burke and Jesse James Burke.

He was a big guy, and he knew how to handle himself. He looked like a fighter. He had a broken nose and he had a lot of hands. If there was just the littlest amount of trouble, he'd be all over you in a second. He'd grab a guy's tie and slam his chin into the table before the guy knew he was in a war. If the guy was lucky, Jimmy would let him live. Jimmy had a reputation for being wild. He'd whack you. There was no question—Jimmy could plant you just as fast as shake your hand. It didn't matter to him. At dinner he could be the nicest guy in the world, but then he could blow you away for dessert. He was very scary and he scared some very scary fellows. Nobody really knew where they stood with him, but he was also smarter than most of the guys he was around. He was a great earner. Jimmy always brought in money for Paulie and the crew, and that, in the end, is why his craziness was tolerated."

On Henry's fourteenth birthday Tuddy and Lenny Vario presented Henry with a card in the bricklayers' local. Even then, in 1957, a job in the construction workers' union paid well ($190 a week) and entitled its members to extensive health care and other fringe benefits, such as paid vacations and sick leave. It was a union card for which most of the hardworking men in the neighborhood would have paid dearly—if they had ever had enough money to buy anything. Henry was given the card so that he could be put on a building contractor's payroll as a no-show and his salary divided among the Varios. He was also given the card to facilitate the pickup of the daily policy bets and loan-shark payments from local construction sites. For months, instead of going to school, Henry made pickups at various construction projects and then brought everything back to the basement of the Presto Pizzeria, where the accounts were assembled.

"I was doing very nicely. I liked going to the construction jobs. Everybody knew who I was. They all knew I was with Paul. Sometimes, because I was a member of the union, they let me wet down all the new brick with a fire hose. I loved doing that. It was fun. I liked to watch the way the brick changed color. Then one day I got home from the pizza joint and my father was waiting for me with his belt in one hand and a letter in the other. The letter was from the school's truant officer. It said that I hadn't been to school in months. Here I was lying to my folks that I was going every day. I even used to take my books like I was legit, and then I'd leave them at the cabstand. Meanwhile I'm telling Tuddy that my classes have already let out for the summer and everything was okay with my parents. Part of my situation in those days was that I was juggling everybody in the air at once.

"I got such a beating from my father that night that the next day Tuddy and the guys wanted to know what had happened to me. I told them. I even said that I was afraid I'd have to give up my brick-layer's job. Tuddy told me not to worry, and he motions a couple of the guys from the cabstand and me to go for a ride. We're driving around, and I can't figure out what's happening. Finally Tuddy pulls the car over. He pointed to the mailman delivering mail across the street. 'Is that your mailman?' he asked. I nodded yes. Then, out of the blue, the two guys got out of the car and snatched the mailman. I couldn't believe it. In broad daylight. Tuddy and some of the guys go out and kidnap my mailman. The guy was crammed in the back of the car and he was turning gray. I was ashamed to look at him. Nobody said anything. Finally we all got back to the pizzeria and Tuddy asked him if he knew who I was. Me. The guy nodded his head yes. Tuddy asked him if he knew where I lived. The guy nodded yes again. Then Tuddy said from now on all mail from the school gets delivered to the pizza parlor, and if the guy ever again delivers another letter from the school to my house, Tuddy's going to shove him in the pizza oven feet first.

"That was it. No more letters from truant officers. No more letters from the school. In fact, no more letters from anybody. Finally, after a couple of weeks, my mother had to go down to the post office and complain."

Henry rarely bothered to go back to school again. It was no longer required. It wasn't even relevant. There was something ludicrous about sitting through lessons in nineteenth-century American democracy when he was living in a world of eighteenth-century Sicilian thievery.

"One night I was in the pizzeria and I heard a noise. I looked out the window and saw this guy running up Pitkin Avenue toward the store screaming at the top of his lungs, 'I've been shot!' He was the first person I ever saw who was shot. At first it looked like he was carrying a package of raw meat from the butcher's all wrapped in white string, but when he got close I saw that it was his hand. He had put his hand up to stop the blast of a shotgun. Larry Bilello, the old guy who was the cook at the pizzeria and did twenty-five years for a cop killing, yelled at me to close the door. I did. I already knew that Paulie didn't want anybody dying in the place. Instead of letting him in, I grabbed one of the chairs and took it out on the street so he could sit down and wait for the ambulance. I took off my apron and wrapped it around his hand to stop the blood. The guy was bleeding so bad that my apron was soaked with blood in a few seconds. I went inside and got some more aprons. By the time the ambulance came the guy was practically dead. When the excitement died down Larry Bilello was really pissed. He said I was a jerk. I was stupid. He said I wasted eight aprons on the guy and I remember feeling bad. I remember feeling that maybe he was right.

"About this time a guy from the South opened a cabstand around the corner, on Glenmore Avenue. He called it the Rebel Cab Company. The guy was a real hick. He was from Alabama or Tennessee. He had been in the army, and just because he'd married a local girl, he thought all he had to do was open his place and compete with Tuddy. He lowered his prices. He worked around the clock. He set up special discounts to take people from the last subway and bus stops on Liberty Avenue to the far reaches of Howard Beach and the Rockaways. He either didn't know how things worked or he was dumb. Tuddy had sent people to talk to the guy. They said he was stubborn. Tuddy went to talk to him. Tuddy told him that there wasn't enough business for two companies. There probably was, but by now Tuddy just didn't want the guy around. Finally one day after Tuddy has been banging things around the cabstand all day long, he tells me to meet him at the cabstand after midnight. I couldn't believe it. I was really excited. For the whole day I couldn't think of anything else. I knew he had something planned for the Rebel cabstand, but I didn't know what it was.

"When I got to the cabstand Tuddy was waiting for me. He had a five-gallon drum of gasoline in the back of his car. We drove around the neighborhood for a while until the lights were out in the offices of the Rebel Cab Company, on Glenmore Avenue. Then Tuddy gave me a hammer with a rag wrapped around its head. He nodded toward the curb. I walked up to the first of the Rebel cabs, squeezed my eyes, and swung. Glass flew all over me. I went to the next cab and did it again. Meanwhile Tuddy was wrinkling newspapers and pouring gasoline all over them. He'd soak the papers and shove them through the windows I had just smashed.

"As soon as he finished, Tuddy took the empty can and started hopping like mad up the block. You'd never know Tuddy lost a leg, except when he had to run. He said it was dumb for both of us to be standing in the middle of the street with an empty gasoline can when the fires began. He gave me a fistful of matches and told me to wait until he signaled from the corner. When he finally waved, I lit the first match. Then I set the whole matchbook on fire, just like I'd been taught. I quickly threw it through the broken cab window in case the gas fumes flashed back. I went to the second cab and lit another matchbook, and then I did the third and then the fourth. It was while I was next to the fourth cab that I felt the first explosion. I could feel the heat and one explosion after another, except by then I was running so fast I never had a chance to look back. At the corner I could see Tuddy. He was reflected in the orange flames. He was waving the empty gasoline can like a track coach, as though I needed anyone to tell me to hurry."

Henry was sixteen years old when he was arrested for the first time. He and Paul's son Lenny, who was fifteen, had been given a Texaco credit card by Tuddy and told to go to the gas station on Pennsylvania Avenue and Linden Boulevard to buy a couple of snow tires for Tuddy's wife's car.

"Tuddy didn't even check to see if the card was stolen. He just gave me the card and sent us to the gas station, where we were known. If I'd known it was a stolen card I still could have scored. If I'd known the card was hot I would have given it to the guy in the gas station and said, 'Here, get yourself the fifty-dollar reward for returning it and give me half of it.' Even if it was bad I would have earned on the card, except Tuddy wouldn't have had any tires.

"Instead, Lenny and I drive over to the place and buy the tires. The guy had to put them on the rims, so we paid for them on the card and drove around for about an hour. When we got back the cops were there. They were hiding around on the side. I walk in the place and two detectives jump out and say that I'm under arrest. Lenny took off. They cuffed me and took me to the Liberty Avenue station.

"In the precinct they shoved me in the pens, and I was playing the wiseguy. 'I'll be out in an hour,' I'm telling the cops. 'I didn't do nothing.' Real George Raft. Tuddy and Lenny had always told me never to talk to the cops. Never tell them anything. At one point one of the cops said he wanted me to sign something. He had to be nuts. 'I'm not signing anything,' I tell him. Tuddy and Lenny said all I had to give them was my name, and at first they didn't believe my name was Henry Hill. I took a smack from one of the cops just because he wouldn't believe a kid running around with the people I was running with could have a name like Hill.

"In less than an hour Louis Delenhauser showed up at the precinct. 'Cop-out Louie,' the lawyer. Lenny had run back to the cabstand and said I had been pinched on the credit card. That's when they sent Louie. They took care of everything. After the precinct the cops took me down for the arraignment, and when the judge set five hundred dollars bail, the money was put right up and I was free. When I turned around to walk out of the court I could see all of the Varios were standing in the back of the room. Paulie wasn't there because he was serving thirty days on a contempt hearing. But everybody else was smiling and laughing and started hugging me and kissing me and banging me on the back. It was like a graduation. Tuddy kept yelling, 'You broke your cherry! You broke your cherry!' It was a big deal. After we left the court Lenny and Big Lenny and Tuddy took me to Vincent's Clam Bar in Little Italy for scungilli and wine. They made it like a party. Then, when we got back to the cabstand, everybody was waiting for me and we partied some more.

"Two months later Cop-out Louie copped me out to an 'attempted' petty larceny and I got a six-month suspended sentence. Maybe I could have done better. Looking back, it sure was a dumb way to start a yellow sheet, but in those days it was no big thing having a suspended sentence on your record. And I felt so grateful they paid the lawyer, so that my mother and father didn't ever have to find out.

"But by now I'm getting nervous. My father is getting worse and worse. I had found a gun in his basement and had taken it across the street to show Tuddy, and then I put it back. A couple of times Tuddy said he wanted to borrow the gun for some friends of his. I didn't want to lend it, but I didn't want to say no to Tuddy. In the end I started to lend Tuddy the gun and get it back after a day or two. Then I'd wrap the gun up just exactly how I found it and put it back on the top shelf behind the pipes in the cellar. One day I went to get the gun for Tuddy, and I saw that it was missing. I knew that my father knew what I was doing. He didn't say anything, but I knew he knew. It was like waiting for the electric chair.

"I was almost seventeen. I went to the recruitment office and tried to sign up. I thought that was a good way of getting my father off my back and keeping Tuddy and Paul from thinking I was mad at them. The guys at the recruitment office said I had to wait until I was seventeen and then my parents or guardian could sign me up. I went home and told my father I wanted to enlist in the paratroopers. I told him he had to sign me in. He started to smile, and he called my mother and the whole family. My mother was nervous, but my father was really happy. That afternoon I went to the DeKalb Avenue recruitment office and signed up. The next day I went to the cabstand and told Tuddy what I'd done. He thought I was crazy. He said he was going to get Paul. Now Paulie shows up, very concerned. He sits me down alone. He looks me in the eye and asks me was there anything wrong, was there anything I wasn't telling him. 'No,' I said. 'Are you sure?' he asked. 'Yeah,' I said. Then he got very quiet. We're in the back room of the cabstand surrounded by wiseguys. He's got two carloads of shooters on the street. The place is as safe as a tomb and he's whispering. He says if I want to get out of it, he can fix it with the recruitment office. He can buy me back the papers.

"'No, thanks,' I said. 'I might as well do the time.'"

Three

When Henry Hill was born on June 11, 1943, Brownsville–East New York was a six-square-mile working-class area with some light industry and modest one- and two-family houses. It stretched from a row of parklike cemeteries in the north to the saltwater marshes and garbage landfills of Canarsie and Jamaica Bay in the south. In the early 1920s electric trolleys and the Liberty Avenue elevated line had turned the neighborhood into a haven for tens of thousands of Italian-American immigrants and Eastern European Jews who wanted to escape the tenement squalor of Mulberry Street and the Lower East Side in Manhattan. The low, flat, sun-filled streets offered only the smallest houses and tiniest backyards, but the first- and second-generation Italians and Jews who fiercely wanted to own those houses worked nights in the sweatshops and factories spotted throughout the area after they had finished their day-time jobs.

In addition to the thousands of hardworking new arrivals, the area also attracted Jewish hoods, Black Hand extortionists, Camorra kidnappers, and wily Mafiosi. In many ways Brownsville–East New York was a perfect place for the mob. There was even a historical ambience. At the turn of the century the New York *Tribune* described the section as a haven for highwaymen and cutthroats and said that it had always been a "nurturing ground for radical movements and rebels." With Prohibition, the area's proximity to the overland liquor routes from Long Island and the countless coves for barge landings along Jamaica Bay made it a hijacker's dream and a smuggler's paradise. Here were assembled the nation's first multiethnic alliances of mobsters that would later set the precedent for organized crime in America. The small nonunion garment factories that dotted the area became ripe for shakedowns and payoffs, and the activities at Belmont, Jamaica, and Aqueduct raceways nearby only added to the mob's interest in the area. In the 1940s, when the 5,000-acre Idlewild Golf Course began its transformation into an airport employing 30,000 people, moving millions of passengers and billions of dollars' worth of cargo, what is now Kennedy Airport became one of the single largest sources of revenue for the local hoods.

Brownsville–East New York was the kind of neighborhood that cheered successful mobsters the way West Point cheered victorious generals. It had been the birthplace of Murder Incorporated; Midnight Rose's candy store on the corner of Livonia and Saratoga avenues, where Murder Inc.'s hit men used to wait for their assignments, was considered a historic landmark during Henry's youth. Johnny Torrio and Al Capone grew up there before going west and taking machine guns with them. The local heroes of Henry's childhood were such men as Benjamin "Bugsy" Siegel, who joined forces with Meyer Lansky to create Las Vegas; Louis "Lepke" Buchalter, whose well-muscled cutters' union controlled the garment industry; Frank Costello, a boss with so much political clout that judges called to thank him for their appointments; Otto "Abbadabba" Berman, the mathematical genius and policy-game fixer, who devised a system for rigging the results of the pari-mutuel tote board at the track so that only the least-played numbers could win; Vito Genovese, the stylish racketeer who had two hundred limousines, including eighty filled with floral pieces, at his first wife's funeral in 1931 and was identified in *The New York Times* story as "a wealthy young restaurant owner and importer"; Gaetano "Three Fingers Brown"

Lucchese, who headed the mob family of which the Varios were a part; and of course the legendary members of Murder Incorporated: the ever dapper Harry "Pittsburgh Phil" Strauss, who was proudest of the way he could ice-pick his victims through the ear in movie houses without drawing any attention; Frank "Dasher" Abbandando, who only a year before Henry's birth went to the chair with a Cagney sneer; and the 300-pound Vito "Socko" Gurino, a massive hit man with a neck the size of a water main, who for target practice used to shoot the heads off chickens running around his backyard.

It was understood on the street that Paul Vario ran one of the city's toughest and most violent gangs. In Brownsville–East New York the body counts were always high, and in the 1960s and 1970s the Vario thugs did most of the strong-arm work for the rest of the Lucchese crime family. There were always some heads to bash on picket lines, businessmen to be squeezed into making their loan-shark payments, independents to be straightened out over territorial lines, potential witnesses to be murdered, and stool pigeons to be buried. And there were always young cabstand tough guys such as Bruno Facciolo, Frank Manzo, and Joey Russo who were ready to go out and break a few heads whenever Paul gave the order, and such young shooters as Jimmy Burke, Anthony Stabile, and Tommy DeSimone who were happy to take on the most violent assignments. But they did this work on the side; almost all of these wiseguys were employed, to some degree, in one kind of business or another. They were small-time entrepreneurs. They ran two-rig trucking firms. They owned restaurants. For example, Jimmy Burke was a hijacker, but he also had a partnership in several nonunion storefront clothing sweatshops in Queens. Bruno Facciolo owned Bruno's, a ten-table Italian restaurant in the neighborhood, and prided himself on his meat sauce. Frank Manzo, who was called "Frankie the Wop," owned the Villa Capra restaurant in Cedarhurst and had been active in the carpenter's union until his first felony conviction. And Joey Russo, a solidly built youngster, was a cabdriver and construction worker.

Henry Hill, Jimmy Burke, Tommy DeSimone, Anthony Stabile, Tommy Stabile, Fat Andy, Frankie the Wop, Freddy No Nose, Eddie Finelli, Pete the Killer, Mike Franzese, Nicky Blanda, Bobby the Dentist (so named because he always knocked teeth out when he punched anyone), Angelo Ruggierio, Clyde Brooks, Danny Rizzo, Angelo Sepe, Alex and Michael Corcione, Bruno Facciolo, and the rest of Paul Vario's sidewalk soldiers lived without restraints. They had always been outlaws. They were the kids from the neighborhood who were always in trouble. As youngsters they were the ones invariably identified as toughs by the police and brought into the precinct for routine beatings whenever some neighborhood store burglary or assault moved the station house cops into action.

As they grew older, most of the arbitrary beatings by cops stopped, but there was rarely a time in their lives when they were not under some kind of police scrutiny. They were always under suspicion, arrest, or indictment for one crime or another. Henry and his pals had been reporting to probation and parole officers since their teens. They had been arrested and questioned so often for so many crimes that there was very little fear or mystery about the inside of a precinct squad room. They were at ease with the process. They, better than many lawyers, knew just how far the cops could go. They were intimately familiar with the legal distinctions between being questioned, booked, or arraigned. They knew about bail hearings and grand juries and indictments. If they were picked up as the result of a barroom brawl or a billion-dollar drug conspiracy, they often knew the cops who arrested them. They had the unlisted telephone numbers of their lawyers and bail bondsmen committed to memory. It was not unusual for one of the arresting cops to call their lawyers for them, knowing that such small kindnesses usually brought hundred-dollar bills as tips.

For Henry and his wiseguy friends the world was golden. Everything was covered. They lived in an environment awash in crime, and those who did not partake were simply viewed as prey. To live otherwise was foolish. Anyone who stood waiting his turn on the American pay line was beneath contempt. Those who did—who followed the rules, were stuck in low-paying jobs, worried about their bills, put tiny amounts away for rainy days, kept their place, and crossed off workdays on their kitchen calendars like prisoners awaiting their release—could only be considered fools. They were the timid, law-abiding, pension-plan creatures neutered by compliance and awaiting their turn to die. To wiseguys, "working guys" were already dead. Henry and his pals had long ago dismissed the idea of security and the relative tranquillity that went with obeying the law. They exulted in the pleasures that came from breaking it. Life was lived without a safety net. They wanted money, they wanted power, and they were willing to do anything necessary to achieve their ends.

By birth, certainly, they were not prepared in any way to achieve their desires. They were not the smartest kids in the neighborhood. They were not born the richest. They weren't even the toughest. In fact, they lacked almost all the necessary talents that might have helped them satisfy the appetites of their dreams, except one— their talent for violence. Violence was natural to them. It fueled them. Snapping a man's arm, cracking his ribs with an inch-and-a-half-diameter lead pipe, slamming his fingers in the door of a car, or casually taking his life was entirely acceptable. It was routine. A familiar exercise. Their eagerness to attack and the fact that people were aware of their strutting brutality were the key to their power, the common knowledge that they would unquestionably take a life ironically gave them life. It distinguished them from everyone else. They would do it. They would put a gun in a victim's mouth and watch his eyes while they pulled the trigger. If they were crossed, denied, offended, thwarted in any way, or even mildly annoyed, retribution was demanded, and violence was their answer.

In Brownsville–East New York wiseguys were more than accepted—they were protected. Even the legitimate members of the community—the merchants, teachers, phone repairmen, garbage collectors, bus depot dispatchers, housewives, and old-timers sunning themselves along the Conduit Drive—all seemed to keep an eye out to protect their local hoods. The majority of the residents, even those not directly related by birth or marriage to wiseguys, had certainly known the local rogues most of their lives. They had gone to school together. A great many of them shared friends. There was the nodding familiarity of neighborhood. In the area it was impossible to betray old friends, even those old friends who had grown up to be racketeers.

The extraordinary insularity of these old-world mob-controlled sections, whether Brownsville–East New York, the South Side in Chicago, or Federal Hill in Providence, Rhode Island, unquestionably helped to nurture the mob. These were the neighborhoods where local wiseguys felt safe, where racketeers had become an integral part of the social fabric, where candy stores, funeral parlors, and groceries were often fronts for gambling operations, where loans could be made and bets placed, where residents made major purchases from the backs of trucks rather than from downtown department stores.

There were other marginal benefits bestowed upon those who were raised under the protective umbrella of the mob. Street muggings, burglaries, purse-snatchings, and rapes were almost nonexistent in mob-controlled areas. Too many eyes were watching the street. The community's natural suspicion was so great that anyone who did not belong in the area was immediately the focus of block-by-block and even house-by-house attention. The slightest change in the street's daily rituals was enough to send a quiver of alarm through every mob club and hangout. An unfamiliar car appearing on a block, a panel truck filled with utility workers no one had ever seen before, sanitation men making pickups on the wrong day—these were precisely the kinds of signals that pressed silent neighborhood alarms.

"The whole neighborhood was always on alert. It was just natural.

You were always looking. Up the block. Down the block. No matter how quiet it looked, nobody missed anybody. Late one night, right after my seventeenth birthday, I was helping in the pizzeria and dreaming about the paratroopers when I saw two of Paulie's guys put down their coffee cups and walk toward the pizza counter window. I went over.

"Outside, Pitkin Avenue was almost empty. Theresa Bivona, who lived down the block, was walking home from the Euclid Avenue subway. There were three or four other subway people, all familiar, people we knew or at least had seen before, walking toward Blake or Glenmore avenues. And then there was this black kid in a sweatshirt and jeans who nobody had ever seen before.

"All of a sudden the kid's got eyes all over him. He was walking very slow. He walked along the curb for a while looking in car windows. He pretended to be looking in store widows, even though the stores were closed. And the stores—a butcher shop and dry cleaner's—didn't have anything a kid like that would be interested in buying.

"Then the guy began to move down the block. I couldn't tell if Theresa knew there was someone about fifty feet behind her. Across the street Branco's Bar looked quiet, but I knew Petey Burns was watching. He used to sit on a stool leaning against the wall at the end of the bar and stare out the window until the joint closed at about two in the morning. I knew guys were watching from Pete the Killer Abbanante's club on the other side of Crescent Street. Frank Sorace, one of Paulie's guys, who was later murdered, and Eddy Barberra, who's now doing twenty years in Atlanta on a bank robbery, were seated in a car parked at the curb. I knew they were armed, because their job was to drive the big winners from Babe's card games home so they didn't get robbed.

"To the guy following Theresa the street must have looked empty, because he never looked around. He just started walking faster. He really began running toward Theresa when she started rummaging around for her keys. As soon as Theresa got inside, the guy was right behind her. It was very fast. He stuck out his hand and caught the door just before it slammed shut. That's when Theresa and the guy disappeared.

"By the time I got to the building it was too late. The guy was supposed to have pulled a knife and was supposed to have been pressing it against Theresa's face, but I never saw anything. All I could see was backs. There were at least three tons of wiseguys crammed in the hallways even before I got there. They had already bashed through the front door. There were so many of them that it looked as though the hallway and stairways were made of rubber. Theresa had squashed herself flat against the mailboxes. All I could see was the top of the guy's head and an arm of his sweatshirt. Then he was swept along with all the other bodies and arms and curses until he was carried up the stairs and out of sight.

"I backed up and went outside. Some of the guys were waiting there. I went across the street, turned around, and looked up. I could make out the small roof wall on the front of the building—it was made of brick—and then I saw the guy launched right over it into the air. He hung there for just a second, flailing arms like a broken helicopter, and then he came down hard and splattered all over the street."

Henry Hill went into the paratroopers just days after his seventeenth birthday on June 11, 1960, and it was a good time to be off the street. There was a lot of heat. The investigation started by the Apalachin meeting in November of 1957 had created a mess. After twenty-five years of saying there was no such thing as the Mafia, J. Edgar Hoover was now announcing that organized crime cost the public over $22 billion a year. The United States Senate had launched its own investigation into organized crime and its links to unions and business and had published the names of almost five thousand hoods nationwide, including members and hierarchy of the five New York City crime families. Henry saw a newspaper with a partial list of members of the Lucchese crime family, but he couldn't find Paulie's name.

Henry Hill turned out to love the army. He was stationed at Fort Bragg, North Carolina. He had never been away from the streets. He hadn't even gone for a drive in the country. He didn't know how to swim. He had never camped out, and he had never lit a fire that wasn't a felony. Other youngsters in boot camp complained and groused; for Henry the army was like summer camp. There was almost nothing about it he didn't love. He loved the rigors of boot training. He loved the food. He even loved jumping out of airplanes.

"I didn't plan it, but I earned in the army. I got myself in charge of the kitchen detail, and I made a fortune selling excess food. The army overbought. It was a disgrace. They would always order two hundred and fifty meals for two hundred men. On weekends sixty guys would show up, and still they bought for two hundred and fifty. Somebody had to be taking care of somebody. Before I got there the kitchen guys were just throwing the extra food out. I couldn't believe it. At the beginning I used to clip a pan of steaks, maybe thirty pounds, and take them to restaurants and hotels in Bennettsville and McColl, South Carolina. They loved it. Soon I was selling them everything. Eggs. Butter. Mayo. Catsup. Even the salt and pepper. On top of selling them the food, I used to drink free in those joints all night long.

"I had it all to myself. I couldn't believe how lazy everybody around me was. Nobody did anything. I began loan-sharking. The guys used to get paid twice a month—the first and the fifteenth. They were always broke just before payday. I could get ten bucks for every five I lent if payday came after a weekend. Otherwise I got back nine for five. I started up a card game and some dice games and then I lent the losers money. The best part was on payday, when the guys would line up to get their money and I'd wait at the end of the line and get paid. It was beautiful. I didn't have to chase after anybody.

"I kept in touch with Paulie and Tuddy. On a couple of occasions they even sent me money when I needed it. Once I got into a bar fight with some farmer and I got locked up. Paulie had to bail me out. I couldn't ask my parents—they'd never understand. Paulie understood everything. After about six months, when I got the sergeant to phony up a double work shift for me in the kitchen, I drove eight and a half hours back to New York. It was great. The minute I drove up to the pizzeria I remembered how much I missed it. Everybody was hanging around. They treated me like a returning hero. They made fun of my uniform, my haircut. Tuddy said I was in a fairy army—we didn't even have real bullets. I brought up lots of booze I got from the officers' club and some bootleg mountain whiskey. It was amazing, I told them. I said I was going to come home more often with a load of nontaxed cigarettes, and also fireworks, which you could buy by the truckload on the streets. Paulie was smiling. It was like he was proud. Before I went back he said he was going to get me a present. He made a big thing out of the presentation. He didn't usually do such things, so everybody showed up. He had a box all wrapped up and made me open it in front of all the guys. They were real quiet. I took off the paper, and inside was one of those wide-angle rearview mirrors that truck drivers use to be able to see everybody coming up behind them. The mirror was about three feet long.

" 'Put it in the car,' Paulie said. 'It'll help you make tails.' "

Four

I t was 1963 when Henry got back to the street. His trips to New York had become more frequent, especially after a new company commander changed the kitchen detail. Henry's mess sergeant had been transferred, skipping out with nearly fifteen hundred dollars of Henry's money. Then, with less than six months to go before his discharge, Henry got into a barroom brawl with three marines. He was drunk. He insisted upon calling them "jar heads" and "jar ears." There were broken bottles and shattered mirrors all over the floor. Blood ran down the front of every khaki shirt and white apron in the place. When the McColl sheriff finally arrived, there was so much chaos that no one saw Henry stagger out of the bar and drive off in the sheriff's car until it was too late. The company commander sent the Fort Bragg chaplain, who was accompanied by three Brooklyn-based MPs, all the way to Pitkin Avenue, Brooklyn, to bring Henry back. Thus Henry Hill spent the last two months of his military career in the Fort Bragg stockade. He lost his pay and benefits for the period. He was also stripped of his rank as a private first class. In Henry's world, of course, getting out of a military stockade was almost as prestigious as getting out of a federal prison.

"When I got out of the army, Paulie's son Lenny was about sixteen, but he looked five years older. He was a big kid, like his father. He had the neck and shoulders of a lineman. He was also Paulie's favorite. Paulie liked him much more than his two older sons, Paul Junior and Peter. Lenny Vario was smart. Paulie was doing six months for contempt at the time I got out of the army and Lenny just gravitated toward me. He was working in the pizza joint, but he was also always fighting with his uncles and his brothers. With Paulie away, his uncles and his brothers wanted to play the boss, but Lenny, even as a kid, used to tell them to go fuck themselves. And every time Paulie heard that Lenny had told everybody off, he loved the kid even more. Paulie would do anything for that kid. Paulie felt that Lenny would go far. Lenny had the nerve to take over a crew. He could run a whole family. Paulie saw great things in Lenny's future.

"So right after the army, with his father away, Lenny became my partner. Wherever I went, he went. I was about four years older than he was, but we were inseparable. Twenty-four hours a day. His brothers, who were also my close friends, were happy I was taking their kid brother off their hands. Still, I needed a job. I didn't want to go back to running errands and doing stuff around the cabstand for Tuddy and the crew. And Lenny became my ticket. Nobody said it that way, but Paulie knew I could watch out for Lenny, and so whatever Lenny got, I got. The next thing I knew, Paulie got Lenny a job as a union bricklayer paying $135 a week. Lenny's sixteen years old at the most, and Paulie got him a man's job. But Lenny says he won't go without me. So now I got a job as a union bricklayer paying $135 a week. I'm just about twenty. Paulie, remember, is in jail during all this, but he can still get us the kinds of jobs that grown-ups from the neighborhood couldn't get.

"Later I found out that Paulie made Bobby Scola, the president of the bricklayers' union, put the muscle on some builders to put us on their payrolls. Bobby then made us union apprentices and gave us cards in the union. I had drifted away from my father during the army years, but he was very happy about my bricklayer's job. He loved union construction work. Everyone he knew was in construction. Lots of the people from the neighborhood worked in construction. It was what people did. But I wasn't expecting to lay brick for the rest of my life.

"Looking back, I can see what a pair of miserable little kids Lenny and I were, but at the time what we were doing seemed so natural. We thumbed our noses at the job and at Bobby Scola. Fuck him. We were with Paulie. We didn't do any work. We didn't even show up regular enough to pick up our own paychecks. We had guys we knew who were really working on the job bring our money to the cabstand or to Frankie the Wop's Villa Capra restaurant, in Cedarhurst, where we hung out. We'd cash the checks, and by Monday we'd blown the money partying or buying clothes or gambling. We didn't even pay our union dues. Why should we? Finally Bobby Scola begged Paulie to get us off his back. He said we were creating a problem. He said there was heat on the job and the builders were getting worried.

"Paulie relented. At first I thought he felt sorry for Bobby Scola and that was why he took us off his hands, but I soon realized differently. Overnight, instead of working as bricklayers, Paulie had us working at the Azores, a very fancy white stucco restaurant next door to the Lido Beach Hotel, in the Rockaways, about an hour from midtown. In those days it was a prime summer eating place for rich businessmen and union guys, mostly from the garment center and construction industry. One phone call from Paulie and Lenny has a job as a service bartender—he isn't even old enough to be in the bar, forget work there—and they got me a tuxedo and made me the maître d' hôtel, a twenty-year-old kid who didn't know the difference between anything.

"In those days the Azores was owned, off the record, by Thomas Lucchese, the boss of the whole family. He used to come in there every night before going home, and that's why Paulie got Lenny the job. It wasn't because he felt sorry for Bobby Scola and his union problems. He wanted Lenny to get to know the boss. And Lucchese had to love us. I mean he got treated beautifully. He walked in the door and his drink was being made. His cocktail glass was polished so hard that a couple of times it broke as Lenny was shining it. The place at the bar where Lucchese liked to stand was always kept empty and it was glossed dry. We didn't care if there were two hundred people in the joint; everybody waited. Very few people in the place knew who he was, but that didn't matter. We knew. He was the boss. In the newspapers he was called Gaetano Lucchese, 'Three Fingers Brown,' but nobody called him that. On the street he was known as Tommy Brown. He was in his sixties then, and he always came in alone. His driver used to wait outside.

"Tommy Brown was the boss of the whole garment center. He controlled the airports. Johnny Dio, who ran most of the union shakedowns at Kennedy and LaGuardia, worked for him. He owned the town. He had district leaders. He made judges. His son was appointed to West Point by the East Harlem congressman Vito Marcantonio, and his daughter graduated from Vassar. Later she married Carlo Gambino's son. Hundreds of million-dollar cloak-and-suiters would drive all the way out to the Azores just because they hoped he might be there so they could kiss his ass. It gave them a chance to nod or say hello. And when these big-money guys saw that I talked to him direct, they would start kissing my ass. They would become real cozy. They'd smile and give me their cards and say if I ever needed anything in ladies' coats or handbags or toppers or better dresses, all I had to do was call. Then they'd stick me with a brand-new twenty or even a fifty that was folded so sharp it felt like it would make my palms bleed. That's who Tommy Brown was. Without trying, he could make the city's greediest rag-trade sharks give money to strangers.

"We first went to work in the Azores in the middle of May. We had an apartment across the street. For a while we lived in Paulie's house in Island Park, about fifteen minutes away, but our own place was more fun. The Azores was ours. The place closed at ten o'clock, and there was a swimming pool at night. We had our friends come in and eat and drink for nothing. It was like our own private club. It was my first taste of the good life. I never had so many shrimp cocktails. After work we went from one night spot to another. I got to see how the rich people lived. I saw the Five Towns crowd from Lawrence and Cedarhurst, mostly all of them wealthy businessmen and professional guys who had lots of cash, wives who looked like Monique Van Vooren, and houses the size of hotels spread out along the south shore, with powerboats as big as my own house tied up in their backyards, which was the goddamn Atlantic Ocean.

"The Azores' owner of record, the guy who ran the place, was named Tommy Morton. Guys like Morton were front men for the wiseguys, who couldn't have their names on the liquor licenses. Front men sometimes had some of their own money in these joints and essentially had the wiseguys for silent partners. Morton, for instance, was a friend of Paulie's. He knew lots of people. He must have fronted for lots of wiseguys. But he also had to pay back a certain amount every week to his partners, and they didn't care whether business was good or bad. That's the way it is with a wiseguy partner. He gets his money, no matter what. You got no business? Fuck you, pay me. You had a fire? Fuck you, pay me. The place got hit by lightning and World War Three started in the lounge? Fuck you, pay me.

"In other words, Tommy Morton only began to see a dollar after he had paid the wiseguys and they'd gotten theirs off the top. That's one of the reasons why Morton hated Lenny and me so much. First, he didn't need a couple of wise-ass kids like us ruining his business. He had to pay us two hundred a week apiece, and for that he could have hired a real maître d' and bartender. Also, we were stealing him blind. Everything we stole or gave away came out of his pocket. I know that we used to drive him nuts, but he couldn't do a thing about it.

"But by the end of the summer we were bored. It was around Labor Day weekend. A tough weekend. We decided to take off. Lenny and I hadn't seen Lucchese for about a month. Everybody was on vacation except us. But we knew our future was secure. Lucchese had said that he had something for us in the garment center after the summer.

"Unfortunately, Tommy Morton had this old German chef. If possible, that guy hated us more than Tommy did. He kept feeding us rice and chicken every night as though we were regular employees. He must have sensed or been told how much Morton hated us, so he was going to twist the screws. Finally, on the Thursday afternoon before the long Labor Day weekend, we were late getting to work. The chef started screaming and yelling at us the minute we walked in the door. He's yelling at us in the dining room. There were people standing around. Early dinner customers. I went nuts. I felt like he was insulting me. The miserable fuck. I couldn't stand it. I ran right at the guy and grabbed him by the neck. Lenny comes over and we picked the guy up by his arms and legs. We carried him into the kitchen and began to shove him into the oven. It must have been about 450 degrees. We couldn't really get him inside, but he wasn't so sure. He screamed and jumped and wriggled until we let him fall out of our grip. The second he hit the floor he was flying. He ran clear out of the joint. He just kept on going, and he never came back. Then Lenny and I walked out and never went back either.

"Paulie was pissed. Tommy Morton must have told him about what we did. Paulie acted as though we had embarrassed him in front of Lucchese. He was so pissed that he made me burn Lenny's car. It was a 1965 yellow Bonneville convertible. Lenny loved that car, but Paulie made me burn it. He put a hit on his own kid's car. He got Tuddy to drive it down the 'hole.' The hole was a body-compacting and car junkyard in Ozone Park that belonged to Jerry Asaro and his son, Vincent. They were with the Bonanno crew. Then Paulie grabs me and he says, 'You go burn the car.' It was crazy. He had given Lenny the car himself. So while he and Tuddy watched me from their own car, I poured half a gallon of gas in the front seat and lit a match. I watched it all burn up.

"The summer was over, but I was already into a million things. A day never went by without somebody coming up with a scheme. We had a neighborhood girl who used to work for the company handling the MasterCharge cards. She used to bring us office memos about security checkups and credit checks. We also bought lots of cards from people who worked in the post office, but then the companies started sending letters to their customers asking if they had received a card yet. But having somebody inside the bank was the best. We had one girl who used to get us duplicate cards, and we'd know the amount of credit attached. Before a card got into an envelope to be mailed, I had a duplicate. If a card had a $500 credit line, for instance, we'd go to stores where we were known or places we had. I'd punch out ten credit-card slips. The guys we knew in the stores would call and get authorization for a $390 stereo, a $450 television, a $470 wristwatch—whatever. The person waiting for the card never got it, and we had about a month before the card was usually reported stolen. I'd try to do all the heavy purchases as soon as I got the card. The guys in the stores didn't care, since they were getting their money. They would just take the authorized slips to the bank and deposit them like cash.

"These days they have traps for this kind of thing in the computer system, but back then I was making a lot of money. If I wanted to, I could have run up $10,000 worth of merchandise in a day. Even working strange stores was easy. There are a hundred items in every store, and you've always got your fake driver's license all typed out and your backup ID. We used to get fake IDs from 'Tony the Baker' in Ozone Park. He was a real baker. He had a bakery that made bread. But he'd also make up fake driver's licenses for you while you waited. He had all the forms. You couldn't believe how good he was. Somehow he had the code from Albany, so that even a state trooper couldn't tell it was wrong. He charged fifty dollars for a set, and that included a driver's license, Social Security card, and voter registration card.

"When I finished with the cards I'd sell them to 'under the limits' people, who would take the banged-out card and go out and buy things that were under the authorization limit. For instance, on some cards the store will call up for authorization if the item being bought is over fifty dollars or over one hundred dollars. 'Under the limit' buyers always make purchases below the call-in figure. They'll go into department stores or shopping malls and bang out forty-five-dollar items on a fifty-dollar card all afternoon. You can go out and buy blenders, radios, cigarettes, razor blades—the kind of stuff that's easy to sell off at half the price—and in two hours make a good payday for yourself. Stacks Edwards, who was a tall, skinny black guy who hung out with the crew, was an 'under the limit' master. He'd do a day at a shopping center with a panel truck until he ran out of room. Then he had an army of people who used to go out and sell his stuff in factories, or he'd take it to small mom-and-pop stores in Harlem, or places in New Jersey that would buy his whole truckload.

"It was Jimmy Burke who put me into cigarettes. I knew about them from having been in North Carolina. A carton of cigarettes was $2.10 in the South at the time, while the same carton would cost $3.75 just because of the New York taxes. Jimmy came by the cabstand one day with his car full of cigarettes. He gave me a hundred cartons and said I should try and sell them. I wasn't sure, but he said I should give it a try. I put the cartons in the trunk of my car and drove over to a nearby construction site. I sold every carton I had in ten minutes. The working guys were saving about a buck a carton. It was worth it to them. But I saw I could make twenty-five cents a carton in ten minutes for my end. That night I went to Jimmy's house and paid him for the hundred cartons he had given me and asked for three hundred more. I took as many as I could fit in the trunk. The next day I sold them in ten minutes again. I said to myself, 'Ain't this nice,' and I went back and got another three hundred for my trunk and two hundred more for my backseat. This was adding up to a hundred twenty-five bucks for a couple of hours' work.

"Jimmy came by the cabstand one day with a skinny kid who was wearing a wiseguy suit and a pencil mustache. It was Tommy DeSimone. He was one of those kids who looked younger than he was just because he was trying to look older. Jimmy had been a friend of Tommy's family for years, and he wanted me to watch out for Tommy and to teach him the cigarette business—help make him a few bucks. With Tommy helping me, pretty soon we're making three hundred, four hundred dollars a day. We sold hundreds of cartons at construction sites and garment factories. We sold them at the Sanitation Department garages and at the subway and bus depot. This was around 1965, and the city wasn't taking it very seriously. We used to sell them on the street, and we'd give a couple of cartons away to the cops just to leave us alone.

"Pretty soon we're importing the cigarettes ourselves. We'd fly down to Washington, D.C., on the shuttle, take a cab to the truck-rental place, use a fake license and ID to get a truck, and then drive to one of the cigarette wholesalers in North Carolina. We'd load up with about eight or ten thousand cartons and drive north. But as more and more guys began doing it, things started to heat up. At first a few guys were pinched, but in those days they'd just give you a summons. The cops were tax agents and they didn't even carry guns. But then they began confiscating the trucks, and the rental people stopped giving them to us. We used every scheme in the world to get those trucks, from bribery to sending local people in to make the rentals. We burned out half the U-Haul places in Washington, D.C. They went bust. Vinnie Beans had the Capo Trucking Company in the Bronx, and so we started renting his trucks. He didn't know what we were going to do with them, so that went along fine until he realized he was missing a dozen trucks. When he found out that they had been seized by the state he dried up our supply. If we hadn't been with Paulie, believe me, we would have been dead. Eventually we had to buy our own trucks—the business was that good. Tommy and I bought a nice twenty-two-footer, and Jimmy Burke was bringing in trailer truckloads. For a while we were all doing great, but then too many guys got into the business. The whole Colombo crew from Bensonhurst, Brooklyn, started glutting the market. They took away the edge. But by then I was already into other things.

"I began stealing cars, for instance. It wouldn't have paid if I hadn't come across Eddy Rigaud, who was an import-export agent for the Sea-Land Service in Haiti. Rigaud owned a small retail store in Queens where he sold Haitian products, and he was somehow related to very influential people in Haiti. I remember one Sunday there was a whole story in *The New York Times Magazine* about his family. The deal was that since he could get hot cars out of the country, I would steal the cars he needed off the city streets.

"It was simple work. I had kids working for me. Kids from the neighborhood. Friends of theirs. Kids who were savvy and knew what was going on. They'd steal the cars for a hundred dollars apiece, and I'd accumulate ten or twelve cars. I'd park them in the rear of parking lots to get them off the street, and I'd get serial numbers for them from cars that were about to be scrapped. If I gave Eddy Rigaud the identification numbers for the cars in the afternoon, I had a manifest for exporting the cars the next day. Then I'd send all the cars down to the dock. The paperwork would just shuttle them through. The cars would be inspected to see if they had spare tires and no dents, just as they were described on the manifest. They were all new cars—little Fords and other compact, gas-efficient cars, because gasoline was a buck and a half a gallon in Haiti in those days. I'd get $750 a car. It was just a couple of hours' work for me, and then every five or six weeks I'd fly down to Port-au-Prince to pick up my money. That wasn't too bad either, because I'd always go down with counterfeit money and stolen traveler's checks and credit cards.

"And all the time I'm moving around with Paulie. I'm driving him here and I'm driving him there. I'd pick him up about ten o'clock in the morning and I wouldn't drop him off until after he had his liver and onions or steak and potatoes at three o'clock in the morning. Paulie never stopped moving and neither did I. There were a hundred schemes in a day and there were a thousand things to watch over. Paulie was like the boss of a whole area, and he watched over the guys who watched over the day-to-day gambling clubs, hot-car rings, policy banks, unions, hijackers, fences, loan sharks. These guys operated with Paulie's approval, like a franchise, and a piece of everything they made was supposed to go to him, and he was supposed to keep some and kick the rest upstairs. It was tribute. Like in the old country, except they're doing it in America.

"But for a guy who traveled all day and all night and ran as much as he did, Paulie didn't talk to six people. If there was a problem with the policy game, for instance, the dispute was presented to Steve DePasquale, who ran the numbers game for Paul. Then, in the morning, when Paulie met Steve, he would tell Paul what the problem was, and Paul would tell Steve what to do. Most of the time Paul just listened to what Steve said, because Steve really knew the numbers business better than Paul. Then he'd tell Steve to take care of it. If there was a beef over the crap games, he'd talk to his brother Babe. Union things would be referred to the union guys, whoever they happened to be, depending upon the specific unions and the kind of dispute. Everything was broken down to the lowest common denominator. Everything was one-on-one. Paulie didn't believe in conferences. He didn't want anyone hearing what he said, and he didn't even want anyone listening to what he was being told.

"The guys who reported to the people who reported to Paulie ranged from regular hustlers to legitimate businessmen. They were the street guys. They kept everything going. They thought up the schemes. They kept everything nice and oiled. And Paulie ran the whole thing in his head. He didn't have a secretary. He didn't take any notes. He never wrote anything down, and he never made a phone call unless it was from a booth, and then he'd only make an appointment for later. There were hundreds of guys who depended upon Paulie for their living, but he never paid out a dime. The guys who worked for Paulie had to make their own dollar. All they got from Paulie was protection from other guys looking to rip them off. That's what it's all about. That's what the FBI can never understand—that what Paulie and the organization offer is protection for the kinds of guys who can't go to the cops. They're like the police department for wiseguys. For instance, say I've got a fifty-thousand-dollar hijack load, and when I go to make my delivery, instead of getting paid, I get stuck up. What am I supposed to do? Go to the cops? Not likely. Shoot it out? I'm a hijacker, not a cowboy. No. The only way to guarantee that I'm not going to get ripped off by anybody is to be established with a member, like Paulie. Somebody who is a made man. A member of a crime family. A soldier. Then, if somebody fucks with you, they fuck with him, and that's the end of the ball game. Goodbye. They're dead, with the hijacked stuff rammed down their throats, as well as a lot of other things. Of course problems can arise when the guys sticking you up are associated with wiseguys too. Then there has to be a sit-down between your wiseguys and their wiseguys. What usually happens then is that the wiseguys divide whatever you stole for their own pockets and send you and the guy who robbed you home with nothing. And if you complain, you're dead.

"The other reason you have to be allied with somebody like Paulie is to keep the cops off your back. Wiseguys like Paulie have been paying off the cops for so many years that they have probably sent more cops' kids to college than anyone else. They're like wiseguy scholarships. Paulie or Babe, who handled most of that for Paul, had been taking care of cops since the guys were rookies on patrol. As they rose in rank, Babe kept taking care of them. When they needed help on a particular case, when they needed some information, Babe would get it for them. It was a two-way street. And when they took money from Babe, they knew it was safe. They developed a trust, the crooked cops and the wiseguys. The same thing went for everybody else. Politicians—not all politicians, but lots of them—needed help here and there. They got free storefront offices, they got the buses and sound systems they needed, they got the rank-and-file workers from the unions to petition when they needed it, and they got lawyers to help them poll-watch. You think that politicians aren't grateful? You think they don't remember their friends? And remember, it's not Paul Vario doing all this. Very few politicians ever meet Paul Vario. Not at all. This is all put together by businessmen connected to Paul. By lawyers indebted to Paulie. By building contractors, trucking company bosses, union guys, wholesale butchers, accountants, and people who work for the city—all the kinds of upstanding people who are totally legit. But behind it all there is usually a wiseguy like Paulie waiting for his payday.

"I was only a street guy and even I was living good. I'm doing everything. I'm stealing and scheming with two hands. When I was doing the cigarettes I was also lending money and I was taking a little book and I was running the stolen cars to Haiti. Tuddy got me a couple of grand setting some fires in supermarkets and restaurants. He and the owners cleaned up on the insurance money. I had learned how to use Sterno and toilet paper and how to mold it along the beams. You could light that with a match. No problem. But with a gasoline or kerosene fire you can't strike a match because of the fumes. The usual trick to start them is to place a lighted cigarette in a book of matches, so when the cigarette burns down to the matches the flash will ignite the room. By then you should be long gone.

"I made a lot of grief for people. I was always in a brawl. I didn't care. I had ten or twelve guys behind me. We'd go into a place in the Rockaways or some place in the Five Towns and we'd start to drink and eat. The places were usually half-assed connected. I mean, there was a bookmaker working out of the place or the owner was half a loan shark or they were selling swag out of the basement. I mean, we didn't go into little-old-lady restaurants like Schrafft's. We'd go to overpriced places with red walls and wall-to-wall carpets—rug joints, we'd call them—places where they had a few bucks invested. Maybe there'd be girls and some gambling. The owners or managers always knew us. We'd spend a buck. We'd really have a good time. We'd run up tabs. We'd sign all over the place. We'd sign over nice tips to the waiters and captains. Why not? We were good for it. We'd throw away more money in a night than a convention of dentists and their wives could spend in a week.

"Then, after a few weeks, when the tabs got to be a few grand, the owner would come over. He'd try to be nice. He'd try to be polite. But no matter how nice he tried to be, we'd always make it into a war. 'You fuck!' we'd scream. 'After all the business we brought you! You got the nerve to embarrass me in front of my friends? Call me a deadbeat? You fuck, you're dead. You miserable bastard cocksucker . . .' And so forth and so forth. You'd curse him and scream and throw a glass or plate and really work yourself up into a fit. I mean, even though deep down you knew you were full of shit, you were still ready to tear the bastard apart. By then somebody would usually pull you away, but you go out threatening to break his legs.

"Now the guy's got a problem. He knows who we are. He knows we could break his legs and he wouldn't be able to do anything about it. He can't go to the cops, because he's got little problems of his own and they'll shake him down for even more money than he's already giving them. Also, he knows we own the cops. If he makes too much noise, he gets his business burned down. There's nothing left for him to do but to go and see Paulie. He won't go direct. He might go to see someone who talks to Paulie. Frankie the Wop. Steve DePasquale. Bruno Facciolo.

"If the guy is well enough connected, there's a meet with Paulie. Let me tell you, Paulie's all heart. He sympathizes. He groans that he doesn't know what he's gonna do with us. He calls us psycho kids. He tells the guy that he talks to us over and over, but we never listen. He's got lots of problems with us. We're making trouble for him all over town. By then the guy knows it's time to say it would be worth his while to get us off his back. And one word leads to another, and pretty soon Paulie is on the guy's payroll for a couple of hundred a week, depending. Also, our bar bill is forgotten. It's so smooth.

"Now the guy's got Paulie for a partner. Any other problems, he goes to Paulie. Trouble with the cops? He can go to Paulie. Trouble with deliveries? Call Paulie. And, of course it goes both ways. Paulie can put people on the payroll for early parole, he can throw the liquor and food buying to friends of his. Plus the insurance. Who handles the insurance? That's always big with the politicians, and the politicians who are close to Paulie get the broker's fees. Plus the maintenance. Who cleans the joint? I mean a wiseguy can make a buck off every part of the business.

"And if he wants to bust it out, he can make even more money. Bank loans, for instance. A place has been in business say twenty, thirty years. It has a bank account. There's usually a loan officer who can come over and give you a loan for some improvements. Of course, if you can, you take the money and forget about the improvements, because you're expecting to bust the place out anyway.

"Also, if the place has a line of credit, as the new partner you can call up suppliers and have them send stuff over. You can call up other new distributors and get them to send over truckloads of stuff, since the place has a good credit rating. Wholesalers are looking for business. They don't want to turn you down. The salesmen want to make the sale. So you begin to order. You order cases of whiskey and wine. You order furniture. You order soap, towels, glasses, lamps, and food, and more food. Steaks. Two hundred filets. Crates of fresh lobster, crab, and shrimp. There is so much stuff coming in the door, it's like Christmas.

"And no sooner are the deliveries made in one door, you move the stuff out another. You sell the stuff to other places at a discount, but since you have no intention of paying for it in the first place, anything you sell it for is profit. Some guys use the stuff to start new places. You just milk the place dry. You bust it out. And, in the end, you can even burn the joint down for a piece of the insurance if it doesn't make enough. And nowhere does Paulie show up as a partner. No names. No signed pieces of paper. Paulie didn't need paper. Back then, in the sixties, aside from busting out joints, I know Paulie must have been getting a piece out of two, three dozen joints. A hundred here, two or three hundred there. He was doing beautifully. I remember once he told me he had a million and a half cash stashed away. He was always trying to talk me into saving a buck, but I couldn't. He said he kept his in a vault. I said I didn't have to save it because I would always make it.

"And I wasn't alone. Everyone I knew was into money schemes, and almost nobody ever got caught. That's what people from the outside don't understand. When you're doing different schemes, and everyone you know is doing these things, and nobody is getting caught, except by accident, you begin to get the message that maybe it's not so dangerous. And there were a million different schemes. You didn't have to sell swag or stick up anybody. One of the guys from the neighborhood was the manager of a local supermarket, one of those giant chain places with ten check-out lanes and a half-a-percent profit margin. He was always very straight, and nobody gave him much credit for anything until the week he went on vacation and the main office sent carpenters to install new check-out lanes. The carpenters got to the supermarket with their blueprints and charts and thought they were in the wrong place. It seemed that the market had eleven check-out lanes instead of ten. It didn't take long for the main office to catch on that someone had created his own check-out lane and that everything rung up on the eleventh register went into somebody else's pocket. When our pal got back from vacation the cops were waiting for him, but he was a local hero. He was fired, but because he dummied up and denied everything he never spent a day in jail.

"Also, hanging around and hustling means gambling. A day

doesn't go by without bets going down on this or that. When I had it, I'd bet a thousand dollars on the point spread of a basketball game, and I wasn't just betting one game. I could have ten thousand dollars riding on the wide, wide world of Saturday afternoon sports. Jimmy bet thirty, forty thousand dollars on football. We were at the track, shooting craps in Vegas, playing cards, and betting on anything that moved. Not a thrill like it in the world, especially when you had an edge.

"And there were guys, like Rich Perry, who could give you the edge. He was a genius. Long before anybody else thought of it, Perry had dozens of people all around the country watching college sports for him. He knew what kind of shape the field was in, the injuries to key players, whether the quarterback had been drunk, all kinds of things that gave his handicapping an edge. He used to find things in small-town college newspapers that never made the wires, and he had people calling him right up to the minute he was ready to bet.

"He was the brain who figured out how to increase the odds on the Superfecta bets at the trotters, so that for a while we were doing so well that rather than alert the track that we were winning all the time, we had to hire ten-percenters just to go and cash our winning tickets. There was so much money involved that some guys—those who had records and didn't want to be seen as the winners—even had cops they knew cashing the tickets for them.

"In the Superfecta races—which they have since banned—a bettor had to pick the first four winners in a race in their exact order. Perry figured that by getting two or three of the drivers to pull back or get their horses boxed in, we could eliminate two or three of the eight horses from the race. Then we could bet multiples of the remaining combinations at a minimal cost. For instance, it would normally cost $5,040 to buy the 1,680 three-dollar tickets to cover every possible combination of winning horses in an eight-horse race. Since the average Superfecta paid off about $3,000, there was no profit. By eliminating two or three horses from the race, we could almost guarantee ourselves a winning ticket, because mathematically there were now only 360 different winning combinations, and they only cost us $1,080 per ticket. When we had a fixed one going, we'd bet $25,000 or $50,000 on the race.

"We usually reached the drivers through 'hawks,' back-stretch regulars who lived and drank with the trainers and drivers. Sometimes they were wives, girlfriends, ex-drivers, retired trainers—people who really knew how the trotting world worked. We got to the hawks by just hanging around, taking their bets, loan-sharking them money, getting them good deals on hot televisions and designer clothes. You'd be amazed at how easy it all was.

"The Off-Track Betting computers eventually figured out that there was something wrong with the payoffs on the Superfecta, and they started an investigation and arrested almost the whole crew. The feds claimed they had made over three million dollars, but that was an exaggeration. There was a trial involving about two dozen drivers, trainers, and wiseguys. Bruno Facciolo and Paulie's son Peter beat the case, but Richie Perry was convicted. He got six months."

Five

I n 1965 Henry Hill was twenty-two, single, and delighted with his life. The days were long, and he enjoyed the continuous action. Hustling and schemes took up every waking hour. They were the currency of all conversation and they fired the day's excitement. In Henry's world, to hustle and score was to be alive. And yet Henry never bothered to accumulate money. In fact, as far as Henry could tell, none of the young men his age were saving any of the money they made. Within hours Henry's financial state would shift dramatically from black to red. Immediately after a score he could find himself with so many inch-thick stacks of new bills that he had to tuck them into his waistband when his pockets were full. A couple of days later he needed cash. The speed with which he and most of his friends were able to dissipate capital was dazzling. Henry simply gave money away. When he went to the bars and supper clubs of Long Beach and the Five Towns and the Rockaways, he overwhelmed the waiters and barmen with cash tips.

Henry spent his money until the cash in his pockets ran out, and then he would borrow from his pals until his next score paid off. He knew some crooked payday was never more than a week away. There were always at least a dozen dirty deals afoot. Aside from his own indulgences, his expenses were almost nonexistent. He had no dependents. He paid no taxes. He didn't even have a legitimate Social Security number. He had no insurance premiums to pay. He never paid his bills. He had no bank accounts, no credit cards, no credit ratings, and no checkbooks other than the phony ones he had bought from Tony the Baker. He still kept most of his clothes at his parents' house, though he rarely slept there. Henry preferred spending his nights at one of the Vario houses, on a sofa at one of the crew's haunts, or even in a free room at one or another of the airport or Rockaway motels where his pals were managers. He never woke up in pajamas. He was lucky to get his shoes off before passing out every night. Like those of most wiseguys, the events of his days were so spontaneously assembled, so serendipitous, that he never knew where the end of the day would find him. He could spend all of his average eighteen-hour day at the pizzeria or cabstand near Pitkin Avenue, or he could find himself in Connecticut with Paulie on a policy game matter, or in North Carolina with Jimmy on a cigarette run, or in Las Vegas with the crew spending the unexpected score he might have made during his totally unpredictable day.

There were girls who cost money, and there were girls who didn't. Neighborhood girls, barmaids, schoolteachers, waitresses, divorcées, office workers, beauticians, stewardesses, nurses, and housewives were always around for a day at the track, a night around the clubs, or a drunken morning in a motel. Some of them liked to dance. Some of them liked to drink. Henry was perfectly happy as a bachelor, taking whatever came up as it came up. His life was utterly unfettered.

HENRY: I was at the cabstand when Paulie junior came running in. He had been trying to go out with this girl Diane for weeks, and finally she had said okay, but she wouldn't go out with him unless she could double-date. Junior's desperate. He needs a backup guy. I'm in the middle of a cigarette deal, I've got some stolen sweaters in the back of the car. I'm supposed to meet Tuddy around eleven o'clock that night for some deal, and now Junior needs me as a chaperone. He says he has a date for the two of us at Frankie the Wop's Villa Capra. The Villa was a big hangout for the crew at the time. When I got there to do Junior a favor I was still in such a hurry to meet Tuddy I couldn't wait to get away.

KAREN: I couldn't stand him. I thought he was really obnoxious. Diane had this thing with Paul, but she and I were both Jewish, and she hadn't ever been out with an Italian before. She wanted to be cautious. Paul seemed nice, but she wanted their first date to be a double date. Little did she know Paul was married. She made me go along. But my date, who turned out to be Henry, was awful. It was obvious he didn't want to be there. He just kept fidgeting. He kept rushing everybody. He was ordering the check before we had dessert. When it was time to go home he was pushing me in the car and then pulling me out of the car. It was ridiculous. But Diane and Paul made us promise to meet them again the next Friday night. We agreed. Of course, when Friday night came around Henry stood me up. I had dinner with Diane and Paul that night. We were a trio instead of a double date. Then I made Paul take us looking for him.

HENRY: I'm walking along the street near the pizzeria when Paul pulls up and Karen comes charging out the car door. It was like a hit. She's really steamed. She comes running right up to me and yelling that nobody stands her up. "Nobody does that to me!" she's screaming on the street. I mean, she's loud. I put up my hands to calm her down. I told her that I didn't show because I was sure she was going to stand me up. I said I'd make it up to her. I said that I thought Diane and Paul wanted to go out without us. Anyway, by the time she finished screaming, we had made a date. That time I went.

KAREN: He took me to a Chinese restaurant in the Greenacres shopping mall on Long Island. This time he was really nice. He was an exciting guy. He seemed a lot older than his age, and he seemed to know more than the other boys I'd been out with. When I asked what he did, he said he was a bricklayer, and he even showed me his union card. He said he'd had a job as a manager at the Azores, which I already knew was a very good place in Lido Beach. We had a nice leisurely dinner. Then we got into his car, which was brand new, and we went to some Long Island nightclubs and listened to music. We danced. Everybody knew him. When I walked into these places with Henry everyone came over. He introduced me to everyone. Everybody wanted to be nice to him. And he knew how to handle it all. It was so different from the other boys I went out with. They all seemed like kids. They used to take me to movies, bowling, the kinds of things you do when you're eighteen and your boyfriend is twenty-two.

HENRY: Karen turned out to be a lot of fun. She was very lively. She liked going to the places, and she was great-looking. She had violet eyes, just like Elizabeth Taylor—or that's what everybody said. We started going out to some of the clubs I knew. We'd go to the 52/52 Club, in Long Beach, near Philly Basile's Rumors Disco. We went to piano bars I knew. Places I had been to with Paulie. Places where I knew the owners and bartenders and managers and they knew me. The first time I went to pick her up at her parents' house for a night at the Palm Shore Club, I got all dressed up. I wanted to make a good impression. I felt great, but as soon as she opened the door, instead of being happy to see me, she screamed. Her eyes bulged out of her head like a monster movie. I looked around. I couldn't figure out what was going on. Then she pointed at my neck. "Turn it around! Turn it around!" she says, really scared. When I looked down I saw that she was pointing at my medal. I had a gold chain my mother gave me and on it was a tiny gold cross.

KAREN: He was going to meet my parents. They knew I had been seeing him, and they didn't like it that he wasn't Jewish. I told them that he was half Jewish. I told them that his mother was Jewish. They still weren't happy, but what could they do? So here he comes to meet them for the first time. The bell rings. I'm so excited. My grandmother is there. She was really Orthodox. When she died they brought the Torah to her house. I was already a little nervous. I go to the door and there he is wearing black silk slacks, a white shirt opened down to his belly, and a powder blue sport jacket. But what I see first is this huge gold cross, I mean it was hanging around his neck. It went from his neck to his rib cage. I closed the door to a crack so nobody could see him and told him to turn the cross around so my family wouldn't see it. When he did, we walked inside, but by then I was in a cold sweat. I mean, they weren't even crazy about him being just half Jewish. And his family wasn't too happy either. He had a sister, Elizabeth, who was studying to be a nun, who really didn't like me. One day when I went to call at his house, she opened the door. Her hair was in curlers. She was kind of stuck-up, and she hadn't expected me. I never saw anybody so angry.

HENRY: Once she took me to her parents' country club. The place had its own nine-hole golf course and tennis courts and swimming pool, and all those rich people walking around and diving off boards, smashing tennis balls, and swimming lap after lap with rubber caps and goggles. I never saw so many rich people jumping around so much for nothing. And then, as I looked around, I realized that there wasn't one thing these people were doing that I knew how to do. Nothing. I couldn't dive. I couldn't swim. I couldn't play tennis. I couldn't play golf. I couldn't do shit.

KAREN: I started going out to places with Henry I had never been before. I'm eighteen. I'm really dazzled. We went to the Empire Room to hear Shirley Bassey. We went to the Copa. The kids I knew went there once, maybe, on their prom night. Henry went there all the time. He was known there. He knew everybody. We always sat up close to the stage, and one night Sammy Davis Jr. sent us champagne. On crowded nights, when people were lined up outside and couldn't get in, the doormen used to let Henry and our party in through the kitchen, which was filled with Chinese cooks, and we'd go upstairs and sit down immediately. There was nothing like it. I didn't think that there was anything strange in any of this—you know, a twenty-two-year-old with such connections. I didn't know from anything. I just thought he knew these people.

HENRY: We were going out every night. Karen had a job working as a dental assistant during the day, but every night we were together. I mean we were really close. I was having a great time with her. I think I loved the idea that she was not from the neighborhood. That she was used to fine things. That she was a very classy girl. We started going to weddings. Some of the Vario kids were getting married at the time, and that sort of threw us together even more closely. In my upbringing, if you took a girl to a wedding it was important. Soon we started to sneak away for weekends on our own. Karen used to tell her parents she was going to Fire Island with some girlfriends, and her parents would drop her at the Valley Stream station. Then I'd pick her up.

KAREN: As soon as I started going steady with Henry, this guy across the street named Steve started coming around. I had known him for years and I never thought anything about him. Then late one afternoon, right after I had come home from work, the guy was near my house and asked if I'd help him pick up something nearby. I don't remember what it was or where we were supposed to go. It was like he needed help on an errand. It wasn't important. He was the guy across the street. I told my mother where we were going. Mostly I wanted to go with him because I liked his car. He had a Corvette. He was very nice, as usual, until we got near Belmont racetrack, about three miles from home. Then he pulled the car over. He started putting his arm around me. I was amazed. I also got angry. I told him to stop. He refused. He said I had grown up. The usual garbage. I got the heel of my hand and I smacked it hard across his face. He was surprised. I hit him again. He got really angry. He started the car up and pulled out onto Hempstead Turnpike. Then he jammed on the brakes, and I almost went through the windshield. He leaned over and opened the door and shoved me out and drove away. I got hit with a spray of gravel and dirt. It was terrible. It must have been about six-thirty, seven o'clock at night. I was terrified. It was the guy who had been bad, but I was ashamed. I was afraid to call home. I knew my mother would be upset. She would start the third degree right there on the phone while I'm still pulling gravel out of my hair. I couldn't stand being yelled at. So instead I called Henry. I told him what had happened and where I was. He came and got me in minutes and he drove me home.

HENRY: I went crazy. I wanted to kill the guy. All the way driving her home Karen is telling me what happened, and I'm getting hotter and hotter. The minute we got to her house she ran inside. I looked across the street. I see the Corvette parked out front. The house was full of miserable rich fucks. There were three brothers. All three of them had Corvettes. I had a hot .22-caliber short-eye automatic. I got a box of shells out of the glove compartment. Looking at the fuck's car, I started to load. I was so mad I was ready to shoot the guy and worry about it later. I walked across the street and rang the bell. No answer. I rang again. Nothing. I had the gun in my pants pocket. Now I walked around the driveway toward the backyard. Steve and his brothers were sitting there. Steve started to come toward me. He must have thought we were going to talk. Man-to-man bullshit. The minute he was in my reach I grabbed him by the hair with my right hand and pulled his face down nice and low. At the same time I took the gun out of my left pocket and I started to smack him across the face. He screamed, "He's got a gun! He's got a gun!" I can feel his face go. I shoved the gun inside his mouth and moved it around like a dinner gong. The brothers are so scared they can't move. Fucks. I swear I would have shot them if they came toward me. Somebody from inside the house said they called the cops. Before the cops arrived I gave Steve a few more belts. I think that when he yelled about the gun it stopped me from killing him. I gave him another couple of smacks in the head and left him crying in the driveway. He had pissed all over himself.

I went back across the street to Karen. She was standing at the side door. I gave her the gun and told her to hide it. She put it in the milk box. Then I pulled my car around the block and tossed the box of shells underneath. When I walked back to Karen's house there were fourteen Nassau County police cars outside. The cops were looking for a gun. I said I didn't have a gun. I said the guy was crazy. The cops searched me and my car from top to bottom. No gun. Then they escorted me out of Nassau County to the Brooklyn line. When we pulled away from the curb, I was afraid they would spot the shells, but they didn't.

KAREN: He came over to the side door. I could see he was hurrying. He said, "Hide it." He had something cupped in the palm of his hand. I took it and looked down. It was a gun. It was small, heavy, and gray. I couldn't believe it. It felt so cold. It was a thrill just to hold it. Everything was so wild I began to feel high. I didn't want to bring the gun into my house, because my mother had eyes all over. She would have found it. So I put it in the milk box right outside the door. In a few minutes Henry comes walking back. The police were waiting. They had spoken to Steve and other people across the street first. It was the biggest thing anyone had ever seen on our block. I was really excited. I loved that Henry had done all this for me. It made me feel important. And then, when the cops asked him if he had a gun, he was so calm. He just said that the guy across the street was crazy. The cops had already heard about what the guy did to me, and Henry was so insistent that he didn't have a gun that when they went back to the guy he began to say that maybe it was a "metallic object." Finally the cops said they would escort Henry out of the neighborhood to make sure there was no more trouble.

HENRY: By this time I'm getting tired of all this sneaking around. Three months I'm going out with Karen every day, and I can't go to her house when her grandmother's there, and her mother keeps telling us we're not meant for each other. My parents are doing the same kind of stuff. It was like we were alone against everybody. Then that business with the guy across the street happened, and I decided we ought to elope. If we were married, then everybody would have to deal with us. Finally, after a couple of false starts, we decided to drive down to Maryland and get married. Just do it. We needed a witness, so I got Lenny to come along. When we got to Maryland we started talking to some kids in a car next to ours waiting at a traffic light. They said there was a three-day wait in Maryland but that you could get married right away in North Carolina. So we went to Walden, North Carolina, instead. We got our physicals and blood tests and then we went right to the justice of the peace. By now our witness, Lenny, has passed out, sleeping in the backseat of the car, so the wife of the justice of the peace was our witness.

KAREN: Henry and I got back and told my parents. First they were stunned, but within half an hour they seemed to come around. We had done it; there was nothing they could do. They were not the kind of people to kick their children out of the house. And I wasn't the kind of young bride who knew what to do. I couldn't boil an egg. We were both kids. They suggested that we stay with them. My parents fixed the upstairs part of the house for us, and we started living at home. It would never have dawned on Henry to get a place of our own. In fact, he liked living in my house. He enjoyed my family. He liked my mother's cooking. He joked with her. He was very warm to her. I could see that he really enjoyed being a part of the family. And slowly my mother and father got to like him. They had three daughters, and now, in a funny way, they had finally gotten their son. He was very sincere about the religious problem and said that he would convert. He began taking religious instructions. He went to work every day. We all thought he was a bricklayer. He had a union card and everything. What did we know? It never occurred to me that it was strange that he had such nice smooth hands for a construction worker. By August, Henry had done so well with the religious instructions that we had a nice Jewish wedding. Even my grandmother was almost happy.

Six

I t took a while before Karen figured out exactly what line of work her husband was in. She knew he was a knock-around guy. She knew that he could be tough. She had once watched him take on three men, who turned out to be football players from New Jersey, with a tire iron outside Jackie Kannon's Rat Fink Room in Manhattan. She knew that some of his friends had been to prison. And she knew that he sometimes carried a gun. But back in the early 1960s, before Mario Puzo's *Godfather* codified the lifestyle, before Joseph Valachi decided to sing, and before Senator John McClellan's Permanent Subcommittee on Investigations listed the names and photographs of over five thousand organized-crime members, wiseguys were still a relatively unknown phenomenon to those outside their tiny world. Certainly Karen Freid Hill, from Lawrence, Long Island, had no reason to believe that she would wind up in the middle of a grade-B movie. All she knew was that her husband's main income came from his job as a bricklayer and low-level union official. There were mornings when she had even dropped him off at various jobs and watched him disappear into the construction site. He brought home $135 a week. They were paying off a bedroom suite at so much a week. He had a new car. But she also knew he had hit the number for a couple of thousand dollars just before they were married. His friends all had jobs. They were construction workers and truck drivers; they owned small restaurants, worked in the garment center or at the airport.

KAREN: Sometimes I think that if my mother hadn't fought it so much I might not have insisted upon being so blind. But she was so set on breaking us up that I was just as determined not to give in. I was going to be as stubborn as she was. I was not going to give him up. I wasn't going to prove her right. I wasn't going to let her win. I made excuses for him to her. And as I gave her those excuses, I found that I was giving them to myself. If he stayed out late, I always said he was with the boys. If he didn't call at a certain time, I'd tell my mother he'd called earlier. And after a while life just became normal. I know it sounds crazy, but it all happened so gradually, day by day, so that you're going along before you know you've changed.

I've talked to people since those days, and I guess I must have had a predisposition for that life in the first place. I know there are women who would have gotten out of there the minute their boyfriend gave them a gun to hide. "A gun!" they would have yelled. "Eek! Who needs you? Get lost!" That's what a lot of girls, a lot of my own girlfriends would have said the minute some guy put a gun in their hands. But I've got to admit the truth—it turned me on.

The first time it really dawned on me about how different his friends were from the way I was raised came when Helene, the wife of Bobby DeSimone, one of his friends, was having a hostess party. We had been married a few months, and I hadn't really seen that much of his friends and their wives without him before. Helene was selling copper-and-wood wall decorations. I had never known anyone who sold things to friends in her own house. Henry said he'd drop me off, spend some time with the guys, and pick me up later. Bobby and Helene's place was in Ozone Park. It wasn't the greatest. A couple of rooms up one flight. Everybody knew each other, I was the new girl in the group, and they were all very, very nice. They really made me feel at home, a part of the crowd. But then, when they started talking, I was shocked by what I heard. One woman, I remember, was talking about waiting three years for her husband, who was away in jail. I couldn't believe it. My God! Three years! I thought I could never wait that long.

It was the first time I had ever had a conversation where the women talked about jail. They made jail very real. They knew the good prisons and the bad ones. They never talked about what their husbands had done to get sent to jail. That just wasn't ever a part of the conversation. What they discussed was how the prosecutors and the cops lied. How people picked on their husbands. How their husbands had done something everybody was doing but had just had the bad luck to get caught. Then in the same breath they would discuss the bus rides up to see their husbands and what they wore on the long trips and how the kids acted up and how hard it was to make ends meet when their husbands were away.

And as they talked I began to look at them, and I saw that they looked bad. Some of them were even disheveled. I saw that they had bad skin. It was obvious that some of them didn't take care of themselves. I mean, they didn't look very good. A few of them had bad teeth. They had missing teeth. You would never see mouths like that where I grew up. Also, they weren't very well dressed. The stuff they wore was unfashionable and cheap. A lot of polyester and double-knit pants suits. And later, when I got to meet their kids, I was amazed at how much trouble the kids gave them. Their kids were always in trouble. They were always in fights. They wouldn't go to school. They'd disappear from home. The women would beat their kids blue with broom handles and leather belts, but the kids didn't pay any attention. The women all seemed to be on the edge of just making it. They were all very nervous and tense. Their younger kids looked dirty all the time. It was that thing some kids have of looking dirty even after their baths. That was the look.

If you listened, you never heard such woe. One of these hostess parties could have kept a soap opera going for years. The first night I was with them, most of the conversation was about their friend Carmen. Carmen wasn't there. Carmen was forty and her husband was away doing time. He was her third husband. She had three sons, one by each of her husbands, and the kids were a nightmare. To make ends meet Carmen was selling stolen credit cards and swag. Just a week before the party Carmen's oldest, a teenager, was in a card game with another kid and an argument began over a ten-dollar bet. Her son got mad, pulled a gun out of his pocket, and it went off. The other kid died, and Carmen's son was arrested. When Carmen's mother, the kid's grandmother, heard that her grandson had been arrested for murder, she dropped dead on the spot, leaving Carmen with a husband and son in jail and a mother in the funeral parlor.

By the time Henry picked me up I was dizzy. When we got home I told him I was upset. He was calm. He said very few people went to jail. He said there was nothing to worry about. He would talk about the money and how hundreds of his friends were doing things that might be against the law, but that they were all making money, and none of them were getting caught. Swag. Gambling. Cigarettes. Nobody went to jail for things like that. Also, he knew the right lawyers. The courts. The judges. The bail bondsmen. I wanted to believe him. He made it sound so easy, and I loved the idea of all that money.

Then one day you read a newspaper story about people you know, and you just can't put the names you're reading together with the people you know. Those I knew were not individuals you thought the papers would write about. I saw one story years ago in the *Daily News* about Frankie Manzo, Paulie's friend. The newspaper misspelled his name as Francesco Manza and said he was an organized-crime soldier. The Frankie Manzo I knew dressed and acted like a working man. He had the Villa Capra restaurant in Cedarhurst, and I had seen him carrying packages of groceries into the kitchen, moving cars from out front, wiping the crumbs off tables, and working day and night in his own kitchen.

To me none of these men looked like big shots. None of them had everything together. There was always something missing. I mean, if they had nice new cars and good clothes, then their houses were in poor areas or their wives looked hard. Tommy DeSimone always drove around in a brand-new car and wore expensive clothes, and he and Angela lived in a two-room tenement slum. I remember thinking, If these are the gangsters they write about in the newspapers, there must be something wrong. I knew Henry and his friends weren't angels, but if this was the Cosa Nostra, it sure didn't feel like it.

It was after Henry and I got married the second time that I really became a part of his world. We had an old-fashioned Italian wedding, except we had a Jewish ceremony and a rabbi. Four of the Vario brothers were there. So were their wives and their sons. It was the first time I was introduced to all of them at once. It was crazy. The five Vario brothers had at least two sons each, and for some unbelievable reason they'd each named two of their sons either Peter or Paul. There had to be a dozen Peters and Pauls at the wedding. Also, three of the Vario brothers were married to girls named Marie, and they all had daughters named Marie. By the time Henry finished introducing me to everyone I thought I was drunk.

Only Paul Vario wasn't at the wedding. I had seen that Paulie was like a father to Henry, much more than Henry's real father, who he rarely saw and almost never spoke to. Henry was with Paulie almost every day. When I asked where Paulie was, Henry just said he couldn't make it. Later I found out that he was serving sixty days for contempt after he'd refused to testify before a Nassau County grand jury looking into a Long Island bookmaking ring. I found out after a while that Paul and his sons Peter and Paul junior were always doing thirty or sixty days for contempt. It went with the territory. It didn't seem to bother them. They just accepted going to jail for a little while. They did their time at the Nassau County jail, where they were very well known and where they had so many people paid off that they eventually wound up getting indicted for bribing the whole jail. I remember that the warden and over a dozen guards were indicted. It was a real mess. It was all over the papers. But by then I knew what was going on. I knew it was not normal, not the way I had been raised, but it didn't seem wrong either. I was in the environment and I just went along.

I'd have to say that Henry's friends were all very hard workers and hustlers. Paulie had the flower store on Fulton Avenue and he had the auto junkyard on Flatlands Avenue. Tuddy Vario had the cabstand. Lenny had the restaurant. Everyone worked somewhere. Nobody loafed. If anything, everyone was always hustling all the time. I never saw people carrying guns. Later I found out that most of the time their wives were carrying them.

I knew Jimmy Burke was smuggling cigarettes, but even that didn't seem like a crime. It was more as if Jimmy was enterprising. He was hustling to make a few extra bucks carting cigarettes. Jimmy's wife Mickey, Phyllis Vario, everyone made it all look so natural. Anyone who wanted to make a few extra bucks had to go out and get it. You couldn't wait for a handout. That was the general attitude. The other women accepted hustling cigarettes, selling swag, and even hijacking as normal for any ambitious guy who wanted to make decent money. It was almost as though I should be proud that I had the kind of husband who was willing to go out and risk his neck to get us the little extras.

HENRY: Then I got arrested. It was a crazy bust. It shouldn't have happened, but none of them should ever happen. They are always more because of your own stupidity than any cop's smarts. There were about twenty of us in Jimmy Burke's basement shooting craps. We were waiting for Tommy DeSimone to arrive from Washington, D.C., with a truckload of cigarettes. It was Thursday, the day we usually got our deliveries and loaded up our own cars and vans. Then on Fridays, between eleven-thirty and two o'clock in the afternoon, we made all our sales. During the morning I'd go to the construction jobs, and by noon or one o'clock in the afternoon I'd go to the sanitation depots and factories, and by two o'clock I'd have made my grand or fifteen hundred dollars for the day.

When Tommy finally got in, it turned out that he only had the big-brand stuff. He had the Chesterfields and Camels and Lucky Strikes, but he didn't have what we called the fill-ins, the less popular brands like Raleighs and L&Ms and Marlboros. Jimmy asked me to go down to Baltimore and pick up the fill-ins. He said if I left right away I could be there early enough to get a load the minute the places opened and be back in plenty of time to sell my stuff before noon. I had a lot of customers who wanted off-brands and I agreed. Lenny, who had been helping me load, wanted to come along. I had about six hundred bucks from the crap game. Jimmy threw me the keys to one of the cars he used and Lenny and I took off.

It was about midnight when we got to Baltimore. The cigarette places didn't open until six in the morning. I had been there before and I knew there were a bunch of strip joints along Baltimore Street. Lenny had never been to Baltimore. We started hitting the joints. We listened to a little jazz. Some B-girls in one place started hustling drinks out of us. We're buying them nine-dollar ginger ales and they're playing with our legs. By two or three in the morning we're pretty smashed. We must have gone for a hundred and fifty bucks with these same two girls. It was very obvious that they liked us. They said that their boss was watching, so they couldn't leave with us, but if we waited outside around back they'd meet us as soon as they got off. Lenny's all excited. I'm all excited. We go around back and wait. We waited for an hour. Then two hours. And then we just looked at each other and laughed. We couldn't stop laughing. We'd gotten taken like chumps. We were two dumb gloms. So we drove over to the cigarette joints and waited for them to open.

The next thing I know somebody's waking us up at eight o'clock in the morning. We'd overslept. Now we were two hours late getting back for eleven. We loaded five hundred cartons in the car, and there wasn't enough room in the trunk. We had to take the rear seat out and leave it at the wholesaler's. We broke up three cartons evenly and placed a blanket on top of them to look like a rear seat. I started going. We're doing eighty, ninety miles an hour during some stretches. I felt if I could make up fifteen minutes here and ten minutes there I'd knock time off the trip.

We made it all the way to the turnpike Exit 14 in Jersey City. I had seen the speed trap and I jammed on my brakes. Too late. I saw one of the radio cars pull out toward us. When I jammed on the brakes the cigarettes in the rear seat were thrown all over the place. As the cop came closer, Lenny scrambled into the rear and tried to rearrange the blanket, but he couldn't manage too well. The cop wanted my license and registration. I told him the car belonged to a friend of mine. I kept looking for the registration to the car, but I couldn't find it. The cop was getting impatient and wanted to know my friend's name. I didn't know whose name the car was in, so I couldn't even tell him that. It was a brand-new 1965 Pontiac, and he couldn't believe that somebody would lend me the car and I wouldn't even know his name. I tried to stall, and finally I mentioned the guy whose name I thought it might be in, and I no sooner gave him the name than I found the registration, and of course it was in somebody else's name.

Now the guy was suspicious. He finally looked in the back of the car, and he saw cigarettes all over the place. He called for a backup car and they took us in. Now I had problems. I'm going to have the distinction of getting Paul Vario's favorite son his first pinch. I could hear the noise from here. I told the cops that I didn't even know Lenny. I said that I had picked him up on the road, that he was hitchhiking. No good. They brought the two of us in. Lenny knew what to do. He had been groomed. He kept his mouth shut except to give his name. He signed nothing and he asked no questions. I called Jimmy, and he got the lawyer and bondsmen.

By two o'clock in the afternoon we came before a local judge and were held in fifteen hundred bail each. Our lawyers and bail hadn't arrived, so they took us upstairs. We got our bedrolls and were put in with a lot of other guys. We had some cigarettes on us and we gave them to the guys and we just sat and waited. In an hour or so we heard a hack yell, "Hill and Vario! Bag and baggage!" We were free, but now I wasn't worried about the cigarettes. I was worried about Paulie. And I was worried about Karen.

KAREN: He called up and said he'd had a little trouble. It turned out he and Lenny were arrested for transporting untaxed cigarettes. It wasn't a big crime, but he was arrested. I still thought he was a bricklayer. Sure, I knew he was doing some things that weren't absolutely straight. I mean, some of my friends and relatives used to buy the cigarettes. Nobody complained, believe me. One time I remember Henry and his friends came up with some imported Italian knit shirts. They had crates of them. There were four different styles in twenty colors, and all of us were wearing Italian knits for a year and a half. It was a matter of all of Henry's friends being involved and all of their girlfriends and wives and children being involved. There were so many of us, and we all tended to only hang out together. There were absolutely no outsiders. Nobody who wasn't involved was ever invited to go anywhere or be a part of anything. And because we were all a part of that life, soon the world began to seem normal. Birthday parties. Anniversaries. Vacations. We all went together and we were always the same crowd. There was Jimmy and Mickey and, later, their kids. There was Paul and Phyllis. There was Tuddy and Marie. Marty Krugman and Fran. We went to each other's houses. The women played cards. The men did their own thing.

But I was mortified by his arrest. I felt ashamed. I never mentioned it to my mother. But nobody else in the crowd seemed to care. The possibility of being arrested was something that existed for anyone who hustled. Our husbands weren't brain surgeons. They weren't bankers or stockbrokers. They were blue-collar guys, and the only way they could ever get extra money, real extra money, was to go out and hustle, and that meant cutting a few corners.

Mickey Burke and Phyllis and lots of the other women kept saying that it was a joke. That nothing was going to happen. That it was just business. Jimmy was taking care of everything. He had friends even in Jersey City. I would see. I would see how dopey I was worrying about such petty stuff. Instead of worrying I should be enjoying myself. Every time I asked Henry what was happening in his case he said Jimmy was handling it. Finally, one day—he must have been home a couple of hours—he asks if I remembered the Jersey incident. "What happened?" I asked, all upset, like I'm Bette Davis sending her husband to the chair. "I got fined fifty bucks," he said. He was laughing.

Looking back, I was really pretty naïve, but I also didn't want to think about what was going on too much. I didn't want my mother to be right. She had been on my back since we eloped. She felt Henry was bad for me, and when she realized I was a couple of months pregnant she had a fit. Morning, noon, and night I heard stories about how he drank too much, hung around with bad people, didn't come home until late, and wasn't a solid kind of man like my father. She didn't like the idea that I kept my job as a dental assistant after I got married. She insisted that Henry made me keep the job for the money. Day after day she was needling me, and day after day I was defending him against her. I would never give her the satisfaction that she was right, but she watched everything he did, and when he was gone she'd bring up the things she didn't like. He slept too late. He came home too late. He gambled. He drank.

We must have been married a little more than a month when one night he didn't come home at all. He had come home after midnight a few times, but this time it was well after midnight and he was still not home. There wasn't even a call. I was waiting upstairs in our apartment. My mother, who was like a shark smelling blood, began to circle. She had been downstairs in bed, but she had apparently been awake waiting to hear what time Henry got home. I'll bet she stayed awake every night waiting to see what time he got home. When it got to be one o'clock in the morning, she was on full alert. By two o'clock she knocked at my door. By three o'clock we're all in the living room waiting for Henry.

My parents' house had a big front door, and my mother, my father, and I were seated in a semicircle right behind it. "Where is he?" she asked. "Your father would never stay out this late without calling," she said. My father was a saint. He never said a word. In the forty years they were married my father never stayed out all night. In fact, he rarely went out at all without telling my mother where he was going. He never once missed the train he was supposed to be on, and when he drove in to work he was never more than five or ten minutes late getting home. And then he'd spend half the night explaining how bad the traffic was and how he couldn't get through.

She kept it up. He wasn't Jewish—what did I expect? By four o'clock in the morning she started to scream that we were keeping my father up. Good thing he didn't have to work in the morning. It just kept going on and on. I thought I was going to die.

It must have been six-thirty in the morning when I heard a car pull up. We were all still sitting in the living room. It was like a wake. I jumped up and looked out the window. It wasn't his car, but I saw him in the backseat. I saw that Paulie's son, Peter Vario, was driving and that one of Lenny Vario's sons was in the car too. My mother had already opened the front door, and the minute he hit the sidewalk she confronted him. "Where were you? Where have you been? Why didn't you call? We were all worried to death! A married man doesn't stay out like this!" She was yelling at him so fast and so loud that I don't think I said a word. I just stood there. I was nineteen and he was twenty-two, but we were such kids.

I remember he stopped, he looked at her, looked at me, and then, without a word, he got back in the car and drove away. My mother just stood there. He was gone. I started to cry. "Normal people don't live this way," she said.

HENRY: I was so smashed that night, all I remember is getting out of the car and seeing Karen's mother standing on the porch screaming at me. So this is being married? I thought and sank back in the car. I went to Lenny's to sleep. I was starting to realize that Karen and I were going to have to move. I waited until later in the day before calling Karen. I told her the truth. I had been at Lenny's son Peter's bachelor party. We'd taken Petey out drinking. We'd been drinking from early afternoon. We'd been to Jilly's, the Golden Torch, Jackie Kannon's Rat Fink Room. I didn't tell her about the hookers on First Avenue, but I did tell her about going for a steam bath at two in the morning to sober up and still being too drunk to drive myself home.

We made a date for dinner. When I picked her up at the house she ran out the door before her mother knew I was there. Having her mother as a common enemy brought us together. It was like our first date.

KAREN: Some of the marriages were worse than others. Some were even good. Jimmy and Mickey Burke got on. So did Paul and Phyllis. But none of us knew what our husbands were doing. We weren't married to nine-to-five guys. When Henry started making the trips for the cigarettes, for instance, I knew he'd be gone a couple of days at a time. I saw the way all the other men and their wives lived. I knew he wasn't going to be home every night. Even when we were keeping company, I knew on Friday night he was going to hang out with the guys or play cards. Friday was always the card-playing night. Later I found out that it was also the girlfriend night. Everybody who had a girlfriend took her out on Friday night.

Nobody took his wife out on Friday night. The wives went out on Saturday night. That way there were no accidents of running into somebody's wife when they were with their girlfriends. One

Saturday Henry took me to the Copa. We were walking to our table when there was Patsy Fusco, big as a pig, sitting with his girlfriend. I really got upset. I knew his wife. She was a friend of mine. Was I supposed to keep my mouth shut? I didn't want to be put in this spot. Then I saw that Henry was going to go over and say hello to Patsy. I couldn't believe it. He was going to put me right in a box. I refused to go. I just stood there between the tables in the lounge and wouldn't budge, at least not in Patsy's direction. Henry was surprised, but he could see I was serious, so he just nodded to Patsy and we went to our own table. It was one of those minor things that reveal a lot. I think that for a split second Henry was going over to see Patsy because he forgot he was with me. He forgot it wasn't Friday night.

Seven

Back in the early 1950s the Idlewild Golf Course in Queens was converted into a vast 5,000-acre airport. Within a few months the local hoods from East New York, South Ozone Park, Howard Beach, Maspeth, and the Rockaways knew every back road, open cargo bay, freight office, loading platform, and unguarded gate in the facility. The airport was a huge sprawling area, the equivalent in size of Manhattan Island from the Battery to Times Square. It came to employ more than 50,000 people, had parking facilities for over 10,000 cars, and had a payroll of over a half a billion dollars a year. Wiseguys who could barely read learned about bills of lading, shipping manifests, and invoices. They found that information about valuable cargo was available from a stack of over a hundred unguarded pigeonholes used by shipping brokers in the U.S. Customs Building, a chaotically run two-story structure with no security, located a mile from the main cargo terminals. There cargo brokers, runners, clerks, and customs officers dealt daily with the overabundance of paperwork required for international shipments. There were over forty brokers employing a couple of hundred runners, many of them part-time workers, so it was not difficult to slip orders from the shelves or copy information about valuable cargo, to pass on to whoever wanted it.

By the early sixties, when cargo worth $30 billion a year was passing through Kennedy Airport, the challenge of relieving airlines of their cargo and freight carriers of their trucks had become the principal pastime for scores of local wiseguys. Jimmy Burke was the king. Furs, diamonds, negotiable securities, even guns were routinely pilfered or hijacked from the airport by Burke and his crew.

Information was channeled to Jimmy from every corner of the airport. Cargo handlers in debt to loan sharks knew they could work off their obligations with a tip on a valuable cargo. One Eastern Airlines truck driver indebted to one of Jimmy's bookies agreed to "accidentally drop" some mail pouches along the road leading from behind the plane loading area to the post office. The pouches turned out to contain $2 million in cash, money orders, and stocks. The airport was also an ideal place to use stolen credit cards to buy thousands of dollars' worth of airline tickets, which could then either be cashed in for full reimbursement or sold at 50 percent discounts to willing customers. The customers were often legitimate businessmen and show business celebrities whose travel costs were high. Frank Sinatra Jr.'s manager, Tino Barzie, was one of the crew's best customers. Barzie, whose real name is Dante Barzottini, bought more than fifty thousand dollars' worth of tickets at half their face value and then used them to transport Sinatra and a group of eight persons accompanying him around the country. Barzie was eventually caught and convicted of the charges.

Incidents of larceny were a daily occurrence at the airport, and those imprudent enough to talk about what was going on were routinely murdered, usually just days after going to the police. Corrupt cops on Jimmy Burke's payroll tipped him off about informants and potential witnesses. The bodies, sometimes as many as a dozen a year, were left strangled, trussed, and shot in the trunks of stolen cars abandoned in the long-term parking lots that surrounded the airport. With Henry Hill, Tommy DeSimone, Angelo Sepe, Skinny Bobby Amelia, Stanley Diamond, Joey Allegro, and Jimmy Santos, an ex-cop who did time for a stickup and decided to join the bad guys, Jimmy Burke raised robbing the airport to an art form.

Occasionally a criminal savant finds a particular field in which he excels and in which he delights. For Jimmy Burke it was hijacking. To watch Jimmy Burke tear through the cartons of a newly hijacked trailer was to watch a greedy child at Christmas. He would rip into the first few stolen crates until his passion to possess and touch each of the stolen items abated. Then he would peer inside the crates, pat their sides, sniff the air around them, lift them in his arms, and begin to carry them off the trucks, even though he always hired neighborhood guys for the heavy lifting. When Jimmy was unloading a truck, there was almost a beatific contentedness glowing on his sweat-drenched face. Henry often thought that his friend Jimmy was never happier than when unloading a freshly hijacked truck.

In addition to his uncanny talent for making money, Jimmy Burke was also one of the most feared men in the city's organized-crime establishment. He had a reputation for violence that dated back to his early years in prison, when he was rumored to have done killings there for mob chiefs who were in prison with him at the time. His explosive temper terrified some of the most terrifying men in the city, and the stories about him left even his friends a little chilled. He seemed to possess a bizarre combination of generosity and an enthusiasm for homicide. On one occasion Jimmy is said to have given the elderly, impoverished mother of a young hood five thousand dollars. The woman's son was said to have owed his mother the money but had refused to pay her. Jimmy was apparently so incensed at this lack of regard for motherhood that he gave the woman the five thousand in the morning, claiming it was from her son, and then allegedly killed the woman's son before dusk. In 1962, when Jimmy and Mickey decided to get married, he discovered that Mickey was being bothered by an old boyfriend, who was calling her on the phone, yelling at her on the street, and circling her house for hours in his car. On the day Jimmy and Mickey Burke were married the police found the remains of his wife's old boyfriend. The body had been carefully cut into over a dozen pieces and tossed all over the inside of his car.

But it was Jimmy's talent for making money that clearly won him a place in the hearts of the mob's rulers. He was so extraordinary that, in an unprecedented move, the Colombo crime family in Brooklyn and the Lucchese family in Queens negotiated to share his services. The notion that two Italian-run crime families would even consider having a sit-down to negotiate the services of an Irishman only added to the Burke legend.

Still, none of his friends ever really knew very much about Jimmy Burke. In fact, even Jimmy didn't know very much about himself. He never knew exactly when and where he was born, and he never knew either of his real parents. According to the records of the Manhattan Foundling Home, he was born July 5, 1931, to a woman named Conway. At the age of two he was designated a neglected child and entered into the Roman Catholic Church's foster-care program. For the next eleven years he was moved in and out of dozens of foster homes, where, psychiatric social workers would later reveal, he had been beaten, sexually abused, pampered, lied to, ignored, screamed at, locked in closets, and treated kindly by so many different sets of temporary parents that he had great difficulty remembering more than a few of their names and faces.

In the summer of 1944, at the age of thirteen, Jimmy was riding in a car with his latest set of foster parents. When he began to act up in the rear seat, his foster father, a stern man with an explosive temper, turned around to slap him. The car suddenly went out of control, crashed, and killed the man instantly. Jimmy's foster mother blamed him for her husband's death and began to beat him regularly, but the Vanguard Childcare Agency refused to move Jimmy into another foster home. Jimmy began running away and getting into trouble. Two months after the accident Jimmy was arrested for juvenile delinquency. He was charged with being disorderly in a Queens playground. The charge was later dismissed, but the next year, at the age of fourteen, he was charged with burglarizing a house near his foster home and with taking twelve hundred dollars in cash. He was placed in the Mount Loretto Reformatory, a juvenile jail for incorrigible youngsters, on Staten Island. It was supposed to have the same isolating effect on young people as Alcatraz was alleged to have on noncompliant adults. In truth, serving time in Mount Loretto's was almost a badge of honor among the youngsters with whom Jimmy Burke had begun to travel.

In September of 1949, after innumerable beatings and arrests at the hands of the police and after a number of stints in various juvenile jails, including Elmira, Jimmy was arrested for trying to pass three thousand dollars' worth of fraudulent checks in a Queens bank. Because of his youth and innocent appearance Jimmy had been used as a "passer" by Dominick Cerami, a Bensonhurst, Brooklyn, hood who headed a gang of professional check cashers. In the squad room on the second floor of the 75th Precinct in Queens, detectives cuffed Jimmy's hands behind his back and began punching him in the stomach in an effort to get him to implicate Cerami in the scheme. Jimmy took the beating and refused to talk. He was sentenced to five years in Auburn for bank forgery. He was eighteen. It was his first trip to an adult prison. The day he walked into Auburn, a huge stone prison with steel gates, set in a frozen stretch of upper New York State, Jimmy was greeted by over a dozen of the prison's toughest inmates. They had been awaiting his arrival in the prison reception area. Two of the men approached Jimmy. They were friends of Dominick Cerami, and they were grateful for what he had done on Cerami's behalf. They told him that if he had any problems in Auburn, he should come to them. Jimmy Burke had met the mob.

"The thing you've got to understand about Jimmy is that he loved to steal. He ate and breathed it. I think if you ever offered Jimmy a billion dollars not to steal, he'd turn you down and then try to figure out how to steal it from you. It was the only thing he enjoyed.

It kept him alive. As a kid he stole his food. He rolled drunks. All those years he was really living on the streets until he'd get picked up and turned over to the foundling home. Then he'd go to another foster home or a reform school until he ran away again. He used to sleep in parked cars. He was a little kid. He had a couple of places to sleep and wash in the backstretch at Aqueduct. Between the ages of sixteen and twenty-two Jimmy had only been out of jail a total of eighty-six days. Jimmy's childhood was spent either behind bars or on the lam and stealing. It got so that the bars didn't bother him. They made no difference to him whatever. He didn't even see the bars. He was invulnerable.

"By 1970 Jimmy owned hijacking at Kennedy Airport. Of course he had Paulie's okay, but it was Jimmy who decided what and when shipments and trucks were worth taking. It was Jimmy who picked the crew for each job, Jimmy who lined up the fences and drops.

"You've got to understand, we grew up near the airport. We had friends, relatives, everybody we knew worked at the airport. To us, and especially to guys like Jimmy, the airport was better than Citibank. Whenever Jimmy needed money he went to the airport. We always knew what was coming in and what was being shipped out. It was like the neighborhood department store. Between boosting cargo and hijacking trucks, Kennedy Airport was an even bigger moneymaker than numbers. We had people working for the airlines, people with the Port Authority, we had clean-up crews and maintenance workers, security guards, the waiters and waitresses at the restaurants, and the drivers and dispatchers working for the air-cargo trucking companies. We owned the place.

"Sometimes a trucking company boss or some foreman would get suspicious that one of their employees was tipping us off and try to fire them. If that happened, we'd talk to Paulie, who would talk to Johnny Dio, who ran the unions, and the guy would always keep his job. The union would make a grievance out of it. They'd threaten a walkout. They'd threaten to close the trucker down. Pretty soon the truckers got the message and let the insurance companies pay."

In 1966, at the age of twenty-three, Henry Hill went on his first hijacking. It was not a true hijacking in that the trucks were parked in a garage rather than traveling along the road when they were robbed, but it was a first-class grade-B felony nevertheless. Jimmy Burke invited Henry along on the heist. Jimmy had found out about three cargo trucks filled with home appliances that were being stored over the weekend in one of the freight garages just outside the airport. He also had a buyer, a friend of Tuddy Vario's, who was going to pay five thousand dollars per truck.

As always, Jimmy had great inside information. The garage had very little security, and on Friday nights there was only one elderly watchman on duty. His job was mostly to prevent vandalism by youngsters. On the night of the robbery Henry had no difficulty getting the watchman to open the gate. He simply told the man that he had left his paycheck in one of the trucks. The moment the gate swung open, Henry poked his finger in the man's back. He then tied the watchman to a chair in a nearby shack. Jimmy knew exactly where the keys were kept and the trucks parked. Within minutes Henry, Jimmy, and Tommy DeSimone were driving the trucks through the industrial roads of Canarsie on their way to Flatlands Avenue, where Tuddy and the fence were waiting. It was simple and sweet. It was the easiest five grand Henry had ever earned. Within an hour he and Jimmy and Tommy were on their way to Vegas for the weekend. Earlier that day Jimmy had made reservations for the three of them in phony names.

"Most of the loads hijacked were sold before they were even robbed. They were hijacks to order. We knew what we wanted and we knew where it was going before the job was done. We used to get two or three jobs a week. Sometimes we'd get two a day if we wanted money bad. We'd get up in the morning and go to Robert's, a bar that Jimmy used to own on Lefferts Boulevard, in South Ozone Park.

Robert's was perfect. There were three card tables, a casino craps table, and enough bookmakers and loan sharks to cover all the action in town. There were barmaids who drank Sambuca in the morning. There was 'Stacks' Edwards, a black credit-card booster who wanted to join the 'May-fia.' He played a blues guitar on weekends. It was a hangout for truck drivers, freight handlers, cargo dispatchers, and backfield airport workers who loved the action and could drop their Friday paycheck before Saturday morning. But a tip on good cargo loads could make up for a lot of paychecks and buy back a lot of IOUs. Robert's was also convenient. It was next to the Van Wyck Expressway and just minutes from the Kennedy cargo area, Aqueduct Racetrack, Paulie Vario's new office in a trailer on Flatlands Avenue at the Bargain Auto Junkyard, and the Queens County courts, where we got our postponements.

"The customers were often legitimate retailers looking for swag. There was also a whole army of fences, who bought our loads and then sold pieces of the loads to guys who had stores or sold the swag off the backs of their trucks or at factory gates or to a whole list of customers who usually retailed the swag themselves to their relatives or to the people they worked with. We were a major industry.

"Lots of our jobs were called 'give-ups'—as opposed to stickups—which meant the driver was in on it with us. For instance, you own the driver who leaves the airport with a $200,000 load of silk. An average score, but nice. Somewhere along the road he stops for coffee and accidentally leaves the keys in the ignition. When he finishes his coffee he discovers that the truck is gone, and he immediately reports the robbery to the police. The 'give-up' guys were the ones we always had to get Johnny Dio to protect when their bosses tried to fire them.

"The guys with the guns who did the actual hijackings usually got a fixed rate. They'd get a couple of grand just for sticking a gun in the driver's face, whether it was a good score or lousy, whether the truck was full or empty. They were like hired guys. They didn't share in the loot. In fact, even Jimmy, who hired most of the guys who did the stickups, didn't share in the ultimate sale of the loot. We would usually sell pieces of the load to different buyers, wholesalers and distributors and discount-store owners, who knew the market and had the outlets where they could get near a retail price.

"On an average hijacking we'd know the truck number, what it was carrying, who was driving it, where it was going, and how to circumvent the security devices, like triple lock alarms and sirens. We usually tailed the driver until he stopped for a light. We'd make sure that he wasn't being followed by backup security. We used two cars, one in front and one behind. At the light one of the guys—usually Tommy, Joey Allegro, or Stanley Diamond—would stick a gun in the driver's face and put him in the car while other guys drove the truck to the drop. Tommy always carried his gun in a brown paper bag. Walking down the street, he looked like he was bringing you a sandwich instead of a thirty-eight.

"The first thing Jimmy would do with the driver was to take his driver's license or pretend to copy his name and address. He'd make a big thing about how we knew where he lived and how we'd get him if he was too helpful in identifying us to the cops. Then, after scaring the shit out of the guy, he'd smile, tell him to relax, and then slip the fifty-dollar bill into the guy's wallet. There was never one driver who made it to court to testify against him. There are quite a few dead ones who tried.

"An average hijacking, including unloading the truck, usually took a few hours. Jimmy always had the unloading drop lined up in advance. It was usually in a legitimate warehouse or trucking company. The guy in charge of the warehouse could pretend afterward he didn't know what was going on. Jimmy would just come in with some stuff to unload. He paid the warehouse operators fifteen hundred dollars a drop, and sometimes we had to store the stuff there overnight. Some warehouse owners were getting five grand a week from us. That's a lot of money. We had our unloaders, who got about a hundred a day. They were local guys we knew and trusted and they worked like dogs. When the truck was empty we'd abandon it and tell the guy babysitting the driver to let him go. The drivers were usually dropped off somewhere along the Connecticut Turnpike.

"I got into hijacking because I had the customers looking for the merchandise. I was a good salesman. Early on, Jimmy told me that I should start using some of the same people who were buying my cigarettes to buy some of the swag. But I was already looking out for big buyers. I had a drugstore wholesaler who had discount stores all over Long Island. He'd take almost everything I had. Razor blades. Perfume. Cosmetics. I had a guy in the Schick razor blade factory in Connecticut who smuggled cartons of blades out for me to resell at twenty percent below the wholesale price. When that was going well, I'd make between seven hundred and a grand a week just on blades. I had a furrier who would buy truckloads of pelts top dollar. Mink. Beaver. Fox. I had Vinnie Romano, who was a union boss down at the Fulton Fish Market, who would buy all the frozen shrimp and lobster I could supply, and we could always supply the bars and restaurants with hijacked liquor at better than half the price.

"It was overwhelming. None of us had ever seen opportunities for such money before. The stuff was coming in on a daily basis. Sometimes I'd go to Jimmy's house and it looked like a department store. We had the basement of Robert's so loaded down with stuff that there was hardly enough room to play cards. Freight foremen and cargo workers used to bring the stuff to us on a daily basis, but still we felt that we had to go out and snatch the trucks ourselves. Waiting for the loads to come to us wasn't cooking on all burners.

"And why not? Hijackings were so public that we used to fence the stuff right out in the open. One of the places I used to go with Jimmy and Paulie was the Bamboo Lounge, a high-class rug joint on Rockaway Parkway, right near the airport. It was owned by Sonny Bamboo, but his mother watched the register. A little old lady, she was at that register from morning till night. Sonny Bamboo's real name was Angelo McConnach, and he was Paulie's brother-in-law. The joint was set up to look like a movie nightclub, with zebra-striped banquettes and barstools and potted palm trees sticking up all around the place. No matter when you walked in the place it was always the middle of the night. Sonny Bamboo's was practically a supermarket for airport swag. It was so well protected by politicians and the cops that nobody even bothered to pretend it was anything but what it was. It was like a commodities exchange for stolen goods. Outside there were big cars double-parked and inside guys were screaming and drinking and yelling about what they wanted to buy or what they needed to have stolen. Fences from all over the city used to show up in the morning. Charlie Flip ran most of the business and he used to buy and sell dozens of 'igloos,' or metal shipping crates, of swag. There were insurance adjusters, truckers, union delegates, wholesalers, discount-store owners, everybody who wanted to make a buck on a good deal.

"It was like an open market. There was a long list of items in demand, and you could get premiums if you grabbed the right cargo. That was another reason for going out and snatching a truck instead of waiting for some cargo guy to steal it for you. Clothing, seafood, fabrics, and cigarettes topped the list. Then came coffee, records and tapes, liquor, televisions and radios, kitchen appliances, meat, shoes, toys, jewelry and watches, on and on, all the way down to empty trucks. When stolen securities got big, we used to have Wall Street types all over the place buying up bearer bonds. They would send them overseas, where the banks didn't know they were stolen, and then they'd use the hot bonds as collateral on loans in this country. Once the stolen bonds were accepted as collateral, nobody ever checked their serial numbers again. We're talking about millions of dollars in collateral forever. We got robbed on those jobs. At that time we didn't have any idea about collateralizing foreign loans. The bankers took us to the cleaners. We got pennies for the dollar."

During the 1960s and early 1970s hijacking was big business. Almost no one went to jail. The airlines were happy to underestimate their losses and pick up the insurance money rather than assume the cost, delays, and inconvenience of additional security. The truckers said they were powerless to fight the union, and the union insisted that the airlines were responsible because they refused to spend enough money to safeguard the drivers. To make matters more complicated, the legislators of the state of New York had never gotten around to codifying the crime of hijacking. When caught, hijackers had to be charged with other crimes, such as kidnapping, robbery, the possession of a gun, or possession of stolen property. And few of these charges ever seemed to stick.

According to a 1960s Joint New York State Legislative Committee on Crime study, at least 99.5 percent of hijacking arrests resulted either in the charges being dismissed or in the defendants receiving small fines or probation. During one year covered by the report the committee traced 6,400 arrests for criminal possession of stolen property and found there were only 904 indictments, 225 convictions, and as few as 30 state prison commitments. A committee case study of eight defendants arrested at the time for the possession of more than $100,000 worth of stolen women's clothing noted that each defendant was fined $2,500 and placed on probation by New York Supreme Court Judge Albert H. Bosch. The men were all part of the Robert's Lounge crew working for Jimmy Burke and Paul Vario. During the next five years, while the eight men were still on probation, they were arrested an additional seventeen times on a variety of charges, including robbery, possession of stolen property, and burglary. But even then, and despite the fact that probation officers recommended that hearings for violation of probation be initiated, Judge Bosch continued the men on probation. He later said that he could not make a final decision concerning the violation of probation until the guilt or innocence of the defendants had been determined.

Eventually Henry was questioned by police so many times and

became so familiar with the process and its loopholes that he no longer worried about getting caught. Of course he tried not to get caught. It was not profitable to get caught. You had to pay the lawyers and the bondsmen, and you had to pay off cops and witnesses and sometimes even the prosecutors and judges. But when he was caught, Henry was not particularly concerned about the addition of yet another charge to those already pending against him. What really worried him was whether his lawyer was adept enough to cluster the court appearances in such a way as to minimize the number of days Henry had to take time away from business and appear in court. Going to court and facing accusers and cops was not the harrowing experience it might be for others; for Henry and for most of his friends it was rather like going to school as kids. Occasionally they were forced to attend, but the experience left little or no impression. More time would be spent figuring out where to eat lunch than was spent on the issues before the court.

"There was no reason to worry. During the pre-trial months and years you just kept throwing money at your lawyer to keep you outside long enough for you or him or one of his friends to fix the case. That's all there was to it. You stayed outside and made as much money as you could so that you had the green to pay your way out. I've never been on a case where somebody wasn't fixed. It's just business. Usually the lawyer has the kinds of contacts that can keep you free on bail as long as you want. They can keep you from running across some hard-nosed judge who sends you inside or rushes the case along. Then you've got the private detectives who work for the lawyers. They are usually ex-cops, and lots of times you know them from the days when you paid them off on the streets. They have good contacts with cops, and arrangements can be worked out so that testimony or evidence is changed just a little bit, only enough to make a tiny hole through which your lawyer can help you escape. Then even if none of this works and you've got to go to trial, you always try to reach the jury.

"Everybody reaches the jury. It's business and it's easy. During the jury selection, for instance, your lawyer can find out anything he wants to know about a juror—where he works, lives, family status. That sort of personal stuff. The 'where he works' is what interested me mostly. Where a guy works means his job, and that always means the unions, and that's the easiest place to make the reach. The whole crew and the lawyers and the private detectives and everyone you know are all going through the list. I know this guy. I know that guy. I know the union boss here. I know the shop steward. I know the delegate. I know a guy who works with this guy's brother over there. Little by little you get closer and closer to the guy, until you go to someone you can trust who can go to someone he can trust, and you make the deal. No big deal. It was business. All you really wanted was to hurry it up so you could get back to the airport and steal some more."

Eight

The first accounting of cargo thefts at Kennedy Airport was released in October of 1967; it revealed that $2.2 million in cargo had been stolen during the preceding ten months. The amount did not include the hundreds of hijackings of airport cargo stolen outside the airport, nor did it include thefts valued at less than one thousand dollars. The total also did not include $2.5 million in nonnegotiable stock taken from Trans World Airlines. The $2,245,868 worth of cargo stolen during the ten-month period had been grabbed right out of the storage bins and security rooms of the Air Cargo Center. At the time, the Air Cargo Center was the largest such facility in the world. It was a thirteen-building complex of warehouses and truck-loading ramps spread over 159 acres. Space in the buildings was leased to twenty-eight airlines, air express agencies, customhouse brokers, federal inspection services, and carting companies. Each of the airlines kept its own valuables in specially guarded security rooms, some of them enclosed by steel or cinder blocks, others by wire cages. In addition, the airlines all had their own guards or hired private detective agencies to protect valuables at the twenty-four-hour-a-day facility.

Besides the airline security personnel, the Port Authority had 113 policemen on duty during the average day. There were also customs inspectors, FBI men, and police from the 103rd Precinct roaming through the facility on a fairly regular basis. But during the ten-month period pinpointed by the survey forty-five major robberies were committed there, including thefts of clothing, palladium ingots, pearls, watches, musical instruments, hydraulic pumps, cigarettes, phonograph records, drugs, wigs, and diamonds—and $480,000 in cash, which was stolen shortly before midnight on Saturday, April 8, from the locked and guarded security room at the Air France cargo building.

"Air France made me. No one had ever pulled that kind of cash out of the airport before, and I did it without a gun. It began around the end of January in 1967. I had been selling cigarettes out at the airport. I had a regular route, and one of my best stops was at the Air France cargo dock. Bobby McMahon, the cargo foreman, was one of my best customers. He also used to come across stuff once in a while, and we'd buy perfume, clothes, and jewelry from him. Bobby McMahon had been with Air France for so long his nickname was "Frenchy," and there wasn't too much about the whole cargo operation he didn't know. He could tell by looking at bills of lading and freight-forwarding orders what was coming in and what was going out. Since he ran the whole operation at night, he could go anywhere he wanted and pick up anything he needed. Nobody watched anybody out there anyway, but Frenchy had carte blanche. Once he came across a small 24-by-48-inch box of silk dresses, which Jimmy unloaded at the garment center for eighteen thousand dollars and which Frenchy got a piece of. Frenchy always got a piece of anything he brought us or pointed us toward.

"Then one day I'm there and Frenchy tells me about money coming in. He said they were building a new strong room with cement blocks where the old wire cage room had been, and in the meantime they were storing all the valuables in the cargo office right up front as you entered the cargo warehouse. Frenchy said the money was in sixty-thousand-dollar packages in large white canvas bags with big red seals over the side flaps. He said there were usually three or four of the canvas bags dropped off by planes coming in from overseas and that they were usually picked up in the morning by armored trucks. Three or four guys with pistols could easily take the load.

"I was really excited. I drove over to Robert's and told Jimmy. He knew Frenchy had great information, so that weekend Raymond Montemurro, his brother Monte, Tommy DeSimone, and me go over to stick the joint up. Johnny Savino and Jimmy were going to wait for us at Jimmy's house. We do the usual thing about getting rented cars and putting on bum plates. We go right up to the cargo office, and immediately we see there are too many people. There must have been about twenty-five, thirty people wandering around. We looked at each other and tried to figure out how we could round them all up, but it was no use. The office was in front, but, then, behind a loading platform there was a whole warehouse full of cargo resting on pallets and crates and boxes piled ceiling-high. There was just too much activity and too much going on we didn't know about. We decided to forget the stickup. We had all gotten a look at the canvas bags. They were just stacked up against the wall where they were building the safe room. All those pretty little bags full of money. Just the sight of it drove me nuts. It was so good we didn't want to blow anything. We did the smart thing and took off.

"When I met with Frenchy I told him we needed another way. He said it was tricky, because he never knew exactly when the money was coming in. Sometimes it wouldn't come in for a couple of weeks, and then there'd be two deliveries at once and they'd leave for the bank the same day. The money came from American tourists and soldiers who converted their American cash into French money. The French would then send all that cash back to the United States and get credited for it in American banks. It was usually in hundreds and fifties, and it was untraceable. It was a dream score.

"Meanwhile, every time I went to the airport to sell cigarettes,

I'd stop by and talk with Frenchy. As we talked I'd watch the work-men get closer and closer to finishing the new storeroom, and then one day the storeroom was finished. There were two keys. Frenchy? No such luck. They gave one of the keys to a guard from a private agency; he had a crewcut and took his job very seriously. He loved being a cop. He loved guarding doors. The guy never let the key out of his sight. If Frenchy had to put something in the room, the guard would never give Frenchy the key—he'd open the door and wait until Frenchy was done and then he'd personally lock the door himself. He wore the key on a key ring attached to his belt. The only other key we knew about belonged to the supervisor of the entire operation, and he worked days.

"The problem with just sticking the guy up and taking his key was that we never knew when the money would be there. We had to have a key of our own so that we could get in there at a moment's notice from Frenchy. If we stuck the guy up and got the key, they'd just change the locks, and we'd also alert them that we knew about the money. I figured we had to get the key, so I asked Frenchy to start making up to the guy. Buy him some drinks. Bullshit a little. Meanwhile Frenchy gave me the guy's address. He lived in a fur-nished room on Rockaway Boulevard, near Liberty Avenue, across from the White Castle hamburger joint. One day when the guard was off, Raymond Montemurro and I waited all day for him to leave, and when he did we burglarized his apartment, looking for the key. The plan was to get the key, make a copy, and put it back so no one knew. Then, when the money arrived, we'd have the key to a fortune.

"We went in and out of every drawer in the place and we couldn't find the key. The sonofabitch must have carried it around with him even on his day off. I couldn't believe it. I had a fortune waiting for me and I'm stuck with a hundred-dollar-a-week nut job for a guard. The other problem was that Jimmy was getting impatient. He was beginning to say the next time Frenchy tells us there's something in the room, we snatch the guy and take the key. I was pretty sure that meant Jimmy would have whacked the guy too. It all made me try harder.

"The guy lived in a typical bachelor's apartment. It was depressing. It was crummy. He had all these detective magazines around, but he also had a lot of girlie magazines. He was a nebbishy-looking guy around forty. He had glasses and was thin. Frenchy was the opposite. Frenchy was a big, gruff, funny guy. He was married and had a nice family somewhere in Hempstead. He was great company. He told funny stories. On the night shift he was the boss. I just knew that would be important to the guard. Company men always like hanging around with the boss. I told Frenchy about the girlie magazines. I said maybe we could butter him up with a girl.

"So now Frenchy took the guy to the Jade East Motel, right across the parkway, for a few drinks. Frenchy started talking about girls, and the guy was definitely interested. Then Frenchy began to talk about this girlfriend he had who was a real swinger. She loved to screw. The guard practically went nuts listening to Frenchy's dirty stories.

"The next day we got a really great-looking hooker from the Bronx. She used to do numbers for Ralph Atlas' clients. Atlas was a top-of-the-line bookmaker, and all his clients were big-money bettors from the garment center and Wall Street. She was about a hundred and a half a night, which was very steep back then. She looked like Natalie Wood. She had black hair, a great figure, and beautiful big eyes. She didn't look like a hook. She looked more like a student or a stewardess.

"That night Frenchy brought the guard to meet his 'girl' at the Jade East. She immediately began to make a play for the guy. Frenchy, playing dumb, made up an excuse that he had to go back to work, and the girl took the guard upstairs to bed. We did not make a move on the key that night. We just wanted to see if it could work. I wanted to know if the guy was vulnerable. He was.

"The next weekend Tommy and I picked her up again, and we

took her to the Jade East. This time the plan was to see if Frenchy and the girl could get the guy away from his key. The Jade East had private steam rooms and whirlpools in the basement, and if we could get them all down there long enough to get the key, make a copy, and put it back, we were home. But first we wanted to do a dry run. Frenchy was supposed to leave the key to the room under the hall ashtray, and we'd know they were going downstairs when he parted the blinds in the room. It worked beautifully. They were down in the steam room for an hour and a half—more than enough time to get a copy of the key made.

"Later that night Frenchy called. He had heard that between four and seven hundred thousand dollars in cash was coming into the airport the following Friday.

"No more dry runs. This was the time to do it. Again, that Friday, Tommy and I picked up the girl, and now she's getting suspicious. She knew we were up to something illegal, but she couldn't figure it out. This time to make things even nicer I bought some terry-cloth robes for the three of them to wear on the way to the steam room. We gave the girl the robes so she could pretend she got them for Frenchy and the guard as presents. She was a great actress. They were all supposed to meet at the motel at around five-thirty.

"It wasn't until about six o'clock when Frenchy and the guard got to the Jade East. By then we're getting nervous. Everything was running late. We had found a locksmith nearby who could duplicate the keys, except he closed at seven. The minute Frenchy and the guard arrived we sent the girl over to rush them along. She hugged the two of them. Frenchy's sweating and rolling his eyes up in his head because he knows we're late. The guard was just a slow and stubborn guy. Every time Frenchy had tried to move the guy along he'd just stand there. He'd get slower. Now at least we had the girl goosing him along, but it still wasn't until six-thirty that they went to their room to get undressed for the steam room.

"The minute they were gone I went right upstairs. I reached

under the ashtray in the hall. The key was there. I opened the door, and right next to the guy's pants was his whole key ring. I grabbed the ring and ran downstairs. Jimmy had the car waiting, and we shot out of the motel to the locksmith's. He was on Rockaway Boulevard, near Jamaica Avenue. We went like hell, but when we got there the guy was getting ready to close. We had to bang at his door and beg. Then we didn't know which of the keys was the one we wanted, so we ordered duplicates of all eighteen keys. The guy started to work and when he was finished he only gave us fifteen duplicate keys. I asked where the other three were and he said he didn't have the blanks. Fifteen out of eighteen aren't bad odds, but in this job I didn't want any odds.

"We drove like mad back to the motel and I went upstairs, put the keys down exactly where I had found them, closed the door, and put Frenchy's door key back under the ashtray. Tommy took half his clothes off and went walking around the steam room until Frenchy saw him. That was our signal that the room was clear.

"First thing Saturday morning I met Frenchy near the cargo area. He took the fifteen keys to make sure we had the one that worked. He came back smiling. Not only did the key work but he had seen the sacks we had been waiting for. Frenchy said the best time over the weekend for the heist would be just before midnight. Lots of guys would be coming and going during the new shift and the guard would be on his coffee break at the other end of the warehouse. Frenchy also said that there was not going to be a bank pickup until Monday afternoon because of a Jewish holiday, and that was music to our ears. The delayed pickup, which would normally have been made on Sunday night, meant the loss wouldn't be discovered until Monday afternoon. It also meant the cops wouldn't know when the money had actually disappeared. People might be able to remember one or two strangers around a place on one night but not over a three-day weekend. It's just too long a time to pinpoint anybody at the scene of the crime.

"We had about twelve hours to go. I kept the key in my hand all day long. I was so happy I went out and bought myself the biggest suitcase I could find so I could put the sacks of money inside. At eleven-forty Saturday night Tommy and I drove into the cargo parking area. We had a rented car with bum plates. We waited until the shift began to change. Frenchy said he would be waiting near the platform and that we should just walk in as though we were returning a suitcase to the office. The plan was that he wouldn't acknowledge that he knew me, but if there was any problem he'd be there to straighten it out. He said chances were that no one would bother me, because there were always lots of people wandering in and out picking up suitcases that had been lost and misdirected. I climbed up the platform ramp and walked into the office area, and I could see Frenchy hovering nearby. I could see the room and walked right up to the steel door. I'd had the key in my hand ever since I left the car. I slipped it in, turned it once, walked inside. The room was just like a big, dark closet. I had brought a pen-size flashlight because I didn't want to turn on any lights. The seven white canvas bags were right on the floor. I could see the red seals. I opened the suitcase and put the seven sacks inside and I walked out the door. The suitcase was so heavy I could hardly walk, but Frenchy later said he thought I was leaving empty, because I practically floated out of the joint."

Nine

As Henry had hoped, the theft was not discovered until Monday afternoon. The *Daily News* story Tuesday said that the money had vanished into "thin air" and that "FBI agents swarmed over Air France cargo building 86 at Kennedy, questioning the employees, searching the area and examining the manifests and bills of lading." *The New York Times* story said: "A thorough search of the building and the cinder block locker where the money was placed failed to turn up the parcels. A work crew of about 20 men as well as an around-the-clock private guard were on duty at the building."

By the time Air France realized its $480,000 was missing, Henry and his pals had already given away $120,000 of it as "tribute" to the mob chiefs who considered Kennedy Airport their turf. They gave $60,000 to Sebastian "Buster" Aloi, the fifty-seven-year-old *capo* who ran the airport for the Colombo crime family, and the other $60,000 to their own *capo,* Paul Vario.

"We took care of Buster because it was insurance. It kept everybody happy. We gave Paulie a piece because he was our boss. That's the way it's set up. He protected us. If there was a beef against us by another crew—and there were always beefs against us—Paulie took care of it. He went to the sit-downs and took our part. The rest of the money we pooled. I could have taken my end and gone home, but what was I going to do with it? Put it in the closet? Jimmy kept it in a couple of bookmakers' safes, and if I needed a few bucks I'd take it out, and he'd keep tabs. It was like having a bank account.

"We wanted to spend some money on ourselves. I wanted a new car and some clothes. Karen needed things for the new apartment and the kids. To justify any new spending, the three of us, Jimmy, Tommy, and I, took a trip to Vegas, dropped about twenty grand, and came back bragging that we had won. Everybody knew we went to Vegas a lot and that Jimmy was the kind of guy who would belly up to the craps table and play until his ankles swole. But even then we didn't overdo anything. I put a down payment on a new 'sixty-seven gold Buick Riviera with a black top and financed the rest, using my brother's name. Tommy did the same, except he bought a beige Cadillac with a black top.

"Our first business proposition came about two weeks after the robbery when Paulie came up to us at the backstretch at Aqueduct and said if we joined him in a deal we could buy a fifty-percent interest in Milty Wekar's bookmaking operation. He had Wekar right there with him in the car. Wekar needed some money. He had been betting heavy on something he had and got burned. It was a great opportunity. Wekar had high rollers and bookmakers for customers. He had garment-center executives, Wall Street brokers, doctors and dentists and lawyers. And he had the guys who took their action. He never took bets for less than five hundred or a thousand dollars a shot, and most of the customers would bet six or seven games at once. Vario said he'd put in fifty thousand if we put in the same. Jimmy and Tommy looked at me and we all agreed. Right there at the track. We didn't need any lawyers. We shook hands and I was in the bookmaking business. I was twenty-four.

"It was an education. Milty was a bookmaker's bookmaker. Most of our action came from bookmakers, not individual bettors. Milty put me on the payroll for five hundred a week and expenses. I used to sit between the two clerks who took the action and I tabbed the bets. I had a yellow legal pad and on it I had all the day's action. I had baseball, football, basketball, the pros, colleges, the tracks, every kind of action going. And I also had the odds on the sheet, and as the bets came in I'd mark a line for every thousand bet, and then I'd draw a line through whenever five thousand was bet. Milty would look at the sheets and adjust the odds. He'd move the odds up or down depending upon whether he wanted action or not. If Milty had a problem and wanted to lay off some of the bets, he had a line to guys in Florida, St. Louis, Vegas, California. Just about anywhere.

"I also helped Milty on Tuesday, the straighten-up day. That's when all the bookmakers and high-line bettors in the city had to straighten up whatever they owed each other for the week. We'd usually straighten up in a garment-center restaurant called Bobby's. On Mondays we'd make up the payout sheet. There were our expenses, like my salary and stuff. There were 'pays' for the winners. There was 'ice'—about seven hundred dollars a week—for the cops. There was 'juice' for when we had a bad week and had to go to the loan sharks for a little extra money ourselves.

"But usually we didn't have to do anything like that. We would just call Paulie, and Paulie would give us twenty-five or thirty grand with no interest. After all, he was a partner. If we couldn't get Paulie and wanted to put off paying for a couple of days, Milty had a great trick. He kept five or six one-thousand-dollar bills around, and he'd give them to me to flash on the winners. Since none of our clients wanted to get paid in thousand-dollar bills, we could always put off paying them for a couple of days. The big bills were just too much trouble for wiseguy bookmakers to cash. Milty must have used those same bills for years.

"We had a great operation. Milty had five different rooms all over the city where we took the action. We had most of the police on the pad. Milty paid off the Borough Command and the Division. Every once in a while we'd have to stand still for an arrest, usually by the police commissioner's Confidential Investigating Unit, but it was a misdemeanor, and all that meant was a fifty-dollar fine. Nobody ever went to jail for bookmaking. Still, we couldn't figure out how the cops always knew where we were. Milty was constantly changing apartments. Sometimes we'd move a couple of times a week, but they always knew our new locations.

"We finally figured it out. Milty had this old guy who used to go around and rent our rooms. That's all the guy ever did. Milty gave him three hundred a week to find the apartments, put down deposits, sign the leases, get the gas and electric lines opened up, and get the phones installed. The guy used to come in on the Long Island Railroad, get off, and take buses and subways as far as he could until he found apartments to rent. Somehow the cops got a line on the guy, and they used to tail him from one apartment to another until they had a list of our places. Then, when they saw one of our cars parked outside, they'd crash through.

"After about four months I took my first pinch for running a wire room. It was in August of 1967, and the cops who broke in said we were doing two million dollars' worth of business a week. I only wish. We'd gotten word from the cops we'd paid off that we were going to get busted. We were due. They just went through the motions. It was done right. No cuffs or anything. After we were booked we took the cops for dinner on Mulberry Street before we went to night court for the arraignment. Al Newman, our bondsman, was already in court when we got there. I grabbed a cab home. The cops dropped Milty off. The next day we were back in action at a different apartment. We had taken a pinch and now we were okay for a while. John Sutter, my lawyer, bounced the case around the courts for a year until I finally pleaded guilty. I got fined a hundred dollars and went home. It was a joke. The city was spending millions of dollars for plainclothes cops to catch bookmakers, but it was obvious that the whole thing was set up so the cops could shake us down. The cops didn't want to put us out of business any more than they wanted to shoot the golden goose.

"It was at this time that another business opportunity arose. There was a terrific supper club and restaurant called The Suite on Queens Boulevard, near Forest Hills. Its owner, Joey Rossano, was a horseplayer and gambler. The guy needed money. We made a deal that I'd take over the place but he'd keep his name on the papers. I paid him some money and I took over his loan-shark debts. I knew some of the guys he owed, and they weren't very strong. They didn't have the weight. So I knew I wouldn't have to pay. I just strong-armed them out of the money—and who could they go to? If you were with Paulie and our crew, you could tell most of the city's half-assed wiseguys to get lost. I made them eat the debts.

"Also, Karen loved the idea of getting a legitimate joint. Our first daughter, Judy, was two and a half and Ruth was about six months old, and Karen had been insisting I keep an eye out for a good business opportunity. She knew about the cigarettes and swag and she knew about Air France. She knew I had some money, and she wanted me to invest it right. The bookmaking business wasn't her idea of a good deal. She knew I had taken the pinch, and she knew I used to gamble away most of the money I made right there in our own office. We all did. We'd get some good action from a trainer or owner on a certain horse and we'd add a few grand of our own money on top of the bet. When you do that as a bookmaker, it's only a matter of time. Show me a bookmaker who bets and I'll show you a guy owned by the sharks.

"Before I thought about taking over The Suite I talked it over with Paulie. He liked the idea. He liked it so much that he ordered the place off limits for the crew. He said we had to keep the place clean. He didn't want to turn it into a joint like Robert's.

"I was in the place every day, morning till night. Karen would bring the kids in and help with the books. All the books. The books for the SLA and IRS and the real books. I got a decent cook in the place, and I got Casey Rosado, who headed the bartenders' and waiters' union at the airport, to send in some of his spies to tell me how much I was getting robbed by my bartenders. The Suite was a big enough place so that I had six bartenders, three of them on at all times. When I got the word from Casey, I fired all of them. Casey said the bartenders were stealing a thousand dollars a night out of the joint, in addition to a hundred a night in tips they were taking home, plus the hundred and a half I was paying them.

"We were doing real well for a couple of months, then, one by one, the guys started to show up. First Jimmy came by to see the place. He brought Mickey and a plant with a good-luck banner on it. Tommy DeSimone came by for a toast. Angelo Sepe came. Marty Krugman, a bookmaker I knew who had a wig shop just two blocks away, began hanging around the bar. Alex and Mikey Corcione started showing up, and so did Anthony and Tommy Stabile, until Tommy went away for a holdup. Little Vic Orena, a lieutenant in the Colombo crime family, became a regular. Even Paulie and the Varios began hanging around."

Within six months The Suite had turned into a gathering place for Henry and his friends. It became an obligatory last stop. The revelers would arrive after midnight, long after they had stuffed their twenties and fifties into the pockets of every bartender, captain, and hatcheck girl in town. As a result, when they got to Henry's place they ate and drank on the tab. Henry once looked at his books and saw that his best friends were drinking him broke. Of course most of the debts were paid off eventually, but payment too often arrived in the form of swag—hijacked liquor, crates of freshly stolen shrimp, phony credit cards, and stolen traveler's checks.

While The Suite never replaced Robert's as the hijacking headquarters, it did begin to function as a bazaar for dirtier deals, con games, and hustles. Henry was soon selling dozens of transatlantic airline tickets run off by crooked travel agents. He steered big bettors to a crooked crap game run by the Varios out of a brand-new apartment house just off Queens Boulevard. Henry would sometimes take the suckers into the apartment himself and pretend to lose five or six thousand alongside his dupes. The next day, of course, Henry got his "lost" money back, plus 10 percent of the suckers' losses.

Also, just having a restaurant and club, with its access to the legitimate credit available in the normal business world, gave Henry endless opportunity for making even more money. He began "banging out" freshly stolen credit cards. The Suite was one of the first places that Stacks Edwards and the other plastic wholesalers went with a newly stolen card. Knowing the card had not yet been reported stolen, Henry would immediately use it to run up hundreds of dollars in phony restaurant bills.

"Instead of making my life simpler, The Suite made it crazier. I had to be there all the time, but I also had to keep an eye on my investment with Milty. I had a million things in the air. I was making it every way I could. And Karen, who was now at home with the kids most of the time, was getting more and more pissed. I had rented a house in Island Park to be closer to Paulie, and, with the kids, she needed somebody to help her around the house. But I was nervous about having some stranger walking around the house. I always had money stashed around the place. Sometimes I had swag stacked up the wall. I also had guns around the place. You'll find that most wiseguy wives do their own housework, no matter how rich they are, because strangers can't be trusted to keep their mouths shut. But Karen wouldn't let up, and finally I asked around The Suite if anyone knew anybody who could be trusted. I didn't want to go to an agency cold.

"Eddy Rigaud, the Haitian who used to buy stolen cars from me, said he had the solution to my problems. He said his family had done it for other friends. They had the right connections in the mountains, where they would buy young girls from their families. The girls were then shipped to Canada on a tourist visa, and their new owners would go to Montreal and pick them up. He said it usually cost thousands of dollars, but he could do it for me at cost. All I needed was the six hundred bucks for the girl's father and I had a slave.

"I remember going home and telling Karen, and she looked at me as though I was nuts, but she didn't say no. I gave Eddy the money, and just before Christmas of 1967 he said that the girl was on her way. He gave me her name and the hotel in Montreal where she would be staying, but when I got to the place and went to her room I almost died. When the slave opened the door, she turned out to be over six feet tall and weighed two-fifty minimum. My knees went. She was bigger than Paul Vario. She was so scary that on the plane back to New York I pretended I didn't know her. When I got home I made her wait outside until I could warn Karen. We couldn't keep her. She made the kids cry. She only stayed a day or two, until I could get Eddy to take her back.

"In addition to this, Karen started getting obscene phone calls. She had been getting them in early December, and we had had the number changed. It was unlisted. Still the calls kept coming. She'd call me at The Suite and tell me about them and I'd go crazy. I told Jimmy about them, and we tried to figure if it was anyone in the crew. It made me suspicious of everybody, except Karen couldn't get his voice. We taped him a couple of times and I couldn't pick him up either. So I decided that the next time he called, Karen should play up a little bit and ask him to meet her someplace. If Karen could act interested enough, maybe the guy was nutty enough to show up. I couldn't wait.

"It was the first week in January when Karen called me at The Suite and says she just talked to the guy and said her husband wasn't home and he should come to the apartment in about an hour. I was home in a second, and we turned out all the lights, except one. I crouched down near the front windows and watched. I had a re-volver in my jacket. I swear I was going to whack the guy right there.

"I waited for over an hour. It was snowing outside. I asked Karen if she thought he'd show. She said she did. I kept looking. Then I realized that there was one car that was driving slowly past the apart-ment for the second time. I waited. Sonofabitch if it didn't cruise by again. Real slow. This time I spot the driver. He's a man and he's all alone. He's looking right at our door. He wants to make sure every-thing's calm. I can't wait to make him calm. He drove around the corner, but I knew he was coming back.

"Instead of taking a chance and losing him I decided to wait for him to pass on the street. I crouched behind a parked car. Karen was watching from the window. The kids were asleep. It's snowing all over my face. And then I see the guy come around the corner again. I couldn't wait. This time he really slows down in front of our house. I can see his face. He rolls down the window and he's squinting at the house numbers.

"Just as he comes to a full stop I slide up alongside his open window and I put the gun in his face. I'm feeling crazy. 'You want something? You looking for something?' I'm screaming and cursing at the top of my lungs. The guy goes to move and I smash him across the face. He's out the door of the car and I'm chasing him. I get him down and start smashing his face with the gun. I don't want to stop. People are screaming. They know me from the neighborhood. I know I'm going to get pinched, but I don't care.

"When I hear the sirens I get away from the bum, and I ditch the gun under the front bumper of a parked car. There's usually a little shelf under the bumper where you can hide things. The cops arrive, and it turned out I beat up the wrong guy. He wasn't the mad caller at all. He was some gay guy looking for his friend's house. Before they took him to the hospital he kept yelling that I had a gun. That didn't help. The cops started looking for the gun in the snow where we had scuffled, and some cop who knew about bumpers found it. I was arrested for assault and possession of a loaded revolver and had to spend the rest of the night at the precinct until Al Newman got me out on bail.

"The phone calls finally stopped when I figured out how the sonofabitch kept getting our number every time we changed it. I went outside the house and looked at it from every angle and realized that with a pair of binoculars you could read the number right off the wall phone we had hanging in the kitchen. We changed the number again and left the number blank. We never got another call. I should have done that the first time instead of getting pinched for assaulting the wrong guy. It was dumb, but that was the way we did things. Whack 'em first and worry about them later."

Ten

For most of the guys the killings were just accepted. They were a part of every day. They were routine. I remember how proud Tommy DeSimone was when he brought Jimmy's kid, Frankie, on his first hit. Frankie Burke was just a timid little kid. Jimmy used to complain that the kid wet his bed all the time and that Jimmy had to beat the shit out of him almost every night. Jimmy even sent him to some military school to toughen him up. Frankie must have been sixteen or seventeen when Tommy took him on the hit, and Tommy said the kid held up great. Jimmy walked around real proud. You'd have thought the kid had won a medal.

"Murder was the only way everybody stayed in line. It was the ultimate weapon. Nobody was immune. You got out of line, you got whacked. Everyone knew the rules, but still people got out of line and people kept getting whacked. Johnny Mazzolla, the guy I used to go cashing counterfeit twenties with when I was a kid, his own son was killed because the kid wouldn't stop holding up local card games and bookmakers. The kid was warned a hundred times. They warned the father to keep the kid under wraps. They told him if the kid had to stick up bookmakers, he should go stick up foreign bookmakers. It was only because of Johnny that they let the kid live until he was nineteen. But the kid apparently couldn't believe he would ever get killed. The dead ones never did. He couldn't believe it until the end when he got two, close range, in the heart. That was out of respect for his father. They left the kid's face clean so there could be an open casket at the funeral.

"Jimmy once killed his best friend, Remo, because he found out that Remo set up one of his cigarette loads for a pinch. They were so close. They went on vacations together with their wives. But when one of Remo's small loads got busted, he told the cops about a trailer truckload Jimmy was putting together. Jimmy got suspicious when Remo invested only five thousand dollars in the two-hundred-thousand-dollar load. Remo usually took a third or fifty percent of the shipment. When Jimmy asked him why he wasn't going in on this load, Remo said he didn't need that much. Of course, when the truck got stopped and Jimmy's whole shipment was confiscated, the fact that Remo had somehow not invested in that particular shipment got Jimmy curious enough to ask some of his friends in the Queens DA's office. They confirmed Jimmy's suspicion that Remo had ratted the load out in return for his freedom.

"Remo was dead within a week. He didn't have a clue what was coming to him. Jimmy could look at you and smile and you'd think you were sitting with your best friend in the world. Meanwhile he's got your grave dug. In fact, the very week Jimmy killed him, Remo had given Jimmy and Mickey a round-trip ticket to Florida as an anniversary present.

"I remember the night. We were all playing cards in Robert's when Jimmy said to Remo, 'Let's take a ride.' He motioned to Tommy and another guy to come along. Remo got in the front seat and Tommy and Jimmy got in the rear. When they got to a quiet area, Tommy used a piano wire. Remo put up some fight. He kicked and swung and shit all over himself before he died. They buried him in the backyard at Robert's, under a layer of cement right next to the boccie court. From then on, every time they played, Jimmy and Tommy used to say, 'Hi, Remo, how ya doing?'

"It didn't take anything for these guys to kill you. They liked it. They would sit around drinking booze and talk about their favorite hits. They enjoyed talking about them. They liked to relive the moment while repeating how miserable the guy was. He was always the worst sonofabitch they knew. He was always a rat bastard, and most of the time it wasn't even business. Guys would get into arguments with each other and before you knew it one of them was dead. They were shooting each other all the time. Shooting people was a normal thing for them. It was no big deal. You didn't have to do anything. You just had to be there.

"One night, right after my arrest for assaulting the wrong guy, we were having a party in Robert's for Billy Batts. Billy had just gotten out of prison after six years. We usually gave a guy a party when he got out. Food. Booze. Hookers. It's a good time. Billy was a made guy. He was with Johnny Gotti from near Fulton Street and he was hooked up with the Gambinos. We're all bombed. Jimmy. Tommy. Me. Billy turned around and he saw Tommy, who he knew from before he went away. Tommy was only about twenty at the time, so the last time Billy saw him Tommy was just a kid. Billy started to kid around. He asked Tommy if he still shined shoes. It was just a snide remark, but you couldn't kid around with Tommy. He was wired very tight. One of Tommy's brothers had ratted people out years ago, and he was always living that down. He always had to show he was tougher than anyone around. He always had to be special. He was the only guy in the crew that used to drink Crown Royal. It was a Canadian whiskey that wasn't imported back when he was a kid. Tommy had it smuggled in. He was the kind of guy who was being so tough he managed to find a bootleg hooch to drink thirty years after Prohibition.

"I looked over at Tommy, and I could see he was fuming at the way Billy was talking. Tommy was going nuts, but he couldn't do or say anything. Billy was a made man. If Tommy so much as took a slap at Billy, Tommy was dead. Still, I knew he was pissed. We kept drinking and laughing, and just when I thought maybe it was all forgotten, Tommy leaned over to Jimmy and me and said, 'I'm gonna kill that fuck.' I joked back with him, but I saw he was serious.

"A couple of weeks later Billy was drinking in The Suite. It was late. I was praying he'd go home when Tommy walked in. It didn't take long. Tommy immediately sent his girlfriend home and he gave me and Jimmy a look. Right away Jimmy started getting real cozy with Billy Batts. He started buying Billy drinks. I could see he was setting Billy up for Tommy.

" 'Keep him here, I'm going for a bag,' Tommy whispered to me, and I knew he was going to kill Billy right in my own joint. He was going for a body bag—a plastic mattress cover—so Billy wouldn't bleed all over the place after he killed him. Tommy was back with the bag and a thirty-eight in twenty minutes. I was getting sick.

"By now Jimmy has Billy Batts in the corner of the bar near the wall. They were drinking and Jimmy was telling him stories. Billy was having a great time. As it got late almost everybody went home. Only Alex Corcione, who was seated in back with his girl, was left in the place. The bartender left. Jimmy had his arm hanging real loose around Billy's shoulder when Tommy came over. Billy didn't even look up. Why should he? He was with friends. Fellow wiseguys. He had no idea that Tommy was going to kill him.

"I was on the side of the bar when Tommy took the thirty-eight out of his pocket. Billy saw it in Tommy's hand. The second Billy saw what was happening, Jimmy tightened his arm around Billy's neck. 'Shine these fuckin' shoes,' Tommy yells and smashes the gun right into the side of Billy's head. Billy's eyes opened wide. Tommy smashed him again. Jimmy kept his grip. The blood began to come out of Billy's head. It looked black.

"By now Alex Corcione saw what was going on and he started to come over. Jimmy glared at him. 'You want some?' Jimmy said. Jimmy was ready to drop Billy and go after Alex. I got between them as though I was going to belt Alex. But I just grabbed Alex by the shoulders and steered him toward the door. 'Get out of here,' I said, real quiet, so Jimmy can't hear. 'They've got a beef.' I maneuvered Alex and his girl out the door and they were gone. Alex was with our own crew, but Jimmy and Tommy were so hot right then they would have whacked Alex and his girl right there if he gave them trouble. I locked the front door, and when I turned back I saw that Billy's body was spread out on the floor. His head was a bloody mess. Tommy had opened the mattress cover. Jimmy told me to bring the car around back.

"We had a problem. Billy Batts was untouchable. There has to be an okay before a made man can be killed. If the Gambino people ever found out that Tommy killed Billy, we were all dead. There was no place we could go. They could even have demanded that Paulie whack us himself. Tommy had done the worst possible thing he could have done, and we all knew it. Billy's body had to disappear. We couldn't leave it on the street. There would have been a war. With no body around, the Gotti crew would never know for sure.

"Jimmy said we had to bury the body where it couldn't be found. He had a friend upstate with a dog kennel, where nobody would ever look. We put Billy in the trunk of the car, and we drove by Tommy's house to pick up a shovel. His mother was already up and made us come in for coffee. She wouldn't let us leave. We have to have breakfast—with a body parked outside.

"Finally we left Tommy's and got on the Taconic. We'd been driving about an hour when I heard a funny noise. I'm in the back half asleep, with the shovel. Tommy was driving. Jimmy was asleep. I heard the noise again. It was like a thump. Jimmy woke up. The banging began again. It dawned on all of us at once. Billy Batts was alive. He was banging on the trunk. We were on our way to bury him and he wasn't even dead.

"Now Tommy really got mad. He slammed on the brakes. He leaned over the seat and grabbed the shovel. Nobody said a word. We got out of the car and waited until there were no more headlights coming up behind us. Then Jimmy got on one side and I got on the other and Tommy opened the trunk. The second it sprang open Tommy smashed the sack with the shovel. Jimmy grabbed a tire iron and he started banging away at the sack. It only took a few seconds, and we got back in the car. When we got to the spot where we were going to bury Billy, the ground was so frozen we had to dig for an hour to get him down deep enough. Then we covered him with lime and drove back to New York.

"But even then Billy was like a curse. About three months after we planted the guy, Jimmy came up to me at The Suite and said Tommy and I would have to dig up the body and bury it somewhere else. The guy who owned the kennel had just sold his property to a housing developer. He had been bragging to Jimmy about how much money he was going to make, but all Jimmy knew was that workmen might find the body. That night Tommy and I took my brand-new yellow Pontiac Catalina convertible and we dug Billy up. It was awful. We had put lime on the body to help it decompose, but it was only half gone. The smell was so bad I got sick. I started to throw up. All the time Tommy and I worked I was throwing up. We put the body in the trunk and took it to a junkyard we used in Jersey. Enough time had passed so nobody was going to think it was Billy.

"I stayed sick for a week. I couldn't get away from the smell. Everything smelled like the body. The restaurant grease. The kids' candy. I couldn't stop smelling it. I threw away the clothes, even the shoes I wore that night, thinking they were the problem. I couldn't get the smell of it out of the trunk of my car. I ripped out all the upholstery and threw it away. I gave the car a real scrubbing. I tossed a bottle of Karen's perfume inside and closed the lid. But I couldn't get rid of the smell. It never went away. I finally had to junk the car. Jimmy and Tommy thought I was nuts. Tommy said if he could have smelled it he would have kept the car just to remind him about how he took care of that miserable bastard Billy Batts.

"I don't know how many people Tommy killed. I don't even think

Jimmy knew. Tommy was out of control. He'd begun carrying two guns. One night Tommy shot a kid named Spider in the foot just because the kid didn't want to dance. It looked accidental, and Vinnie Asaro, who's with the Bonanno crew, took Spider to a neighborhood doctor to get the kid fixed up. We let Spider sleep in Robert's for a couple of weeks. He was walking around with his leg in bandages. But crazy Tommy kept making the kid dance. Tommy said he was using the kid for target practice.

"One night we're playing cards in the cellar—Tommy, Jimmy, me, Anthony Stabile, Angelo Sepe—when the Spider walks in. It's three o'clock in the morning and we're all smashed out of our minds. All of a sudden Tommy wants him to dance. 'Do a dance,' Tommy says. For some reason Spider tells Tommy to go fuck himself. Now we started getting on Tommy. Jimmy is joking and he says to Tommy, 'You take that shit from this punk?' We're all egging Tommy on, joking with him. He's getting mad, but he's still playing cards. Then, before anyone has any idea what he's going to do, he puts three shots into Spider's chest. I didn't even know where he had the gun, except for a second we're all deaf. I can smell burn. Nobody says a word, but now I'm convinced Tommy is a total psychopath.

"Finally Jimmy yelled at him, 'All right, you dumb fuck, if you're going to be a big fucking wiseguy, you dig the hole.' That was it. Nothing else. Nobody said anything else. Jimmy just made Tommy dig the hole right there in the cellar, and all the while Tommy was grousing and pissed off that he had to dig the hole. He was like a kid who had been bad and had to clean the erasers after school.

"Every day was some kind of war. Every day was another sit-down. Every time we went out bouncing, somebody got bombed and there was a war. Everybody was getting very hot all the time. One night Paulie, who was usually calm, came into Robert's crazy mad. He wanted everybody. Call Jimmy. Call the cabstand. Get Brooksie from the junkyard. I thought it was a full-scale war. It turned out that he and Phyllis had gone to Don Pepe's Vesuvio Restaurant, on Lefferts Boulevard, just a few blocks south of Robert's. Don Pepe's was a great restaurant, but the owner was a real pain. There were no menus, and he wouldn't take reservations. Everybody waited on line, even Paulie.

"It turned out that Paulie and Phyllis had waited on line for half an hour while a new maître d' kept seating one doctor after another in front of Paulie. When Paulie complained, the guy finally gave him a table, but he was pissed at Paulie. When Paulie ordered some wine, the maître d' came to pour and, maybe by accident, spilled it all over Phyllis. By now Paulie's coming out of his skin. But when the maître d' pulled out a dirty rag and started putting his hands all over Phyllis' dress, Paulie turned over the table, and he started to slap the guy around. Paulie only managed to get one or two swings at the guy before he ran into the kitchen. When Paulie told him to come out, a half dozen waiters with heavy pans and knives blocked the kitchen door.

"I never saw Paulie so angry. He said if the waiters wanted to protect their friend, then they were all going to get their heads broken. Within an hour we had two carloads of guys with baseball bats and pipes waiting outside Don Pepe's. By eleven o'clock the waiters and kitchen help got off. The minute they saw us waiting for them they started to run. A few jumped in cars. We were chasing waiters and breaking heads all over Brooklyn that night.

"It was so easy. Lump them up. Whack them out. Nobody ever thought, Why? What for? Nobody thought about business. The truth was the violence began to damage the business. The hijackings, for instance, had been going beautifully, but all of a sudden everyone began getting very loose with their hands. 'Whack 'em!' 'Fuck 'em!' That's all they knew.

"I didn't usually go out on the actual hijackings. There was Tommy, Stanley, Joey Allegro, and other guys who enjoyed sticking a gun in a driver's face. I usually dealt with the distribution of the stuff. I had the buyers. I lined up some of the deals. Sometimes, however, if we got shorthanded I'd go on the heist myself. On this occasion we had a two-hundred-thousand-dollar cigarette load. It was going to be easy. It was half a 'give-up,' which meant one of the two drivers was in on the deal.

"We grabbed them right near their garage at the Elk Street warehouse. They were making the turn onto the Brooklyn-Queens Expressway when Tommy and Stanley jumped on the running boards, one on each side. They showed guns. Joey Allegro and I are in the backup car. Stanley made the driver who's with us give up the dashboard code. Big trucks with valuable loads usually had a keyboard under the dash with three buttons. You need to know the code to start the engine, or even open and close the doors, or the truck's burglar alarm would go off.

"Tommy put the drivers in the car and got in with Joey, and I got in the truck with Stanley, and we headed for the drop, which was a legitimate truck warehouse near the General Post Office on West Thirty-sixth Street. Jimmy was waiting there with five unloaders. He had long rollers, and we started running the cigarette cartons out of the trailer and into other trucks. There were other trucks being unloaded at the same time, and of course none of the workmen knew we were unloading a hot truck. We were in the middle of the job when this big burly guy comes over and wants to see our union cards. We don't have union cards, we've got guns.

"He was a big, chesty guy and he didn't know Jimmy and he didn't give a fuck. He started a beef that Jimmy's unloaders were not members of the union. He was going to close the whole place down. Jimmy tried to talk to him. No good. Jimmy tried to take care of him with a few bucks. No good. The guy wanted to see our union cards. He was a real pain, and Jimmy had another two hundred thousand dollars' worth of cigarettes lined up to be unloaded in the same place the next day.

"By now we've got the truck pretty well cleaned out, except for twenty cases of Laredo roll-your-own cigarettes we left in the truck because nobody wanted them. Jimmy motioned to me and Stanley to move the truck out of there. Stanley, thank God, remembered the dashboard code to start the engine without the alarm going off, and within seconds we're heading down Ninth Avenue toward the Lincoln Tunnel and New Jersey to dump the truck.

"We hadn't gone a couple of blocks before I noticed that people were waving at us. They were screaming at us. They're pointing to the back of the truck. I stick my head out the window and I realize that Jimmy and the crew forgot to lock the back of the trailer and we've been dropping cartons of Laredo cigarettes along Ninth Avenue. It's unbelievable. People were screaming at us and we were pretending not to hear them, but when we got to the next corner, parked right in front of us was a police radio car. That was it. I looked at Stanley and said, 'Pull over and let's close it.' Stanley just looked at me, blank. I said, 'If I don't lock that rear door, we're going to get stopped.' But he looked really sad and said I couldn't lock the back door because I couldn't get out of the truck without triggering the alarm. He said he had been trying to remember the dashboard code for opening the doors, but he couldn't. If I got out of the truck in the middle of Ninth Avenue all the alarms would go off.

"I remember we just looked at each other for a minute, said 'Fuck it,' and wiggled out the truck windows. We must have looked pretty peculiar. As soon as we hit the pavement we took off. We made sure we weren't followed and went back to the drop, where Jimmy's really steaming because the union guy is still busting his chops. The guy was threatening Jimmy. He said there wouldn't be another truck unloaded unless the workers were union. The guy was hopeless.

"That night Jimmy sent Stanley Diamond and Tommy DeSimone to New Jersey, where the guy lived, to straighten him out. They were just going to rough him up a little bit. Just get him to mind his own business a little bit. Instead, Stanley and Tommy got so carried away with the ball buster that they killed the guy. They were so pissed that the guy wouldn't listen to Jimmy, that he lived in the boondocks of Jersey, and that they had to go all the way out there just to talk to him, they got themselves so worked up that they just couldn't keep from killing him."

Eleven

In 1969, at the age of twenty-six, Henry was living in a rented house in Island Park, just two blocks from Paulie's. He and Karen both had brand-new Buick Rivieras and closets bursting with new clothes. He had fifteen Brioni suits, for which he had paid one thousand dollars each, over thirty custom-made silk shirts, and two dozen pairs of alligator and lizard shoes dyed to match his suits and cashmere sports jackets. There were so many clothes that the two of them used to fight over hangers. There were bureau drawers jammed with bracelets, wafer-thin platinum and gold watches, sapphire rings, antique brooches, gold cuff links, and tangled webs of silver and gold chain necklaces.

Karen had a maid for the house and four fur coats—"She went to the supermarket in mink"—and when she needed cash she used to separate her thumb and index finger to indicate whether she needed a half inch, an inch, or an inch and a half of money. The baby's room was filled with the bounty of FAO Schwarz, and the knotty-pine basement overflowed with gifts—yacht-size prams, cashmere comforters, embroidered pillows, imported children's clothes, sets of sterling silver spoons, and a zoo full of huge stuffed animals.

Henry had it all—cash, cars, jewelry, clothes, and, after a while, even a girlfriend. For most wiseguys, having a steady girl was not unusual. Almost all of his friends had them. You didn't leave a wife or abandon a family for one, but you did swank them around, rent them apartments, lease them cars, and feed them regularly with racks of swag clothes and paper bags of stolen jewelry. Having a steady girl was considered a sign of success, like a thoroughbred or a powerboat but better: a girlfriend was the ultimate luxury purchase.

HENRY: I first met Linda by accident. It was late in 1969. I was getting ready to do a sixty-day bit on Riker's Island for untaxed cigarettes. She and her girlfriend Veralynn were having dinner in Michael's Steak Pub, in Rockville Centre, where I was having dinner with Peter Vario, Paulie's son. All of a sudden Peter started a conversation with Veralynn, so I started talking to Linda. She and Veralynn worked in Queens and shared an apartment on Fulton Street, in Hempstead. After dinner we all went to Val Anthony's, a little supper club on the north shore, where we had more drinks and danced. Linda was twenty at the time and she had just come back from California. She was all tan and blond. She was beautiful. We just hit it off right away. It was one of those nights when everything worked. Peter and Veralynn split, and Linda and I kept talking and dancing. When I drove her home we noticed Peter's car. We drove around some more, and when we got back, Peter's car was still there. By now Linda and I are into it pretty good, so we decided to spend the night together at a Holiday Inn. The next day when I drove her home, Peter's car was still in the parking lot.

A couple of days later Paulie comes by and he wants to know about the two girls we met. He said that Peter was acting dopey. Paulie said Peter hadn't talked about anything but Veralynn for days. It was Veralynn this and Veralynn that, and Paulie said he was sick of it. Paulie wanted to meet this Veralynn. I knew there had to be more to all this than he was letting on, and the next Saturday afternoon, when we were driving over to the girls' apartment, I learned why Paulie was so nervous.

"They're cops," he said. "The two of them are fucking cops." I was amazed. I said, "Paulie, are you crazy or what?" But he just kept repeating, "You'll see. They're the FBI. You'll see." I knew Paulie was under a lot of pressure from Nassau grand juries. He had just done thirty days for contempt. The juries were asking him about his numbers operation with Steve DePasquale, about a meeting at Frankie the Wop's restaurant, and about who really owned his boat. Paulie was getting the feeling that the cops were all over the place. He actually set up a closed-circuit television camera outside the window of his Brooklyn apartment. He used to sit on the bed in his underwear for hours trying to spot G-men. "There's one," he'd say. "The guy behind the tree. Didja see him?" As far as I was concerned, Paulie was acting nuts.

When we got to Linda's and Veralynn's apartment, Paulie was so certain they were cops he wouldn't go upstairs in case the place was wired. He wanted Veralynn to come down. I made up some bullshit story about just dropping by to say hello over the building's intercom. Linda said Veralynn was shopping, but she'd be right down. She came out smiling. She kissed me hello. She invited us up, but I said we were in a hurry. Paulie just grumbled. He was looking at the windows. He was looking for cops. Linda was perfect. She was smart. Charming. She wasn't pissed that I hadn't called her after our date. She wasn't upset that we'd barged in on her unannounced. She was terrific. I could see there were no dues to pay with Linda.

Meanwhile Paulie is whispering, "She's FBI. She's FBI." He's saying it under his breath so Linda can't hear him. I got so tired of his craziness that I decided to bring the question out in the open. We're all standing around Paulie's Fleetwood Cadillac, and I asked Linda point-blank if she or Veralynn were cops. Paulie looked at me like I was out of my mind, but Linda broke up laughing. She said she worked in Bridal Land, on Queens Boulevard. It was perfect. It was like sticking a pin in Paulie's balloon, because he knew the place. Bridal Land was owned by a half-assed wiseguy named Paul Stewart, who was mostly a front man for Vinnie Aloi, Buster Aloi's son. Buster was a boss with the Colombo crew.

As we talked, even Paulie saw that Linda had no idea who we were. And, more important, she didn't care. By now Paulie was looking to go home. He was bored. Before we left I told Linda that I was a CPA. She believed me for weeks. She believed that I was a CPA and that Paulie was a fat, old, crazy fuck.

After that I started seeing Linda almost every day. She was fun. Whenever I would show up, she was happy. There were no strings attached. I was living a crazy life and she went right along with me. No bullshit. No hassle. By now Karen was used to my not getting home some nights, and Linda and I were having a great time. Three or four nights a week we're out. She begins screwing up at work. She's not getting to the store until after eleven in the morning. She's having a ball, but Paul Stewart, her boss, started to get pissed. One day he yelled at her, so I went over to straighten him out. I just abused him a little. I didn't want to hurt him or anything. But the next time I call her, instead of putting her on the phone, Stewart hangs up. I called back. He hangs up again. That was it. Now I'm hot. I grabbed Jimmy, who was at the bar, and said, "Let's go!" This time I was going to do more than just threaten him a little bit. I wanted to loosen his head. When he saw us coming he started to run, but we got him in the back of the store and slapped him around a little bit. "Hang up on me, you fuck?" And I started to tie the telephone cord around his neck. He's begging and yelling and the customers are screaming to let him go.

Next thing I know there's a beef. We had a sit-down with the guy's partner, Vinnie Aloi, and Vinnie's father, Buster. I had Paulie at the table, and Jimmy was my witness. Buster started right out kissing me. The old man had loved Jimmy and me ever since we gave him a sixty-thousand share out of Air France. Buster started right away begging me not to kill the guy. He said the guy fronted for his son. I could see Vinnie Aloi sitting there hating me. The old man said Vinnie got a paycheck out of the place and had his cars registered there.

Big-shot me, I pretended I was thinking about it—like I had any intention of doing anything to the guy. I didn't care, it was already out of my system. But I played it out, and I agreed, for Buster's sake, that I wouldn't kill the rat bastard. Next thing I know, Stewart comes out of the kitchen. They had him waiting in there during the sit-down. He's shaking, and right away he apologizes to me in front of everybody. He started begging and crying. He swore that he didn't know who I was with and that he'd do anything he could to make up for the insult.

Now Linda doesn't even have to go to work. We started seeing more of each other. Pretty soon I was living two lives. I set Linda up in an apartment around the corner from The Suite. I'd get home three or four nights a week, and I'd usually take Karen out to a show or club on Saturday night too. Karen always looked forward to Saturday nights. The rest of the week she was usually busy with the kids and I did my bouncing with the crew and took Linda along. Everybody got to know her. Linda became a part of my life.

LINDA: I first met Henry when Peter Vario started to see my roommate, Veralynn. Henry and I met, and we just hit it off. We both liked to laugh and to enjoy ourselves. He was a very sweet guy. He was kind. I could see the way he did things for people without taking credit and without even letting them know what he did.

I think I was his escape, and that wasn't so terrible. He was always under tremendous pressure. He and Karen were always fighting. They couldn't say two words to each other without a war. Every time he had a fight with her he'd come over to see me. Once she threw away all their car keys, and he got on a bike and had to pedal four miles to my place. Karen was a very strong, demanding person. She put a lot of pressure on him. When they got married, for instance, she had him convert. He was twenty or twenty-one at the time, and she made him get circumcised. It was horrible. He was walking around with a diaper for a month.

He was very different from the guys he hung around with. He was a taming influence. He used to be able to get them to do normal things. When we first took the apartment near The Suite, for instance, the furniture store wouldn't deliver my stuff immediately, so Henry got Jimmy and Tommy and a truck, and they all went to the store in Hempstead on a Saturday and picked up the stuff themselves.

They were like big, noisy kids. That's what they reminded me of. Always laughing. Always looking to have fun. Especially Jimmy. I knew him as "Burkey" back then. I never heard anybody call him "Jimmy the Gent." He was the biggest kid of them all. He loved water fights. At Robert's Lounge or The Suite he would rig up pails of water, and when someone walked in the door, he'd dump the buckets all over their heads. Robert's was incredible. It was like a clubhouse for high school kids, except they had a terrazzo floor in part of the basement and a huge barbecue in the backyard. There were cherubs and sconces all over the walls. Tommy had an apartment on the second floor. Paul loved to cook, and everyone was always trying this or trying that and complaining that he put in too much salt or not enough garlic.

Henry and I went out for a long time, and I felt I had become a part of his life and close to his friends and their families. I understood he had the children. I knew it was hard for him to leave. But I loved being with him so much, it was worth it to me. I went from week to week and month to month, and there was always the thought that maybe this time he would stay and not go back.

The holidays were the worst. Christmas. New Year's. They were awful. I was always alone. Waiting for him to get out of his house and meet me for half a date. He was always late, and lots of times he never came. He'd make sneak phone calls, and that just made me madder. A couple of times he'd send me away just before the holidays. He'd book me on a plane to Vegas or the Caribbean and say he'd meet me on Christmas Day or right after he took care of his kids. I'd go with some of the other girls. I'd go with Tommy's sister, who was also seeing a married guy. When he wouldn't show up I'd get so mad that I'd stay an extra week and run his bill sky-high.

But meanwhile I was usually with him and with his friends and we were all very close. After a while everything began to feel almost normal.

KAREN: I first began to suspect that Henry might have been fooling around just before he was sent to Riker's Island on an earlier cigarette case. I knew, because I was just pregnant with Ruth, and I felt that something was wrong. I suppose there had already been a million clues, but under the circumstances, who was looking? I had to get hit with it in the face before I wanted to look. During that summer a girlfriend of mine called and said she and her husband were driving past The Suite when they saw us in the doorway next to the restaurant. She said she was going to stop, but her husband said that he thought we were having a real fight, and so they just kept on going. I didn't say anything to my friend, but I knew I was never in any doorway fighting with my husband. I knew it had to be somebody else.

And then there were the couple of times when I'd call The Suite and ask for Henry without saying who I was. Once or twice whoever answered the phone said, "I'll get him, Lin," or "Hold on, Lin." Lin? Who's Lin?

Every time I brought this up to Henry it would create a fight. He'd get angry and start yelling that I was a witch, and sometimes he'd just walk out and I wouldn't hear from him for a day or two. It was very frustrating. I would yell and accuse him, and he'd act like he couldn't hear me and just go about the house packing his bag. He said I was making stuff up and that he had enough headaches without me driving him crazy. But he never denied anything, he just got mad.

That's why I made us move back from Island Park to Queens.

After the Nassau DA raided the pizzeria and arrested Raymond Montemurro in a roundup, I spotted two men in a car taking pictures of me and the kids. That was all the excuse I needed. That night I told Henry about the photographers. I said that Nassau was too hot. He agreed. Within weeks we were living just three miles from The Suite in a three-bedroom apartment with a terrace in Rego Park.

The Suite was Henry's office, and I began to drop in there for an hour or so every couple of days. I said I wanted to keep an eye on the books, but I was keeping an eye on everything. There were lots of people hanging around the place all the time. There was one girl, Linda, who worked in the bridal shop nearby, and she'd come in for lunch and stay. She was such a sad sack that I never put two and two together. I never picked her. I remember the first time I saw her was at a Halloween party in a friend's apartment. I was there with Henry, and she was pretending to be with the host's brother. Again she was crying her eyes out. She followed me into the bathroom at the party, and I told her if anybody was giving her this much trouble, she should leave him. She was still crying. I was so dumb I gave her a Kleenex.

But she kept right on mooning around The Suite. Lots of nights when Henry and I were going out, she'd be at the bar crying in her drink. I just thought she was a drunk. Little did I know that she was crying because Henry was going home with me.

One day the Chinese chef finally straightened me out. I had called the place looking for Henry, and again somebody called me "Lin." This time I went tearing over there. I must have been hysterical. I had Judy with me, and I was as big as a house with Ruth. And I was mad. I went right to the kitchen and I grabbed the poor chef. He hardly spoke English. I wanted to know who Lin was. He kept saying there wasn't any Lin. "No Lin, no Lin!" he kept saying. "Linda is Lin! Linda is Lin!"

I was a wild woman. I got her address from the kitchen, because they used to send food around to her apartment. She never cooked or cleaned. I snatched up the baby and went to her building. She buzzed me in from downstairs, not knowing who I was, but when I got to her apartment and told her we had to talk, she pretended she wasn't home. She wouldn't open her door. I rang her bell. She still wouldn't open. I rang her bell continuously for two hours, and she kept on hiding.

LINDA: I've got a crazy person screaming at the door. She was hysterical. She thought Henry was in my apartment. She kept yelling that she could hear him going out the fire escape. I didn't even have a fire escape. She was desperate to keep him, and she was driving him crazy.

She knew something was up. That's why she started hanging around all the time, but Henry and I still got away. Once, just before she tried to break down my door, Henry took me to Nassau, in the Bahamas. He wanted to sneak Paulie out of the country for a long weekend just before the old guy had to go to jail for a while.

Henry got Paulie and his wife phony papers, and we had a great time. Paulie was so nervous away from his own world that he wouldn't leave us for a second. He's got so much money, but he's never been anywhere or done anything. Paulie lived through Henry.

We went to the casino on Paradise Island and Paulie and Henry had a credit line. We caught Billy Daniels at LaConcha and became his guests. We spent the night looking for a hooker for him.

When we got back, customs decided to go through my luggage and clothes with a full search. Paulie and Henry were on the floor in hysterics.

I think Karen heard about all this and that's why she was hanging around and why she decided to make her move. She was losing him. He was taking me and not her away with Paulie. She was desperate, and she could ring my bell until her finger turned blue.

HENRY: That night I got home late. Everything looked normal. The baby was in bed. I was a little loaded and tired. Karen was doing some stuff around the house. I got in bed and collapsed. I must have been half asleep when I felt this pressure on my arms and shoulders. I was groggy and smashed and I opened my eyes just a bit and saw that Karen was straddling me in the bed. She had a thirty-eight aimed right between my eyes. I always kept a loaded gun in the bedroom closet and I knew it worked. I could see the bullets in the cylinder. She was shaking and panting. She pulled back the hammer on the gun. She had me pinned. I sobered up immediately. She was screaming about Linda and Lin and the restaurant and the chef, and I can feel she's getting hysterical.

I started talking. I thought maybe somehow she was in some control of herself. She hadn't said a word when I got home. She'd kept it all in until now. I thought maybe she was just being slick. So I started talking to her, and after a while I managed to move her hand very gently and got the gun away. Now I was mad. I was so mad I belted her. I didn't need this bullshit. I had to worry about getting shot by wiseguys; I didn't have to worry about getting shot by my wife. I told her I'd be back when she calmed down. I packed a bag and moved in with Linda for a couple of weeks. It was the first of a dozen times over the next few years when I moved out, and there were a couple of times when Karen moved out on me.

KAREN: That first night when I got the gun I was really mad. I felt used. At first I thought, Oh, boy, am I going to scare him! But once I had the gun in my hand my palm began to sweat. I felt so powerful it was frightening. The gun was heavy. I'd never held a gun that heavy before, but once I had it I began to feel that I could use it. I felt that I could have killed him. I put it between his eyes. I called his name softly. Like I was waking him up from a nap. He opened his eyes, slowly. Then I cocked the gun. I pulled back the hammer. I wanted him to know how desperate I had become. But still I couldn't hurt him. How could I hurt him? I couldn't even bring myself to leave him.

The truth was no matter how bad I felt, I was still very, very attracted to him. He could be incredible. He had a side that was so nice you wanted to bottle it. He was sweet, considerate, sincere, soft. He had no sharp edges. He wasn't like the other guys around him. He was young, and I was just attracted. My sisters used to say I was obsessed with him, because whenever he and I split up for a few days or even a couple of weeks, I never talked about anything else. Also, whenever we got back together after a brief separation, he always swore it was forever. No more Linda! I wanted to believe him. I think he wanted to believe it.

I suppose if I wrote down the pros and cons of the marriage, lots of people might think I was nuts to stay with him, but I guess we all have our own needs, and they're not added up in the columns. He and I were always excited by each other, even later, after the kids and all those years together. We turned each other on. Sometimes in the middle of a real brawl we'd look at each other and laugh, and the war was over.

I would listen to my friends talk about their marriages, and I knew that for all my troubles, I still had a better deal than they did. When I looked at him I knew I had him, because I saw how jealous he got. Once he threatened to burn down some guy's business just because the guy was making a play for me. I loved to watch him get mad.

But still, when I first found out what was going on, it was very tough. I was married to him. I had Judy and the baby to worry about. What am I supposed to do? Throw him away? Throw away somebody I was attracted to and who was a very good provider? He wasn't like most of his friends, who made their wives beg for a five-dollar bill. I always had money. He never counted money with me. If there was anything I wanted, I got it, and it made him happy. Why should I kick him out? Why should I lose him just because he was fooling around? Why should I give him up to someone else?

Never! If I was going to kick anybody, it was the person who was trying to take him away from me. Why should she win?

And besides, the minute I started checking her out with the other wives, I heard that every time he was with her he was drunk. I heard that he was abusive and made her wait in the car all night like a dope while he played cards with the guys. The way I began to see it, she was getting the worst side of him and I was getting the best.

HENRY: I'd be with Karen and the kids most of the time, but when Karen would start screaming or driving me nuts, I'd go over to Linda's. I'd be there for a few days, and I'd go back to Karen. This madness went on even when I was in jail. I remember on Riker's Island, Karen tore into the visitors' lounge screaming like a gorilla. She was crazy. It turned out one of the rat stool pigeon hacks had showed her Linda's name on my visitors' list. Karen made me take Linda's name off the list or she wouldn't vouch for my strong family ties and healthy homelife when she was interviewed by the social workers and parole officers about my getting an early release. It meant a couple of months to me on the street, so I told the warden to take Linda's name off the list.

KAREN: When he was on Riker's I visited him as often as possible, and that place was really a pigsty. The guards treated the wives awful. Visitors had to drive to a parking area near the island and then take a prison bus over a guarded bridge to one of the trailers, where they were picked up and taken to the various buildings for their visits. I was so big I could hardly get in and out of the buses, but the other women had to take lots of abuse and a lot of pawing from the guards. It was really disgusting, but what could the women do? They couldn't yell at the guards, because they'd never get their visits, and they didn't want to tell their husbands or boyfriends, because that would only make things worse. And all of this for visits that only lasted twenty minutes, and you had to talk over a telephone through a filthy glass partition nobody ever cleaned. Also, you couldn't visit whenever you wanted. I had to go on Saturdays, then I couldn't go again until the following Sunday, and then I had to wait until Saturday again.

I was working with the lawyer to get him out as early as possible. For instance, there was a rule that you got ten days off a month for good behavior. That would have taken one third off his sixty-day term. I went right to the fines-and-release window, and they told me the rule had just been changed to only five days off. I had a fit. I went to our lawyer and got the papers that showed Henry had been committed under the old rules. I wrote letters to the commissioner. I wrote letters to the Board of Corrections. I wrote to everybody. I got our lawyer to write. I fought it and I won. They decided to give Henry twenty days off his term instead of ten.

But even with the twenty days off, he still couldn't get out until December 28, and I had made myself the promise that I'd get him home for Christmas. I just had it in my head. That's one of the things that kept me going. I went back to the window at Riker's. I said that since the twenty-eighth was a Sunday, and I knew they let people out before the weekend, Henry would normally be released on Friday, the twenty-sixth. They agreed, but they said it still came up one day after Christmas. I remember the guy said, "I can't get the day from the air." Then I asked, "What about the two days when he was arrested?" I had learned that they can count arrest time toward incarceration time. Henry hadn't been under arrest for two days, but the guards just looked at each other. I was making a lot of work. That's when one of them went to check something and left the visitor's book right there at the desk. That's when I saw her name on his list. I was so furious by the time the guard came back with the approval, I couldn't hear him. I went wild, because here I was knocking myself out trying to get him home for Christmas and he's got his girlfriend visiting him on my visiting day. I just wanted to kill him. I was so mad when I saw him that all I did was yell at him. I didn't even tell him that he was getting out early. Let him suffer.

HENRY: After Karen made me take Linda off the list I had Linda pissed at me. Linda was so mad that the first day I was back on the street she caught up with me at The Suite. We had a real fight. She took off a seven-carat black opal ring I had bought her and threw it at me so hard she split the stone. Then she slapped me right in front of everybody in the joint. I grabbed her by the throat and pushed her right out the door. We're on the street, and she's still yelling. She was wearing a white mink stole I had given her. She went to the curb and took off the mink and shoved it right down the sewer. Then I belted her. She quieted down and looked hurt. Now I felt shitty. I felt so bad for what I did that I got a busboy to fish the stole out of the sewer, and I took her home and we made up. After a couple of nights with Linda, Karen called Paulie and Jimmy, and they came by and said it was time for me to go home.

My life was a constant battle, but I couldn't bring myself to leave either one. I couldn't leave Linda and I couldn't leave Karen. I felt like I needed them both.

Twelve

I

t always struck Henry as grossly unfair that after a lifetime of major crimes and petty punishments his longest stretch—a ten-year sentence in a federal penitentiary—came about because he got into a barroom brawl with a man whose sister was a typist for the FBI. It was as if he had suddenly hit the Superfecta of bad luck. He had been caught in a barroom brawl, and they had literally made a federal case out of it.

It had started as a lark, a spur-of-the-moment trip to Florida with his pals Jimmy Burke and Casey Rosado, the president of Local 71 of the Waiters and Commissary Workers at Kennedy Airport. Casey wanted company—he was going down to Tampa to see his parents and pick up some gambling money that was owed him. Tommy DeSimone had been scheduled to go, but he had been arrested on a hijacking the night before, and he wasn't going to get bailed out early enough to make the flight. So Jimmy asked Henry if he wanted to go.

"Why not? A little vacation. The union had already paid for a first-class round-trip ticket, and the flight would get me away from battling with Karen and Linda for a couple of days. Time out. That's the way I looked at it. I called Karen from The Suite and told her to pack me a bag. Jimmy and I picked it up on our way to the airport.

"We got to Tampa late that night and were met by Casey's cousin in a car. We went straight to Casey's parents' house, where there was a lot of hugging and kissing. Finally we left our suitcases there and went to the Colombia Restaurant, in Ybor City, the old Cuban section of town, where Casey and his cousin turned out to be local celebrities. Everybody knew them.

"We were just going to have a good time. At dinner Casey said that the guy who owed him the money was named John Ciaccio and that he owned the Temple Terrace Lounge, just outside Ybor City. Casey said he had a meeting with the guy later that night. Jimmy said he and I would tag along.

"When we got to Ciaccio's place I saw that it was a pretty big, one-story, cement block lounge surrounded by a giant parking lot. There was a liquor store right next to it which was also owned by Ciaccio. I saw that the place was near an intersection. I made a note that if there was trouble we could drive away from the bar real fast and disappear on either of two four-lane highways.

"Before we went inside, Casey's cousin came over to me and out of nowhere handed me a huge thirty-eight revolver. It was an antique. It was bound to explode if you tried to use it. I put it in my jacket and forgot about it. Casey and his cousin walked in first. After a minute Jimmy and I walked in. The room was very dark. It took a few seconds to see anything, but I could hear that the place was jumping. Casey was already talking to the guy near the bar, and when they walked over to a table, Jimmy and I sat down about four tables away.

"Pretty soon Casey and the guy were yelling at each other in Spanish. We didn't know what they were yelling about. But all of a sudden the guy and Casey both jumped up. When they jumped up, we jumped up. I had the gun in my hand, and we walked over to their table. Jimmy grabbed the guy's tie and twisted it around until the guy's eyes bulged. Jimmy had his fist right under the guy's chin, pressing it into his throat. Jimmy said, 'Shut your mouth and walk out the door.'

"I watched the room to see if anyone made a move. There must have been twenty-five people in the place, but nobody did anything. Later they were all witnesses at the trial, and the bartender, a retired New York cop, got our license plate when we pulled away. It turned out that Casey's cousin had rented the car for us in his own name. I still can't get over that.

"Casey and his cousin were in the front, and Jimmy and I had the guy squeezed between us. The bum was screaming that he wouldn't give up any money. He was yelling that we would have to kill him before he paid. A real tough guy. I whacked him across the face with the gun a few times. I didn't really want to hurt him too bad. After about two blocks he changed his mind. He said he'd pay but he only owed half the money—the rest was owed by a doctor who had been in on the bet. All this negotiating was going on in Spanish. Casey's cousin said he knew the doctor and the guy was probably telling the truth. Casey said he didn't care who paid just as long as they paid him the money they owed.

"I could see that all of these people knew each other very well. I felt like I was in the middle of some hotheaded family feud. Jimmy and I were the strangers. I decided to keep the gun just in case. We drove to a bar owned by Casey's cousin, but by now the guy was bleeding so badly that we had to pull his jacket up over his head when we walked him inside so that he wouldn't attract too much attention. We hustled him right into a small storage room in the rear of the bar, but there were still enough witnesses, including a couple of waitresses, who later testified against us in court. Casey called the doctor.

"It took half the night, but they finally came up with the dough. We cleaned up the guy as best we could and turned him over to his brother. That was it. Case closed. No big deal. Jimmy and I spent the rest of the night and most of the weekend drinking rum and brandy with Casey and his cousin.

"About a month after I got back I was driving down Lefferts Boulevard on my way to Robert's Lounge when I saw eight or twelve cars blocking the street. They were parked all over the sidewalk. I saw Jimmy Santos standing near the corner. 'Get out of here,' he said. 'Put on your radio.' I did what Santos said and I heard that the FBI was 'arresting union officials' and that 'Jimmy Burke and others are being sought.'

"I still didn't know what was going on. I thought it might have had something to do with our having broken up an airport restaurant for Casey the night before. Until I knew more about what was happening I didn't want to go home. I didn't want to go to The Suite. I went to Linda's and watched the television news. That's the first I knew that they were talking about Florida. It was a big thing. They even interrupted shows with news flashes. I couldn't believe it. They said we were an organized-crime, interstate gambling ring. They made it sound like we were part of some big syndicate.

"It didn't make any sense. For some crazy reason the feds had decided to play our little case up big. Jimmy and I met with Casey and all of our lawyers, and none of us could figure the damn thing out until just before the trial. That's when we found out that John Ciaccio, the guy we'd roughed up, had a sister who was a typist for the FBI. Nobody knew that was where she worked. Even her family just thought she had some ordinary job with the government.

"She had apparently gone to see him on the night we beat him up, and she got hysterical. She was afraid her whole family was going to get beaten up and killed. She cried the whole weekend. Monday she went in to work and burst into tears in the middle of the Tampa office of the FBI. She was surrounded by agents. Of course they asked her why she was crying and of course she gave it all up. Her brother. His friends. The bars. The bets. The doctor. And, naturally, us. The agents went wild. They had an organized-crime case in their own backyard.

"We were first indicted by the state of Florida for kidnapping and attempted murder, but we beat that case because Casey took the stand and convinced the jury that Ciaccio was a liar. Casey was the only one of us whose record was clean enough so he could take the stand and not get picked apart by the prosecutor in the cross-examination.

"But after we beat the state case, the feds came after us with an extortion indictment. Just before we were going to trial, Casey Rosado, the only one of us who could take the stand, dropped dead one morning while putting on his shoes. He was forty-six. His wife said he was sitting on the edge of the bed and just bent over to tie his laces and he never got up. He collapsed. A heart attack.

"I almost had a heart attack myself when I heard what happened, because I knew with Casey gone our chances for beating the case were gone. And was I right. The trial, which took twelve days, was over on November 3, 1972. It took the jury six hours to bring in a verdict. Guilty. It was unanimous. The judge gave us ten years like he was giving away candy."

Thirteen

A ten-year sentence—it was more time than Karen could conceive of. When she first heard about it, she planned to move in immediately with her parents. Then she planned to kill herself. Then she planned to kill Henry. Then she planned to divorce him. She worried about how she would support herself and the children. She awoke every morning to greater and greater anxiety. And yet she felt compelled to stay with him for the time being—from day to day, she used to tell herself, or until he was taken behind the wall and it was finally over.

But Henry didn't go off to prison right away. In fact, as a result of the appeals his lawyers filed, almost two years elapsed between the time of his sentencing in Tampa and the day he finally surrendered in New York and actually began serving his ten-year term. In those twenty-one months Henry completed the time he owed Nassau County for his misdemeanor plea, opened a restaurant in Queens, and hustled as he had never hustled before. He was practically a one-man crime wave. He borrowed money from loan sharks that he never intended to pay back. He moved truckloads of swag at discount rates (below the usual 30 percent of wholesale), and reorganized his stolen-car gang for the chop shops, looking for spare parts. He traded stolen and counterfeit credit cards with his old pal from Robert's Lounge, Stacks Edwards. He started buying Sterno in bulk to keep up with the demand for his services as an arsonist. As the prison date drew near, he busted out The Suite, running up huge bills with creditors, selling off liquor and fixtures to other bar owners, even after the IRS had padlocked his door. One night, just before the end, Henry burglarized his own place so thoroughly that when the IRS agents went to auction, they found that every glass, dish, chair, Naugahyde banquette, bar stool, lighting fixture, and ashtray had disappeared.

"The day before I went in I took Linda to the top of the Empire State Building. It was the first time in my life I had ever gone up there. I told her that I was going away in the morning. She hadn't known exactly when I had to start my sentence. I told her that if I had half a million dollars I'd take her away with me to Brazil in a minute, but I didn't have half a million, and, anyway, I was a bum. I said that it was better if she went her own way. I told her it was time for her to move on. Don't waste any more time with me. It was the end. I kissed her good-bye. We were both crying, and I watched her go down in the elevator."

Henry had been preparing for prison for almost two years. He was going to make his stay as soft as possible. After all, he had been hearing about prisons all his life, and now he sought out the experts. Mob lawyers, for instance, often employ ex-cons as paralegals, and many of these ex-jailhouse lawyers are encyclopedic on the subject of prison and the latest wrinkles in the Bureau of Prisons' rules and regulations. Henry found that of all the maximum-security prisons to which he could be sent, Lewisburg Federal Penitentiary in Lewisburg, Pennsylvania, was probably the best. It was close to New York, and that would make it easier for Karen, lawyers, and friends to visit. It had enough corrupt guards and key officials to make his stay reasonably bearable. And Lewisburg had a large population of organized-crime members inside at the time, including Paul Vario, who was doing two and a half years for income tax evasion, and Johnny Dio, who had been given a long stretch for the acid blinding of newspaper columnist Victor Riesel. In order to get to Lewisburg himself Henry paid an assignment officer at the West Street jail two hundred dollars.

Henry also figured out how he could use the various special rehabilitation programs offered by the prison to shorten his sentence. For instance, prisoners got time subtracted from their sentences for everything from sweeping their cells to going to college. In fact, it seemed that prison authorities were so anxious to get rid of prisoners that nearly three quarters of all adults sentenced to correctional institutions were not inside but on parole, probation, furloughs, work-release, or out early. The Bureau of Prisons automatically deducted five days a month from every sentence as part of its mandatory "good time" provision. Since Henry had received a 10-year, or 120-month, sentence, he was automatically entitled to have 600 days, or 20 months, deducted from his original sentence; thus his original sentence really amounted to 8 years and 4 months. The bureau would also deduct 2 or 3 days a month from his sentence if he took on a work detail and another 120 days (one day off for every month he had been sentenced) if he attended classes offered in the prison.

Henry would be eligible for parole after he had served one third of his sentence, which meant the parole board could free him after he had served 39 months, or a little more than 3 years. Since his file had been stamped "OC" (Organized Crime) in big red letters, it was unlikely that the parole board would free him at the first opportunity. But he learned that their rejection could be appealed to Washington and that a letter-writing campaign by his family, clergymen, and politicians could overturn the prison's decision. When Henry finally got on the bus for Lewisburg, he knew he would probably end up serving between 3 and 4 years.

There was a going-away party for him the night before at Roger's Place, a Queens Boulevard restaurant Henry had started in order to help provide some income for Karen and the kids while he was gone. Paulie, Jimmy, Tommy DeSimone, Anthony Stabile, and Stanley Diamond were already doing time, but there were more than enough wiseguys around to fuel an all-night blast. By eight o'clock in the morning Henry had taken an exhausted Karen home, but he kept going. The crew—made up of only the guys now—moved to the bar at the Kew Motor Inn, and at ten o'clock, with only two hours of freedom remaining for Henry, they all left in a limousine, hired by his pals, for the trip to check in with the marshals. On the way to the jail Henry decided he wanted a drink at Maxwell's Plum. It would be his last drink on the street for a long time. At eleven o'clock Henry and his pals were at the bar at Maxwell's drinking Screaming Eagles—shot glasses of white Chartreuse dropped into large goblets of chilled champagne. Soon some women who were early for their own luncheon dates joined Henry's party. His noon check-in was toasted by all, and the party continued.

By five o'clock in the afternoon Henry was being advised to run away. One of the women, a Wall Street analyst, insisted that Henry was too nice to go to prison. She had a place in Canada. He could stay there for a while. She could fly up on weekends. By five-thirty Karen called. She had been able to track him down by calling the wives of the men with whom he had been partying. Al Newman, the bondsman who had been carrying Henry on the fifty-thousand-dollar appeal bond, had received a call from the prison authorities threatening to revoke the bond. They were going to declare Henry a fugitive. Newman told Karen the insurance company would not cover the loss. Al would have had to get up the fifty thousand himself. He was desperate for Henry to turn himself in. Karen was frantic about having to support herself for the next few years, and now she was afraid she would also have the burden of paying off Henry's forfeited bond. When Henry hung up after speaking with her on the phone, he realized that everyone—with the possible exception of his friends at the bar—wanted him to go to prison. He had one last Eagle, swallowed some Valiums, kissed everyone good-bye, and told the limo driver to take him to jail.

The Lewisburg Federal Penitentiary is a massive walled city of twenty-two hundred inmates set amid the dark hills and abandoned coal mines of central Pennsylvania. It was raining the day Henry arrived and he could barely make out a huge, bleak castle with its Warner Brothers wall, mounted gun towers, and searchlights. Everything surrounding Lewisburg was cold, wet, and gray. From his seat inside the dark-green prison bus Henry saw the great steel gates swing open. He and about a dozen other prisoners had been cuffed and shackled ever since they left New York. They had been told that there would be no food or toilet stops during the six-and-a-half-hour journey. There had been two armed guards seated behind locked metal cages—one in the front of the bus and the other in the rear—and upon arrival at Lewisburg they both began snarling orders about when and how Henry and the other prisoners were to leave the bus. Henry saw concrete, iron mesh, and steel bars everywhere. He watched a whole wall of steel, streaked with rain, slide sideways, and he heard it slam behind him with the finality of death. This was Henry's first time in a real prison. Until now all of his stints had been in jails—places such as Riker's Island and Nassau County, places where wiseguy inmates would spend a few casual months, usually on work-release. For Henry and his crew doing thirty or sixty days in a jail was little more than a temporary inconvenience. This was different. Prisons were forever.

"The bus stopped at a cement building just inside the walls. The guards were all screaming and yelling that we were in prison and not at some country club. As soon as we got off the bus I saw at least five guards with machine guns, who watched us while some other guards removed our cuffs and leg shackles. I was wearing tan army fatigues I'd gotten at West Street when I signed myself in, and

I was freezing. I remember looking down at the floor—it was wet red tile—and I could feel the damp come right up through the soles of my shoes. The guards walked us through a long cement tunnel toward the reception area, and it echoed and smelled like the basement of a stadium. The reception room turned out to be little more than a wider cement hallway, surrounded by thick wire mesh, with a long, narrow table where we handed over our papers and were given a thin mattress bedroll, one sheet, one blanket, one pillow, one pillow case, one towel, one washcloth, and a toothbrush.

"When it was my turn to get the bedroll I looked up. Right there in the reception area, standing next to the guards, I saw Paulie. He was laughing. Next to Paulie I saw Johnny Dio, and next to Dio was Fat Andy Ruggierio. They're all laughing at me. All of a sudden the guards who had been screaming shut up like mice. Paulie and Johnny came around the table and started hugging me. The guards acted like Paulie and Johnny were invisible. Paulie put his arm around me and walked me away from the table. 'You don't need that shit,' Fat Andy said. 'We got nice towels for you.' One of the guards looked up at Paulie and nodded toward my bundle. 'Pick it up,' Paulie said, and then he, Fat Andy, and Johnny Dio walked me to the Assignment and Orientation room, where they got me a single cell for my first couple of weeks.

"After they checked me in, Paulie and Johnny walked me into the main reception room, and there were a dozen guys I knew waiting for me. They were clapping and laughing and yelling at me. It was a regular reception committee. All that was missing was the beer.

"Right from the beginning you could see that life in the can was different for wiseguys. Everybody else was doing real time, all mixed together, living like pigs. Wiseguys lived alone. They were isolated from everyone else in the prison. They kept to themselves and paid the biggest and meanest black lifers a few bucks a week to keep everybody cool. The crew owned the joint, or they owned a lot of the guys who ran the joint. And even the hacks who wouldn't take money and couldn't be bribed would never snitch on the guys who did.

"After two months of orientation I joined Paulie, Johnny Dio, and Joe Pine, who was a boss from Connecticut, in their honor dorm. A fifty-dollar connection got me in there as soon as Angelo Mele was released. Fifty dollars could get you any assignment in the joint. The dorm was a separate three-story building outside the wall, which looked more like a Holiday Inn than a prison. There were four guys to a room, and we had comfortable beds and private baths. There were two dozen rooms on each floor, and each one of them had mob guys living in them. It was like a wiseguy convention—the whole Gotti crew, Jimmy Doyle and his guys, "Ernie Boy" Abbamonte and "Joe Crow" Delvecchio, Vinnie Aloi, Frank Cotroni.

"It was wild. There was wine and booze, and it was kept in bath-oil or after-shave jars. The hacks in the honor dorm were almost all on the take, and even though it was against the rules, we used to cook in our rooms. Looking back, I don't think Paulie went to the general mess five times in the two and a half years he was there. We had a stove and pots and pans and silverware stacked in the bathroom. We had glasses and an ice-water cooler where we kept the fresh meats and cheeses. When there was an inspection, we stored the stuff in the false ceiling, and once in a while, if it was confiscated, we'd just go to the kitchen and get new stuff.

"We had the best food smuggled into our dorm from the kitchen. Steaks, veal cutlets, shrimp, red snapper. Whatever the hacks could buy, we ate. It cost me two, three hundred a week. Guys like Paulie spent five hundred to a thousand bucks a week. Scotch cost thirty dollars a pint. The hacks used to bring it inside the walls in their lunch pails. We never ran out of booze, because we had six hacks bringing it in six days a week. Depending upon what you wanted and how much you were willing to spend, life could be almost bearable. Paulie put me in charge of the cash. We always had two or three thousand stashed in the room. When the funds were running low

I'd tell him, and the next thing I knew some guys would come up for a visit with the green. For the first year or so Karen would come up every weekend with the kids. She used to smuggle in food and wine, just like some of the other guys' wives, and we'd pull the tables in the visiting room together and make a party. You weren't allowed to bring anything into the prison, but once you were in the visiting area you could eat and drink anything, just as long as you drank the booze out of coffee cups.

"Our days were spent on work details, going to rehabilitation programs and school, assembling for meals, and recreation. Almost everybody had a job, since it got you time off and it counted a lot with the parole board. Even so, there were guys who just wouldn't work. They usually had so much time or were such bad parole risks that they knew they'd max out no matter how hard they worked. Those guys would just sit in their cells and pull their time. Johnny Dio never did anything. He spent all his time in the priest's office or meeting with his lawyers. Dio was doing so much time for having Victor Riesel blinded that he was never going out on a program or parole. He spent all his time trying to overturn the conviction. He didn't have a prayer. Most of the other wiseguys had jobs. Even Paulie had a job. He used to change the music tapes on the public-address system that was piped into the place. He didn't actually do it himself. He had somebody do it for him, but he got the credit for the job. What Paulie really did all day was make stoves. He was a genius at making stoves. Since you weren't supposed to cook in the dorms, Paulie had the hot-plate elements smuggled in. He got the steel box from the machine shop, and he wired and insulated the whole thing. If you were okay, Paulie made you a stove. Guys were proud to cook on his stoves.

"Dinner was the big thing of the day. We'd sit around and drink, play cards, and brag, just like outside. We put on a big pot with water for the macaroni. We always had a pasta course first and then meat or fish. Paulie always did the prep work. He had a system for doing

the garlic. He used a razor, and he sliced it so fine that it used to liq-
uefy in the pan with a little oil. Vinnie Aloi was in charge of making
the tomato sauce. I felt he put in too many onions, but it was a good
sauce anyway. Johnny Dio liked to do the meat. We didn't have a
grill, so Johnny did everything in pans. When he panfried steak you'd
think the joint was on fire, but still the hacks never bothered us.

"I enrolled to get a two-year associate degree in restaurant and
hotel management from Williamsport Community College. It was a
great deal. Since I was a veteran, I got six hundred a month in veteran's benefits for going to school, and I had that money sent home
to Karen. Some of the guys thought I was nuts, but they weren't
vets and couldn't get the money. Also, Paulie and Johnny Dio used
to push me to go to school. They wanted me to become an ophthal-
mologist. I don't know why, but that's what they wanted me to be.

"I took sixty credits each semester, and I was hungry to learn. When
I went inside I was only half literate. I had stopped going to school as a
kid. In prison I learned how to read. After lock-in at nine o'clock, while
everybody else bullshitted all night long, I used to read. I read two or
three books a week. I stayed busy. If I wasn't in school, taking bets, or
smuggling food, I was building and maintaining tennis courts in the
recreational area. We had a beautiful red clay court and one cement
court. Tennis got to be my game. I never played a sport before in my
life. It was a tremendous outlet. Paulie and his old wiseguys used to
play boccie near the wall, but the young guys like Paul Mazzei, Bill
Arico, Jimmy Doyle, and some of the shooters from the East Harlem
Purple Gang all started showing up in tennis whites. Even Johnny Dio
got interested. He learned to play, except he always swung his racquet
like an axe.

"At the beginning Paulie took me around and introduced me to
everyone. Within three months I started booking in jail. Hugh Ad-
donizo, the former mayor of Newark, was one of my best customers.
He was a sweetheart of a guy but a degenerate gambler. On Saturday
he used to bet two packs of cigarettes a game, and he'd bet twenty

games. If there were twenty-one games, he'd bet twenty-one. He bet college football on Saturday and the pros on Sunday.

"After a while I was booking lots of guys and guards from the prison. I had Karen outside running around and straightening up for me. She was making the payouts or collecting. Guys would bet or buy things from me on the inside and have their wives or pals pay up on the outside. It was safer than keeping too much cash in the joint. If the cons didn't take it, the guards would. Since everybody knew who she was and who she was with, she had no problem making the collections. I was making a few dollars. It passed the time. It helped me to keep the guards happy."

After two and a half years Henry got himself assigned to the prison farm, about a mile and a half outside the prison wall. Getting to the farm had been Henry's dream. A riot in the Lewisburg cellblocks, where there had been nine murders in three months, had created a very tense situation. Prisoners, including the wiseguys, had refused to leave their cells and go to work details. During the height of the riot the guards went to the honor dorm and marched all of the wiseguys into solitary, where they would be safe.

Karen had begun a letter-writing campaign to the Bureau of Prisons in Washington about getting Henry assigned to the prison farm. She would write to top bureau officials, knowing that they would pass the letters down through the bureaucracy. She knew that if she wrote directly to the Lewisburg officials her letters could be disregarded. But if Lewisburg received letters about Henry Hill from the main office in Washington, D.C., the local prison officials had no way of knowing whether Henry's case might not be of more than casual interest to the brass. Every time Karen got a congressman to write the Bureau of Prisons, the bureau would forward the letter to Lewisburg, where Henry's case manager was notified about the congressional inquiry. It was never clear whether the congressional letters were routine responses to constituent requests or whether Henry had some special relationship with a politician. It wasn't that the prison officials felt compelled to do anything extralegal as a result of the political interest in Hill, but they were certainly not going to ignore Hill's rights as a prisoner.

Karen also got businessmen, lawyers, clergymen, and members of the family to write follow-up letters to both the congressmen and the prison on Henry's behalf. She made phone calls to follow up on her letters. She was unrelenting. She kept files of her correspondence and tracked friendly bureaucrats through the system, continuing her correspondence with them even after they had been promoted or transferred. In the end the combination of the wholesale transfers that followed the riot, an excellent prison record, and Karen's letter-writing campaign got Henry assigned to the farm.

To be assigned to the farm was like not being in prison at all. The farm was a two-hundred-acre working dairy that supplied milk to the prison. The men assigned there had extraordinary freedom. Henry, for instance, would leave the dorm every morning at five and either walk to the farm or drive one of the tractors or trucks to it. Then Henry and three other prisoners would hook up about sixty-five cows to a milking and pasteurizing tank and fill five-gallon plastic containers with the milk and ship it into the prison. They also supplied the Allenwood Correctional Facility, a minimum-security federal jail for white-collar criminals, about fifteen miles away. After seven or eight in the morning Henry was free until four in the afternoon, when the milking process began again. He usually got back to the dorm only to sleep.

"The first day I walked into the dairy and saw the guy who ran the place sitting at a table with a scratch sheet I knew I was home. The guy—his name was Sauer—was a junkie gambler. He was getting divorced from his wife, and he went to the track every night. I gave him money to bet for me. I pretended I thought he was a great handicapper, but he couldn't pick his nose. It was a way of slipping him the money so he got to depend upon my cash when he went to the track. Pretty soon I had him bringing me back Big Macs, Kentucky Fried Chicken, Dunkin' Donuts, bottles of booze. It used to cost me between two and three hundred a week, but it was worth it. I had a gofer.

"I knew I could make lots of money. There was so little supervision on the farm, I could smuggle anything into the place. I had the job of checking the fence, which meant I had the wire clippers and tractor and rode around the perimeter of the farm to make sure the cows hadn't crashed through anywhere. I could be gone three or four hours a day. After my first day I called Karen from the dairy phone. That was Wednesday night. That Saturday night I met Karen in the fields behind the pasture, and we made love for the first time in two and a half years. She brought a blanket and a duffel bag full of booze, Italian salami, sausages, special vinegar peppers—the kinds of things that were hard to find in the middle of Pennsylvania. I got it all behind the wall by putting it in a plastic liner that went inside the five-gallon milk containers we delivered to the prison kitchen, where we had other guys unpacking.

"Within a week I had people bringing up pills and pot. I had a Colombian named Mono the Monkey, who lived in Jackson Heights, bringing in pot in compacted cylinders. I buried milk containers out in the woods and began to store the stuff. I had cases of booze out there. I had a pistol. I even had Karen bring up some pot in the duffel bags when my supplies were low. When I hit the farm I was in business.

"But I was also working eighteen hours a day. If there was calving, I'd get up at four in the morning. I'd be there late at night if the pipes or tubes needed cleaning. I was the hardest-working, best farmhand the dairy ever had. Even the guards gave me that.

"In the meantime I went into partnership on the marijuana and pills with Paul Mazzei, a Pittsburgh kid who was inside because of selling pot. He had good local sources, and I got the stuff inside the wall. Bill Arico, one of the Long Island crew, was also at Lewisburg, on a bank robbery, and he did most of the selling. In fact, in no time at all Arico was the biggest dope supplier in the joint. Bill sold about a pound of pot a week. He'd sell five hundred to a thousand dollars' worth of grass a week. There were other guys selling pills and acid. Lots of guys did their time on acid. The prison was a marketplace. The gates would open up and it was a businessman's dream.

"I used to bring the cocaine in myself. I didn't trust anybody with coke. I put the pot into handballs I used to split in half and retape. Before tossing the balls over the wall onto the handball court I'd call the clerk at the hospital, who was a dope fiend, and he would alert my distributors to start congregating around the handball court. The pot was so compacted that I used to get a pound or two of stuff over the wall in just a few handballs.

"The only problem was with the bosses. Paulie had gone home by now, but Johnny Dio was still there, and he didn't want any of the crew playing around with dope. He didn't give a damn about dope on moral grounds. He just didn't want any heat. But I needed the money. If Johnny gave me money to support myself and my family, fine. But Johnny didn't give up anything. If I was going to pay my way through the can, I had to earn my own money, and selling dope was the best way around. Still, I had to do it pretty much on the sly. Even so, there was an explosion. One of my distributors used to store his stuff in a safe in the priest's office, and he got caught. Johnny Dio used to use the place as his office—making calls to his lawyers and pals—and now it was off limits. He went nuts. I had to get Paulie to talk to his son on the outside before we could convince him not to have me killed. Paulie wanted to know if I was selling dope. I lied. Of course not, I told him. Paulie believed me. Why shouldn't he believe me? Until I started selling stuff in Lewisburg I didn't even know how to roll a joint."

Fourteen

For almost two years Karen visited Henry in jail once a week. By the third year, however, she cut down to once or twice a month. Henry was assigned to the far less onerous farm detail, and the children found the arduous journey—six hours' drive each way—unbearable. Judy had begun to suffer from severe stomach cramps whenever they visited the prison, and for a long time neither Karen nor her doctor could trace the cause of her pain. It was only after two years, when Judy was eleven years old, that she finally confessed she found the toilet in the prison visiting area so filthy that she was unable to use it during the interminable ten- and twelve-hour visits. Ruth, who was nine at the time, remembers long stretches of unrelieved boredom while her parents and their friends talked and ate at long picnic tables in a large, bare, cold room. Karen brought small toys, coloring books, and crayons for the children, but there was little else for them to do. The prison had no facilities for children, although dozens of youngsters showed up on weekends to see their fathers. Judy and Ruth were so desperate for diversion after the first couple of hours that Karen would let them feed a roll of quarters into the line of overpriced commissary vending machines—despite the fact that cash was a problem.

KAREN: When Henry first went away, the money just dried up. It was impossible. I worked part-time as a dental technician. I learned how to clip and groom dogs, mostly because that was the kind of work I could do at home and keep an eye on the kids. The money owed to us by most of Henry's friends from The Suite never got paid. Most of those guys didn't have two nickels to rub together until they made a score, and then it would be gone before we got to see any of it. There was one bookmaker who made a fortune working out of The Suite. Henry had done everything for the guy. He had a wife and kids in Florida and ten girlfriends in New York. A friend of mine suggested that maybe he should kick in some money for me and the kids now that Henry was away. His suggestion was that I go sit in a precinct house with the kids until the cops got me on welfare.

That's the mentality of those people. I sold some of the fixtures we stole from The Suite to Jerry Asaro, a regular big shot. He was a friend of Henry's and a member of the Bonanno crew. I'm still waiting for the money. He took the fixtures and never paid me a cent. I've read about how these guys take care of each other when they're in jail, but I've never seen it in life. If they don't have to help you, they won't. As much as I felt we were a part of the family—and we were—there was no money coming in. After a while Henry had to make money inside. It must have cost him nearly $500 a week just to live inside the prison. He needed money to pay off the guards and for special food and privileges. He sent me the monthly $673 Veterans Administration check he got for going to school, and later I'd get some money from him after he started smuggling and selling stuff behind the wall, but they were hard dollars and we were both taking chances.

For the first couple of years I had an apartment with the kids in Valley Stream, but we were always at my parents' house. We usually ate dinner there, and Henry used to call me long-distance every night and talk to the girls. The girls knew he was in jail. But at first all we told them was that he had done something against the law. I said that he hadn't hurt anybody, but he had been unlucky and had gotten caught. They were only about eight and nine at the time, so I told them he had gotten caught playing cards. They knew you weren't supposed to play cards.

Even later, when they got older, the girls never thought of their father or any of his friends as gangsters. They weren't told anything. They just seemed to accept what their father and his friends were doing. I don't know exactly what they knew as kids, but I know they didn't think of Uncle Jimmy or Uncle Paulie as racketeers. They saw Jimmy and Paulie like generous uncles. They only saw them at happy times anyway—at parties or weddings or birthdays—and they always arrived with lots of presents.

They did know that their father and his friends gambled and that gambling was against the law. They also knew that there were things in the house that had been stolen, but as far as they were concerned, everybody they knew had things in their houses that were stolen.

Still, they knew their father was doing things that were wrong. Henry never talked about what he was doing as though he was proud. He never boasted about what he did the way Jimmy talked in front of his kids. I remember one day Ruth came home from Jimmy's, where she had been watching television with Jesse, Jimmy's youngest son. She said that Jesse—who Jimmy named after Jesse James, for God's sake—used to cheer the crooks and curse the cops on television. Ruth couldn't get over it. At least my kids weren't being raised to root for robbers.

My mother seemed to accept Henry's going to prison very calmly, but she could never figure out why I had to go visit him all the time. She thought I was crazy. She saw how much work was involved in preparing for my trips. She saw me buy all kinds of different foods, soaps, razor blades, shaving creams, cologne, and cigarettes. To her the trips didn't make sense. But of course she didn't know that I was helping Henry get stuff into the prison so he could make a few extra dollars.

I was nervous as hell at the beginning, but Henry explained exactly how I should do it. He said everybody's wife was bringing in supplies. I started bringing his special olive oil, imported dried sausages and salamis, cigarettes, and pints of brandy and Scotch, but I was soon bringing in small envelopes of pot, hash, cocaine, amphetamines, and Quaaludes. Henry arranged for suppliers to drop the stuff off at the house.

To get past the prison check-in, I sewed food in sacks and strapped them to my body. The guards would search our bags and make us walk through the metal detectors, looking for knives and guns, but that's all they did. As long as you didn't wrap anything in aluminum foil, you could walk in with a grocery store under your coat. I used to wear a big poncho, and I had sandwiches and salami and stuff from my feet to my chin. I used to put pint bottles of brandy and Scotch in a pair of extra-large and extra-wide boots I bought just for getting past the gate. I got a giant-size forty-two-DD bra and a pair of leg girdles to carry the pot and pills. I used to walk into the visiting room as stiff as the Tin Man, but the guards didn't mind. I'd go straight to the ladies' room and take all the stuff off me and carry it out to one of the long tables where Henry and the girls would be waiting. We weren't supposed to bring anything to eat from the outside into the visiting room, but every table had mounds of food that the wives had cooked at home. Once we got the stuff on the table inside, we were safe. The guards wouldn't bother you. It was like a game. When I saw the setup I realized that I didn't have to worry too much about getting caught, because, as Henry said, most of the visiting-room guards were already on the payroll. They each got fifty dollars a day on visiting days just to look the other way.

Still, lots of wives were nervous. One woman was so terrified trying to get stuff inside that she actually shook. I had to make the delivery for her. She stayed outside with the kids and I made the delivery. I tucked her stuff inside my own stuff and walked through. She was practically in tears from fear that I'd get caught. When we got in I looked to see what she'd brought. I couldn't believe it. A package of ginseng tea, a jar of shaving cream, and some after-shave lotion. For that she was trembling.

I'd arrive at the prison around eight in the morning. I'd wake the girls at three, pack their dolls, blankets, pillows, and medicine, and then drive along turnpikes for about six hours. I tried to get to Lewisburg early so that after the long drive I'd at least get to spend a full ten-hour day with Henry before heading home. But no matter how early I arrived, dozens of wives and kids were already on line ahead of me. Visiting days were like big family picnics. The wives dressed up the kids and brought food and photo albums to show their husbands. There were also two prisoners who wandered around taking Polaroids—one had been an army spy for the Russians and the other a bank robber—and they got two dollars for the pictures.

Finally, in December of 1976, after a little more than two years, Henry got assigned to the farm. It was a godsend. It was also easier to smuggle in larger amounts of stuff. Since he worked on the farm from before dawn until late at night, he was pretty free to move around outside the wall with almost no supervision. He used to say he was going out to check the fence, and he'd meet me around the back end of the farm. That's when I started to load up duffel bags with extra food, whiskey, and dope. One of the other wives, whose husband was in with Henry, would drop me off with the two duffel bags along the narrow dirt road. It had to be pitch black outside, because one of the guards lived nearby and he used to look out his window with binoculars.

The first time I was dropped off I was really nervous. I was alone in the middle of this dark farm road. I waited in the blackness for about five minutes, but it seemed like hours. I couldn't see a thing. Then all of a sudden I felt this hand grip my arm. I think I jumped to the stars. It was Henry. He was dressed all in black. He grabbed the duffel bags and handed one of them to another guy. Then he grabbed my hand and we took off into the woods. He had a bottle of wine and a blanket. It was scary. I was very jumpy, but I soon calmed down. I hadn't made love with him in two and a half years.

When Henry first got to Lewisburg he was very angry with Karen. She would show up on visiting days with the kids and grouse about money. She harped on the fact that a lot of the guys weren't paying the money they still owed in bar bills at The Suite. She complained that his friends pleaded poverty and drove around in new cars and meanwhile she had to clip poodles at night. As far as Henry was concerned, Karen just couldn't understand that when a wiseguy went away he stopped earning. It was a fact. All bets and all debts were off. No matter what it said in the movies, a wiseguy's friends, former partners, debtors, and ex-victims whined, lied, cheated, and hid rather than pay money owed to a man behind bars, much less to his wife. If you wanted to survive prison you had to learn how to earn money on the inside.

For two years Henry made between a thousand and fifteen hundred dollars a month selling booze and marijuana Karen had smuggled inside. When Henry finally landed his job on the Lewisburg farm, his smuggling operation (which had grown to include a number of guards as well as Karen) expanded greatly. Now he could meet Karen and her duffel bags of whiskey and dope along the farm road about once or twice a month. Not that this meant that Henry suddenly began to accumulate great wealth. Prisoners like Henry do not keep the money they make behind the walls. Almost all of Henry's profits were simply passed on to Karen and to the guards and prison officials who allowed him to operate. In return for the bribes, Henry was protected from the usual perils encountered behind the wall and was also permitted to maintain his relatively comfortable and unfettered prison life.

Henry had few complaints about the way he was treated. He was not confined behind the wall, he had the dormitory roommates of his choice, his meals were well above prison fare, he had the unlimited use of the farm manager's office and telephone, and in the spring and summer he had so little supervision that he could take Karen for picnics in the woods. Once he and Karen both caught poison ivy. Sometimes, when Henry was able to sneak away for a while, they would run off for a few hours to a nearby Holiday Inn. But Henry was still in a maximum-security prison, and it looked as if he was destined to stay there for at least another two and a half years, or until June of 1978, when he would finally become eligible for parole.

Henry had been on the farm exactly eight months when he first realized he might be able to get out of Lewisburg legitimately. In August of 1977 Henry heard that G. Gordon Liddy, the jailed Watergate conspirator, who was being held about fifteen miles down the road at the minimum-security Allenwood Correctional Facility, had organized a food strike. It was only a rumor at first; Henry learned about it from the drivers who delivered milk from the Lewisburg farm to Allenwood. It seemed that Liddy had managed to get sixty of Allenwood's white-collar criminals and corrupt politicians to follow his lead. Henry also heard that after a few days of this nonsense the Bureau of Prisons decided to transfer Liddy and his sixty food resisters.

"As soon as I heard about the possible transfers I started scheming right away. I knew if they were going to move sixty people out of Allenwood, there were going to be sixty empty bunks at Allenwood. At all costs I wanted one of those bunks. For me the difference between doing time in a place like Lewisburg—where I really didn't have it too bad—and Allenwood would be like not being in jail at all. I got Karen and told her to start calling up her contacts in the Bureau of Prisons immediately. I told her, 'Don't write, call!' I told her to call Mickey Burke and have Mickey try and get Jimmy, who was then in Atlanta, into Allenwood too. If we could get into Allenwood, it was the next best thing to being home. It was the country club of the Federal Bureau of Prisons. No walls. No cells. It was supposed to be like a summer camp for naughty grown-ups. There were tennis courts, a gym, jogging tracks, a nine-hole golf course, and, best of all, extremely liberal and enlightened rehabilitation programs.

"Just as I suspected, about a week after the food strike began, the Bureau of Prisons decided it had had enough of Mr. Liddy and his bullshit. They loaded up six buses with all the guys who didn't want to eat—G. Gordon Liddy number one—and they sent forty of them over to Lewisburg and twenty of the dumb bastards to Atlanta, where the Muslims and the Aryan Brotherhood were stabbing each other over the doughnuts.

"Within days the warden's office began moving guys out of Lewisburg and sending them to Allenwood, but my name wasn't on the list. When I asked my people in the warden's office, some of them said I couldn't get on the list because my folder was labeled 'Organized Crime.' Others said it was because I had injured my wrist in a softball game and Allenwood didn't want to accept injury cases. It was maddening. I felt like I'd set the whole thing up and they were transferring all these people and not me. Karen must have called Washington twenty times. No good.

"Finally I went to see the secretary to my counselor. She took pity on me. I had always been nice to her, even though she was awful-looking. She used to watch me play tennis. I'd joke around with her. I'd cook things and bring them over. I brought her flowers.

"Now I was desperate. I was begging. She knew what I wanted, and I think my years of kindnesses paid off. One day, after the warden had gone home, while they were transferring the last batch of bodies to Allenwood, I went to make another pitch at getting transferred. She looked real sad. 'Please don't say anything,' she said, and then she took one poor bastard off the list and put another poor bastard on. Me.

"I couldn't believe it. In a couple of days I was in Allenwood. It was a different world. It was like moving into a motel. There were five large dormitories, with about a hundred guys in each, and everyone had his own little private cubicle. The administration building, the dining room, and the visiting rooms were at the foot of the hill, and except for a roll call twice a day—once when we got up for breakfast at seven o'clock and another time about four-thirty in the afternoon—everything was on the honor system. By the time I was there a week I was going downtown to the hospital to check on my injured wrist by myself. No guards. No spying. No nothing.

"The place was filled with a nice class of people. Guys ran their businesses from the dorms. We had phone rooms next to the television rooms in each dorm, and you'd see guys on the phone all day and night doing deals. We had four stock swindlers whose wives would show up for visits just about every day. Allenwood had unlimited visits, and some of these guys stayed in the visiting rooms from nine in the morning until nine at night. The stockbrokers' wives used to arrive in limousines with maids who would cook a whole filet of beef right there in the kitchen. On weekends people showed up with their kids and nannies, and there was even a day-care center in the prison where kids could play and rest.

"There were about forty Jewish guys in the joint when I arrived. They had just gotten the right from the Bureau of Prisons in Washington to have a separate kosher kitchen. I immediately volunteered to work in the kosher kitchen. I wanted to establish right away that I was a religious person so that I could get religious furloughs that would entitle me to seven days at home every three months.

"I soon figured out how to get home even more often. I got Karen to contact a rabbi we knew, who then wrote letters to the Allenwood authorities asking that I be permitted to leave the facility for three-day religious instruction weekends once a month. Prison officials were always terrified of requests from the clergy. That's how we got two kitchens in Allenwood and that's how the black prisoners got their special Muslim diets and Islamic prayer days.

"Once I got my religious instruction weekends approved, there was a local rabbi who arranged everything. He was slick. He had been working with Allenwood inmates for a couple of years, and you got the kind of instruction you paid for. There were about a dozen guys at Allenwood who were in his program, and he actually took them to a local motel meeting room where they received religious instructions and relaxed. I knew that he could do better for a price. Within a couple of weeks I had it set up so he used to pick me up in a 98 Olds early Friday afternoon, and we'd drive like hell to Atlantic City, where I'd meet Karen and some of the crew and spend the weekend gambling and partying. The guy took a grand for the weekends and I had to pick up the tab for his room and meals. He was so anxious to please that after a couple of trips I got Jimmy included on the Jewish religious weekends. I hadn't seen too much of Jimmy after he got to Allenwood because he had been assigned to one of the other dormitories and he was on the grounds-keeping crew. But I did get him in on the religious weekends, and come Friday, when we started to take off for Atlantic City, it was like old times.

"I also joined the local Junior Chamber of Commerce because they took us out on five-day rehabilitation furloughs every month. And they had 'Toastmaster Weekends' one Sunday a month, where we'd be signed up at a local motel and listen to lectures about starting out in business again. Most of these JCs were well-meaning and legit, but a few of them weren't, and it didn't take me long to find out who was willing to take a hundred dollars a day to look the other way. Pretty soon I was signed up for everything. One month I managed to string together so many furloughs, days off, and religious holidays that the joint wound up owing me a day.

"Also, if I had to get out to pick up some pills or pot, I could always pay one of the guards fifty dollars and he would take me out of the place after his tour and the four-thirty count and then bring me back when he returned to work before the seven o'clock morning count. Nobody questioned the practice. The guard didn't have to sign any papers. It was just a way that some of them made a few extra bucks, and nobody was going to blow the whistle. I would usually arrange for Karen to have a room in one of the motels nearby. I liked the ones with indoor swimming pools.

"On the longer, five-day furloughs I just went home. Why not? Karen or one of the crew would meet me at whatever motel the Junior Chamber was having its seminars, and my guy would just wave me good-bye. I'd be home in a few hours. After a while I was getting home so often that there were lots of people in the neighborhood who thought I was out of jail a year ahead of time."

On July 12, 1978, Henry Hill was granted an early parole for being a model prisoner. According to the report of the Bureau of Prisons, he had been the ideal inmate. He had availed himself of the prison's self-improvement and educational programs. He had maintained a clear-conduct record throughout his entire incarceration. He had adjusted well to rehabilitation and had entered into community-service and religious programs created to assist inmates. He had been courteous and cooperative during interviews with prison personnel, social workers, and psychologists. He appeared self-confident and mature. He had strong family ties and, upon release, he had been guaranteed a $225-a-week job as an office manager for a Long Island company near his home.

Of course the prison officials had no way of knowing how expertly Henry had manipulated and misused their system. Nor did they know that his new job was essentially a no-show affair that had been arranged for him by Paul Vario. Henry's prospective employer, Philip Basile, was a mob-controlled rock promoter and Long Island disco owner who had once hired Henry to burn some buildings. To the Bureau of Prisons, however, Henry Hill's file read like a testimonial for the modern penological approach to rehabilitation. When he signed out of Allenwood for the last time, the Bureau of Prisons noted that his prognosis was good and that it was very unlikely he would ever return to prison again.

Fifteen

Henry Hill walked out of Allenwood on July 12, 1978. He was wearing a five-year-old Brioni suit, he had seventy-eight dollars in his pocket, and he drove home in a six-year-old car, a four-door Buick sedan. Karen and the children had been living in a cramped, shabby, two-bedroom ground floor apartment in a run-down section of Valley Stream. Henry's lawyers, prison guards, and weekend furloughs had swallowed up almost all of his money, but he told Karen to start looking for a house. He had prospects.

In anticipation of his release, Henry had discussed dozens of potential money-making schemes during his weekend furloughs home. That, in fact, was one of the main reasons that furloughs were so important: They helped Henry to feel he was on the way back into action even before he was out of prison. After four years behind bars Henry had no intention of going straight. He couldn't even conceive of going straight. He needed to make money. For Henry it was a simple matter of getting out and getting over.

Within twenty-four hours of his release Henry flew to Pittsburgh (in violation of his parole) to pick up fifteen thousand dollars, his share of the marijuana partnership he had started in Lewisburg with Paul Mazzei. Henry planned to use the money as a down payment for a house. Unfortunately, when he got to Pittsburgh he found that

Mazzei had just bought a garage full of high-grade Colombian grass and had only two thousand dollars in cash. Henry couldn't wait for Mazzei to raise the money; he had an appointment in New York the next day with his parole officer, and he had promised his daughter Ruth that he would take her to FAO Schwarz on her eleventh birthday and buy her the biggest doll in the store. Henry borrowed Mazzei's largest suitcase, filled it with bricks of marijuana, and headed back to New York.

Henry had been in prison and away from the street so long that he was uncertain about the procedures for examining luggage before boarding planes. Rather than chance the airlines he went back on an all-night Greyhound bus. It took over twelve hours and made dozens of stops, and he had to get off the bus at every stop and guard the luggage compartment to make sure nobody walked off with his suitcase. Henry wasn't sure where he could unload the grass. He had never sold or even smoked grass before he went to prison. He could not use sources within his own crew, because Paul Vario had outlawed any kind of drug dealing among his men.

It took Henry at least a week of sneaking around before he was finally able to unload the suitcase. Nevertheless, when he did, he made twelve thousand dollars in cash. It was fast and sweet. He had a down payment. He took Ruth to FAO Schwarz, and even though she cried and said that they couldn't afford it, he bought her a two-hundred-dollar imported porcelain doll. Then he called Pittsburgh and told Mazzei to send him a hundred pounds more. Within a month Henry began wholesaling uppers, Quaaludes, some cocaine, and a little heroin. Soon he had a drug crew of his own, including Bobby Germaine, a stickup man who was on the lam and pretending to be a freelance writer; Robin Cooperman, a clerical worker at an air freight company, who soon became Henry's girlfriend; and Judy Wicks, a courier who never made a delivery unless she was wearing a pink-and-blue hat.

In addition, Henry started a little sideline operation in automatic rifles and pistols, which he bought from one of his Quaalude users and part-time distributors who worked in a Connecticut armory. "Wiseguys like Jimmy and Tommy and Bobby Germaine loved to have guns around them. Jimmy would buy them in shopping bags. Six, ten, a dozen—you never had too many pistols for those guys." Also, Henry started to fence stolen jewelry through a jeweler in the West Forty-seventh Street diamond exchange. Most of the large pieces came from William Arico, another Lewisburg pal, who had joined a gang that specialized in robbing swank hotels and the homes of wealthy people. "Arico worked with Bobby Germaine, Bobby Nalo, and that crew. They were strictly stickup guys. Bobby used to get his information from a woman furrier and designer who used to get into rich people's homes and then give Bobby the layout." One night Arico's gang tied up cosmetic queen Estée Lauder in her Manhattan townhouse and got away with over a million dollars in jewels, which Henry fenced. "They got in by Arico pretending to be a chauffeur. He left my house all dressed up in his uniform and hat. Karen even drew a mustache across his face. It went very smoothly, but then the jeweler ruined almost all of the pieces by scratching the stones taking them out of their settings. You always take hot stones out of the settings as soon as you can so they can't be traced. They're then sold off and reset in new pieces. The gold and platinum settings are sold off separately and melted down."

Henry started to muscle his way into a liquor-distribution route, through which he planned to supply whiskey to all the bars and restaurants where Jimmy Burke and Paul Vario had clout. And, most important of all, he made sure to collect his $225-a-week paycheck for the no-show job as a disco manager with Phil Basile that Paul Vario had arranged for him. Henry needed the weekly pay stub so he could show his parole officer that he was gainfully employed.

It was on one of his increasingly frequent trips to Pittsburgh that Henry met Tony Perla, a local bookmaker and close friend of Paul Mazzei's. Over drinks at Mazzei's apartment discussing the drug business, Perla told Henry that he had a Boston College basketball player willing to shave points for the upcoming 1978–79 season.

"Tony Perla had been cultivating this kid, Rick Kuhn, for over a year. Kuhn was a Boston College rebounder, who had grown up with Perla and Perla's brother, Rocco. He was a big kid who wanted to make money. Perla had already given the kid a color TV, money for repairs on his car, and even some grass and cocaine. When I said that Kuhn alone couldn't guarantee the points, Perla said Kuhn would bring in his best friend, Jim Sweeney, the team captain. Perla said that with Kuhn and Sweeney and a third player, if we needed one, we could probably control the game points for twenty-five hundred dollars per game.

"The players loved it, because they were not dumping games. They could keep their honor. All they had to do was make sure that they didn't win by more than the point spread. For instance, if the bookies or the Vegas oddsmakers said the line was Boston by ten, our players had to muff enough shots to make sure that they won by less than the bookies' ten points. That way they'd win their games and we'd win the bets.

"Perla needed me in the scheme because of my connections with Paulie. Perla wasn't able to place the large numbers of big-money bets you'd have to put down with bookmakers across the country to maximize your profits on every game. Also, Perla wanted to be sure of protection in case the bookies got suspicious and refused to pay. In other words, if one of the bookmakers came up to Perla with a serious beef, he wanted to be able to say that any questions should be taken up with his partners—namely me, Jimmy Burke, and Paul Vario.

"Some people might not know it, but betting lots of money on college basketball is a very difficult thing to do. Very few bookmakers get into the baskets seriously. In fact, most bookies will handle college basketball action only as a favor for someone who is also betting a lot on football or baseball. And even then, all they'll usually put you down for is fifty, or maybe a thousand dollars tops.

"That's why I would have to line up a string of maybe fifteen or twenty bookmakers, and I would have to let a few of them in on what was going on so that they'd be able to help me spread the bets around even more. I already knew the guys I had in mind. Some guys, like Marty Krugman, John Savino, and Milty Wekar, would make money with us, while other guys would lose.

"When I got back and told Jimmy and Paulie about the scheme, they loved it. Jimmy loved to beat bookmakers, and Paulie loved to beat anybody. We were standing in Geffkens Bar, and Paulie kissed me on both cheeks. I was back a couple of months and I was already bringing in one score after another. That's what I did and that's what made Paulie happy.

"When I had the thing set up, Mazzei and Perla flew into the city for a meeting at Robert's with Jimmy and Paulie. By then Paulie had turned the basketball deal over to his son Peter, and Peter and I flew up to Boston with Mazzei and Perla to talk to the players. I had never met the players before. Perla had been the contact, but now we were going to be betting heavy money on these kids, and I wanted to make sure they understood the seriousness of what they were doing.

"The meeting was set in the Sheraton at the Prudential Center, in Boston. Kuhn and Sweeney looked nervous at first. Before I would talk to them I took them, one at a time, into the bedroom and searched them for wires. Then they ordered the most expensive stuff on the room-service menu. They talked about their careers, and both said they felt they were either too small or not good enough to make the pros.

"They knew who I was and why I was there. They knew I was the one with the connections to get the bets down, and they kept asking me to make sure to get bets down for them in addition to the twenty-five hundred we promised them for every game. They talked about shaving points and betting lines and the odds so casually I had the feeling they had been doing this stuff since high school.

"I asked which of the upcoming games they felt we could shave. Sweeney took out one of those little schedule cards, circled the games he thought we could fool around with, and gave the card to me. They kept saying that they liked the idea of just shaving points and not blowing the games.

"I remember going to the first game we tested. I wanted to see them on the court for myself. It was the December 6 game against Providence. It was really a dry run, but Jimmy and I put a few bucks down to see how it would work. Boston College was favored to win by seven. Kuhn got me the tickets, and I found myself sitting right behind Sweeney's parents, in the middle of the Boston College rooting section. They were cheering like mad. When we got ahead by a few extra points, I began to relax. We were home. Providence was dead. We're racking up some points.

"Sweeney is having a great night. His parents are jumping up and down. Sweeney started hitting from all over the court. I'm cheering right along, but toward the end of the game I see that we're too far ahead. I see that I'm cheering for my own disaster. Everything Sweeney threw in the direction of the basket went in. Bang! He'd hit for two and run back up court looking so proud of himself. I'm holding the wrong end of a bet and this jerk is looking for a prize. Bang! Two more. Bang! Bang! Two free throws. I'm watching this shit. I want to scream, 'Miss the free throw!' but I got his folks in front of me smiling and cheering. I've got a disaster on my hands. Toward the end I thought I saw Rick Kuhn throw the ball away three or four times, trying to get us below the spread. I thought at least he was trying. On one play I saw him foul this Providence guy in such a way that the basket counted and the guy got a free throw. Typical for the night, the guy missed the free throw. But Kuhn was thinking. By jumping too late Kuhn let the ball bounce over his head, and the same Providence guy who had just missed the free throw grabbed it. The guy drove around Kuhn, who was standing there like a lamppost. The guy scored. Still, that idiot Sweeney is dropping shots in. I'm supposed to be puffing cigars on my way to the bank, but Sweeney has blown the bet. He wouldn't stop.

"All they needed to win by was seven. They would have won the game and I would have won the money. Instead they won by 19 points—83 to 64. Some scheme. A waste. They took a perfectly good no-lose deal and threw it away. It was ridiculous. If we had bet big money on the game we would have been dead. I didn't want to go near the kids. I talked to Perla and Mazzei and said I was pissed and Jimmy was going to be even more upset. We were serious people. If the kids wanted to shave points, fine. It was business. But if they didn't, then let's forget the whole thing. No hard feelings, just good-bye. I told them, don't screw around—you can't play ball with broken fingers.

"Later Kuhn said that just before the Providence game he had gone over to Sweeney to tell him the spread was seven, but Sweeney didn't say anything. During the game, when Sweeney began scoring, Kuhn said he asked Sweeney what he was doing. Sweeney said he was playing to win. Kuhn said that after the game he had told Sweeney he was crazy, that he had just blown twenty-five hundred dollars. We had a Harvard game coming up that weekend, and I told Perla it was their second chance, but I was going to need some assurances. Kuhn said he had already recruited Ernie Cobb, the team's best player, into the deal. It was a lock.

"At the December 16 Harvard game everything was perfect. We only bet about $25,000 on it because of the Providence disaster. We bet on Harvard. Our bet was that Boston couldn't beat Harvard by more than the 12-point spread. This time the players did well. They threw away dozens of shots to keep the winning score low. Boston wound up winning by only 3 points, and we cleaned up. Then, on December 23, we got bold and bet more than $50,000 on the UCLA game, where the guys were the big underdog. That time we bet that

Boston would get beaten by more than the 15-point spread. Again the guys did fine. They managed to lose by 22 points, and I began to think that the thing might really work.

"We were riding high. The next game, against Fordham, on February 3, we had trouble laying off enough bets in New York, and we sent Mazzei to Las Vegas to bet $55,000 with the bookmakers. This time we were betting on the underdog, Fordham. We bet that Boston could not beat them by the 13-point spread. Since Boston was the easy favorite, it was just a matter of how much our guys decided to win by.

"It should have been beautiful. We should have cleaned up. Except that just before the end of the game we got a call from Paul Mazzei. He said that he had been driving into Vegas from the airport with the money for our bet when he got into some kind of a traffic jam, and by the time he got to town he was too late to get the bet down.

"Guys got killed for missing the window on winning bets, but Mazzei was smart enough to call before the game was over to make sure we didn't think he was holding out on us. We should have made a couple of hundred thousand dollars, but we wound up holding nothing.

"It was an omen. We got some money down on the next game, February 6, against St. Johns, but that turned out to be a 'push,' or a game where the point spread balances itself out and nobody wins and nobody loses. We let the money ride on the next game, February 10, which was against Holy Cross.

"In that game Holy Cross was the favorite, and all our guys had to do was make sure they were beaten by at least 7 points. We, of course, bet Holy Cross to win by the 7-point spread. It was our big-money game. We bet with both arms. The bookies already had our money from the 'push' game the week before, and we dumped even more green on top of that.

"I was at Jimmy's watching the game on television. It was a party.

Everything was going as you'd expect. Holy Cross was winning all through the game, but toward the end our guys seemed to get all fired up. It looked as though they didn't want to lose by too much.

"Pretty soon, before anyone even realized it, they had come within a few points of the lead. As the clock began the final countdown, our guys tried to pull back, but by then the Holy Cross players went cold. Our guys are just standing there, but Holy Cross couldn't hit from anywhere on the court. Then the other Boston College players, the ones who weren't in on our scheme, started scoring from all over. They must have smelled an upset. It was awful. Of course Holy Cross finally won, but they only won by 3 points instead of the 7-point spread, and Jimmy and I went down the tubes.

"Jimmy went nuts. He was furious. He put his foot through his own television set. I know he lost about fifty thousand dollars all by himself. I finally got Perla on the phone and he said that he had talked to Kuhn right after the game and that Kuhn had said they just couldn't bring themselves to lose by too much against Holy Cross.

"That was it. No more. The end of the point-shaving scheme. Jimmy was so mad at losing the cash that he said he wanted to shake those kids up. At one point during the night he said, 'Let's go up to Boston and put their heads through hoops,' but we never went anywhere. By then Jimmy had bigger problems than money."

Sixteen

Henry was out of prison only two months when he first heard about Lufthansa. His bookmaker pal Marty Krugman first told him about the possibility of the Lufthansa score. Marty and his wife, Fran, had come by to see Henry and Karen's new house, in Rockville Centre. It was a three-bedroom brick ranch house with a sunken living room, but Marty hardly looked at a wall. He kept motioning for Henry to talk with him on the side. Marty was so distracted during the visit that he kept grimacing at Henry to cut the house tour short whenever their wives were not looking. Finally, when Fran and Karen were in the kitchen making sandwiches, Marty told Henry about Lufthansa. He said that there were millions upon millions of dollars in untraceable fifty- and hundred-dollar bills sitting out there in a cardboard vault at Kennedy Airport just waiting to be robbed. He said it was the ultimate score. A mountain of cash. Marty said that the money, which was flown in about once a month as part of the routine return of U.S. currency that had been exchanged in West Germany by American tourists and servicemen, was sometimes stored overnight in the Lufthansa cargo vaults before it was picked up by armored trucks and deposited in banks.

Marty's information had come from Louis Werner, a pudgy, forty-six-year-old Lufthansa cargo supervisor, who owed Marty about

$20,000 in gambling debts. According to Marty, Lou Werner was one of those long-shot bettors who had spent the past eleven years trying to support an estranged wife, a girlfriend, a loan shark, three children, and a $300-a-day gambling habit on a $15,000-a-year salary. Like many airport bookies, Marty Krugman had carried Werner on the rim for months in the hope of a jackpot tip on a hijacking score.

Henry, Jimmy, and the crew at Robert's had picked up thousands of tips from Kennedy's indentured cargo handlers over the years, but Lou Werner's tip to Marty was unique. Werner's information held out the promise of more money than anyone in the crew had ever robbed before. And Werner was so desperate to get started that he actually had a plan. He had methodically worked out the details: how many men would be needed, the best time for the heist, how to bypass the elaborate security and alarm system. Werner had even figured out where the holdup men should park. Most important, the score was in cash—clean, easy-to-spend, unmarked money. For professional crooks that kind of cash is better than diamonds, gold, or even negotiable securities; it doesn't have to be cut, melted down, recast, or resold. There are no treacherous middlemen, insurance adjusters, or wiseguy fences involved. A guy can spend it walking out the door.

After meeting with Marty, Henry became obsessed with Lufthansa. The timing was perfect. Jimmy Burke was about to be released from Allenwood and temporarily assigned to the Bureau of Prisons' Community Treatment Center, a seedy hotel that had been converted to a halfway house on West Fifty-fourth Street, near Times Square. Jimmy would sleep at the center, but he would be free to roam around the city during the days and evenings. Tommy DeSimone was also due to be released to the halfway house at about the same time. Henry realized that he, Jimmy, and Tommy could beat by ten times their glorious $480,000 Air France score of 1967. It was the best welcome-home present any of them could ever receive.

There was only one problem: Jimmy Burke hated Marty Krugman. Jimmy had not trusted Marty since the early 1970s, when Marty was just starting out as a bookmaker and owned For Men Only, a men's hair-styling shop and wig salon next door to The Suite, Henry's Queens Boulevard nightclub. Marty did well enough in the wig business to star in his own late-night television commercial, in which he would be seen swimming vigorously across a pool wearing his wig while an announcer proclaimed that Krugman's wigs always stayed put. Henry always found Marty Krugman amusing, but Jimmy saw him as a mark. He felt that Krugman was booking out of his store and paying nothing in tribute or protection. Jimmy kept insisting that Henry shake down Marty for at least two hundred dollars a week, but Henry kept trying to placate Jimmy with stories about how Marty wasn't doing well enough yet to be shaken down. The situation was exacerbated by the fact that Jimmy was a part-time insomniac, and when he couldn't sleep he turned on the television. Whenever he saw Marty's wig commercial at four in the morning he felt duped. "That fuck has the money to go on television," he would complain to Henry, "but no money for anybody else?" Eventually Jimmy had Tommy DeSimone and Danny Rizzo work over one of Marty's employees as a warning, but instead of giving in, Marty threatened to go to the DA.

"Jimmy never trusted Marty after that, so when I finally got to run the Lufthansa thing down for him I emphasized how much money was involved, and I made sure I put in all the zeroes before I said the tip came from Marty Krugman. As I expected, Jimmy lit up over the idea. Still, he didn't want anything to do with Marty. He said he'd think about it. All he thought about was the money. After a week he finally told me to bring Marty down to Robert's.

"Jimmy was at the bar drinking, feeling good, and he had Marty run the score down for him. Jimmy was friendly and kept smiling and winking at Marty. When Marty had finished, Jimmy got me on the side and told me to get Lou Werner's telephone number from

Marty. Jimmy was still so suspicious of Marty that he didn't even want to ask him for Werner's number. That's when I realized that during their meeting Jimmy hadn't said more than a couple of words. He just let Marty talk. In the old days, before we both went away, Jimmy would have been up to his elbows in the heist himself. He would have had Werner sitting in Robert's drawing pictures on the bar. Looking back, I think it was my first sign that Jimmy was a little different. A little more cautious. One step removed. But why not? Marty had never been his buddy. And, anyway, Marty was so keyed up just leaning his elbow on the bar at Robert's with Jimmy Burke that he didn't notice a thing.

"Jimmy started running the Lufthansa heist right out of Robert's. He'd go to the halfway house at night and then get picked up every morning by one of the guys, who drove him to Robert's. It was Jimmy's office. He first called Joe Manri, who was also known as Joe Buddha because of his big belly, and told him to take a look at Lou Werner's plan. Joe Buddha came back all excited. He said that Werner's plan was great. He said there might be so much money involved that we'd need two panel trucks just to carry the bags away.

"By the middle of November Jimmy had most of the crew lined up. He needed five or six men to go inside and two men on the outside. First, he had Tommy DeSimone and Joe Buddha lined up to go into the place with the guns. He also had Angelo Sepe, who had just gotten out after five years for bank robbery, and Sepe's ex-brother-in-law, Anthony Rodriquez, who had just been freed after assaulting a cop, lined up as inside gunmen. Another guy was Fat Louie Cafora, who Jimmy met in Lewisburg, and Paolo LiCastri, an illegal Sicilian shooter, who used to say he was in the air-conditioning business because he put holes in people. Stacks Edwards, the black guy who had hung around for years and worked our credit-card scams, had been assigned to get rid of the vans after the robbery.

"There were other guys in on the deal, but by now I was flying back and forth so often to Boston and Pittsburgh between the basketball and the dope deals that I lost track. I heard, for instance, that Jimmy was going to send his eighteen-year-old son, Frankie Burke, on the heist under Tommy, but I never asked and nobody ever mentioned it. Later I heard LiCastri wasn't on the job. Frenchy McMahon, another stickup guy, who first helped us with the Air France robbery years ago, was also hanging around all the time, but I wasn't sure where he was going to fit in. Frenchy was a good guy and he was very tight with Joe Buddha, so wherever you saw Joe Buddha you saw Frenchy. When you've got something like Lufthansa coming up, you don't ask questions and you don't talk about it. You don't want to know. Knowing what's not necessary is only trouble.

"By early December everything was ready and we were just waiting for the word from Werner that the money had arrived. Jimmy told Paulie about what we had coming, and Paulie assigned his son Peter to pick up his end. Jimmy also had to give up a share to Vinnie Asaro, who was then the Bonanno family's crew chief out at the airport. The Bonannos ran half the airport in those days, and Jimmy had to show respect to them to maintain the peace. 'To Christmas,' Jimmy used to say after a day at Robert's and before getting a ride back to the halfway house at night. We were all counting the days."

On Monday, December 11, 1978, at 3:12 in the morning, a Lufthansa security guard patrolling the cargo terminal's parking area spotted a black Ford Econoline van pulling into a garage bay near the vault loading platform. The guard, Kerry Whalen, walked toward the van to see what was up. As he approached he was suddenly hit across the forehead with the barrel of a .45 automatic. A short, wiry man wearing a knitted black cap paused a moment and then hit him again. Blood began to pour from the guard's wound just as the man pulled his cap down over his face like a ski mask. Whalen felt another man grab his holster and disarm him. The two gunmen then ordered Whalen to deactivate a silent alarm near the gate. Stunned as he was, Whalen nonetheless wondered how they knew about the alarm. Whalen's hands were then pulled behind his back and he was handcuffed. He saw several men with ski masks, all carrying pistols or rifles. His wallet was removed by another gunman, who said they knew where his family lived, and if Whalen did not cooperate they had men ready to visit his house. Whalen nodded to indicate that he would cooperate. It was difficult for him to see because he could not wipe away the blood pouring down his face.

A few minutes later Rolf Rebmann, another Lufthansa employee, thought he heard some noise on the ramp. When he opened the door to investigate, a half dozen armed men wearing ski masks pushed into the building, forced him back against a wall, and handcuffed him. The gunmen then took a set of one-of-a-kind magnetic keys from Whalen and walked directly through a maze of corridors into a high-security area, in which they seemed to know exactly where two other Lufthansa employees would be working.

When those two had been rounded up, two of the gunmen remained downstairs to make sure there were no unexpected visitors to disturb the robbery. The rest of the gang marched the handcuffed employees up three flights to a third-floor lunchroom, where six other employees were on their 3:00 A.M. meal break. The gunmen burst into the lunchroom brandishing their guns and propelling the bloodied Whalen before them as an indication of their seriousness. The gunmen knew each of the employees by name and ordered them to lie on the floor. They asked John Murray, who they knew was the terminal's senior cargo agent, to call the Lufthansa night supervisor, Rudi Eirich, on the intercom. The gunmen knew that Eirich, who was working somewhere else in the vast building, was the only employee on duty that night who had the right keys and combinations to open the double-door vault.

On the pretext of reporting trouble with a cargo shipment from Frankfurt, Murray asked Eirich to meet him in the cafeteria. As Eirich, who had been employed by Lufthansa for twenty-one years, bounded toward the cafeteria, he was greeted with two shotguns at the top of the stairs. He looked into the cafeteria, not twenty feet away, and saw his employees on the floor with thick plastic tape across their mouths. He was quickly convinced that the gunmen were dangerous, and he decided to cooperate. While one of the gunmen stood guard over the ten bound employees in the cafeteria, the other three hoods took Eirich down two flights of stairs to the vaults. They seemed to know everything. They knew about the double-locked two-door security arrangements in the four-foot-thick cinder-block vault rooms. They knew about the silent wall alarm system inside the safe, and they even cautioned Eirich about accidentally touching it.

The gunmen had Eirich open the first vault door to a 10-by-20-foot room. They then ordered him to lock it behind them. They knew if he opened the door to the second vault, where the money and jewels were stored, without closing the outer door, a silent alarm would be sounded at the Port Authority's police office about half a mile away. Once the inner vault was opened, Eirich was ordered to lie on the floor while the men went through what appeared to be copies of invoices or freight manifests. They were apparently trying to identify the correct parcels in a room filled with hundreds of similarly wrapped packages. Finally the gunmen began to toss some of the parcels out the door. One of the first was thrown just inches from Eirich's head. He looked at it for a second, and then the heel of a work boot smashed the package open and he could see what looked like neatly bound stacks of bills under the thick paper wrapping.

The gunmen carried at least forty parcels out of the inner vault into the outer vault. They then ordered Eirich to reverse the procedure and lock the inner vault door before he opened the outer vault door. Two of the gunmen were designated to load the parcels into the van while the other gunmen took Eirich back upstairs to the cafeteria. There they gagged him with plastic tape, just as they had done with the rest of his employees. Suddenly one of the gunmen who had been loading the parcels onto the van came puffing into the cafeteria. He was sweating and excited. He had taken off his ski mask and was wiping his brow. One of the other gunmen yelled at him to put on his mask but not before several employees had managed to sneak a glimpse of his face.

The gunmen ordered the employees to remain where they were and not to call the police until 4:30 A.M. It was then 4:16, according to the cafeteria wall clock. Exactly fourteen minutes later the Port Authority police received their first call. Five million dollars in cash and $875,000 in jewels were gone. The single most successful cash robbery in the nation's history had taken exactly sixty-four minutes.

Seventeen

ufthansa should have been the crew's crowning achievement. A dream come true. The ultimate score for anyone who had ever hijacked a truck or moved swag out of the airport. It was the heist of a lifetime. The one robbery where there should have been enough for everyone. Six million dollars in cash and jewels. And yet, within days of the robbery the dream score turned into a nightmare. What should have been the crew's happiest moment turned out to be the beginning of the end.

Henry had been running around so frantically that weekend trying to keep his point-shaving scheme afloat that he didn't even know that there had been a robbery until ten o'clock Monday morning when he woke up, turned on the radio, and got into the shower:

". . . and nobody knows for sure just how much was taken in that daring predawn raid at Kennedy Airport. The FBI says two million dollars, the Port Authority police say four million dollars, the city cops say five million. How much maximum? That they won't say. So far Lufthansa has not said anything, but they've promised to break their silence soon with a press conference, and WINS will be there to cover it live from the scene of the heist at JFK when they do. It looks like a big one, maybe the biggest this town has ever seen. Stay tuned . . ."

"I didn't even know they were going to take the place that night. I was drunk out of my mind. I was with Marty Krugman all night. We were drinking at the Spice of Life, in Cedarhurst, not two miles from the airport, and we didn't know a thing. When I got home that night I had an argument with Karen. I got so pissed I packed my clothes and took the Long Island train to the place of a girl I knew, on East Eighty-ninth Street.

"About ten o'clock in the morning Jimmy calls me up. He says he wants me to meet him at the Stage Delicatessen that night just before he checks into the halfway house.

"I go over to the Stage. Tommy was there, smiling. Fat Louie Cafora was there. He weighed three hundred pounds, owned a parking lot in Brooklyn, and was going on trial for extortion and arson, but he was happy. He was marrying his childhood sweetheart, Joanna. He had just bought her a white Cadillac for a surprise wedding present.

"Lufthansa was all over the television and radio that day. Everybody knew about it, but I didn't say two words. Jimmy and Tommy were on their way back to the halfway house to check in. Jimmy was half drunk and feeling good.

"He was concerned about whether I was going home to Karen that night. Karen had come to his house looking for me that morning. In fact, he had had to call around just to get the girl's number where I was staying. Karen didn't know where I was.

"He asked if I was going home. I said in a couple of days. He said okay. I now see that he didn't want anything out of line. He wanted everything to appear normal. He didn't want angry wives running around from house to house looking for their lost husbands.

"He asked me if I needed money. I said no. I asked him if he needed money. He laughed. He took out an envelope stuffed with fifty- and hundred-dollar bills—there must have been ten thousand dollars there—and he counted out about five hundred to Tommy and five hundred to Fat Louie.

"With that he says that he'll meet me in the morning at Moo Moo Vedda's dress factory, next to Robert's.

"The next morning I meet Jimmy at Moo Moo's, and we started driving to Bobby's Restaurant, in the garment center. We have a meeting with Milty Wekar about betting the Harvard game we'd rigged for the next Saturday. Later that afternoon we had the same kind of meeting set up with Marty Krugman back in Queens. Milty and Marty were two of the bookmakers we used to get our bets down in the point-shaving games.

"We were on the expressway, getting close to the tunnel, when Jimmy let go of the steering wheel, turned toward me, and gave me a big, one-armed hug around the shoulders. 'We got it!' he said. 'We got it!' Then he started driving again like he hadn't said a word. I was so surprised by his sudden move that he almost broke my neck, but I knew it was his way of telling me that we had taken Lufthansa.

"But the next thing he said made me feel sick. He was looking ahead, driving, and he asked, almost casually, if I thought Marty had told his wife, Fran, about Lufthansa.

"At that point I knew that Jimmy was going to whack Marty. I knew Jimmy better and longer than most people. Sometimes I knew what he was going to think about something before he did. I could tell whether Jimmy was going to like something or hate it. And now I knew Jimmy was thinking about murdering Marty Krugman.

"I shrugged. I didn't want to look as though I even considered Krugman important enough to think about. We kept driving. I didn't say anything. After a minute or two Jimmy said that when we got to Bobby's he wanted me to call Marty and make an appointment with him for later that night. Now I said that I was certain Marty had told Fran everything. I wanted to sound like Marty probably talked with lots of people. That it was no big deal. Nobody could prove anything. I was scrambling to try and keep Marty alive. Jimmy didn't listen. He just said that after our meeting with Marty I should figure out a way to get Marty to go somewhere with me later that night.

"Now, I know where to find Marty every hour of the day. I had been with him all night Sunday, but since the robbery early Monday morning I had been purposely ducking him. Marty must have called my house a million times. I knew what he wanted. He wanted to know when he was going to get his money. And now I began to suspect that he had been busting Jimmy's balls about money too.

"I called Marty from Bobby's and said that Jimmy and I would meet him at the Forty Yards at four-thirty. I didn't say anything about later. When I got back to the table I saw that Tommy DeSimone was sitting there with his sister Dolores, and so was Milty Wekar. Jimmy started talking to Milty about the basketball bets, and then he turned to me and said that I should work out with Tommy where we were going to take Marty later that night.

"That's how it happens. That's how fast it takes for a guy to get whacked. It was getting crazy, but I still had from two in the afternoon until eight or nine o'clock that night to talk Jimmy out of killing Marty. Meanwhile I'm going along with the program.

"Tommy said that he and Angelo Sepe would meet me at the Riviera Motel. There was a big parking lot in the rear of that place. Tommy said, 'Just bring Marty to the back of the parking lot. Tell him you got to meet some broads downstairs. Just get out of the car and leave him there. Me and Angelo will take it from there.' Tommy loved it. To Jimmy whacking people was just business, but Tommy got enjoyment out of it. I told Tommy that I'd be there between eight and eight-thirty.

"In a little while Jimmy and I were on our way to the Forty Yards to see Marty about the baskets. I could see for the first time that Jimmy was a nervous wreck. His mind was going in eight different directions. All the way to the Forty Yards I talked about what a pain in the ass Fran Krugman would turn out to be if we whacked Marty. That she'd pester everybody until she found out what happened. I also reminded him that we needed Marty to lay off some of our bets.

I didn't use the words, but I was trying to say that killing Marty was like taking bread off our table.

"When we got to the Forty Yards, Marty was waiting. On the way in the door Jimmy said, 'Forget about tonight.' It was like a load off my mind. And in a few minutes Jimmy's drinking and joking with Marty like they were the best of friends. We drank for the rest of the afternoon, and there was no mention of Lufthansa and no mention of the money. I thought maybe Marty was wising up. Maybe he had a chance.

"Jimmy left, and while Marty waited for Fran to pick him up he started his song. 'When do I get my money?' he asked. 'What are you asking me for? Ask Jimmy,' I said. I was almost joking. He said, 'I did, and Jimmy says my end is $500,000.' Now I know why Jimmy wants to whack Marty. It's a matter of a half a million bucks. No way Jimmy was going to deny himself half a million dollars because of Marty Krugman. If Jimmy killed Marty, Jimmy would get Marty's half a mill.

"Meanwhile Marty was asking me how much my end would be. I told him not to worry about my end. But he wouldn't stop. He said that he'd talk to Jimmy. That he'd give me $150,000 and then get Jimmy to give me $150,000. He was screaming that he'd make sure I wasn't cheated. The poor bastard, he didn't have any idea how close he had just come to being killed, and I couldn't even tell him. He wouldn't have believed me.

"Thursday afternoon, about three days after the robbery, we were all in Robert's having our Christmas party. Paulie had come up from Florida, and we'd kicked everybody out of the place who wasn't with us. Paulie looked good. Jimmy was running around making sure Paulie was happy. Paulie's brothers Lenny and Tommy were there. Fat Louie was there. Everybody was there except Tommy DeSimone, because Paulie didn't like Tommy being around.

"There was this big spread of food, and I took out some money to pay. We're all having a good time when Stacks Edwards sees my

wad and starts to do his 'black dude' number. 'How come I'm fucking broke and all you whities from the May-fia got the money?' He
starts joking about the 'May-fia' guys who got all those millions from
the airport.

"Stacks was crazy. That day in the papers the cops had found the
truck, and it had prints all over it. The papers said they found the
ski masks, a leather jacket, and a footprint from a Puma sneaker.
I knew Stacks was supposed to have taken the truck to a guy we
knew in Jersey and compacted it. Finished it. Instead he had gotten
stoned and left the van on East Ninety-eighth Street and Linden
Boulevard, in Canarsie, about a mile and a half from the airport.
Then the jerk went home to sleep. The next day the cops found it,
and now it's in the papers. Stacks should have been running for his
life, but instead he's in Robert's screwing around. The guy either
had a death wish or he couldn't believe he was in trouble. The truth
is that nobody ever knows just how much trouble he's in, and here's
Stacks, and there's a chance his prints are all over the truck, and
he's carrying on about how the 'May-fia' was getting all the money.

"Then Lenny Vario, Paulie's brother, butts in on the joke and he
starts talking about how the guys who made the airport score must
all be down in Puerto Rico or Florida basking in the sun, while we're
all up here busting our humps.

"I look at Lenny like I can't believe he would kid around about
a thing like this, and then suddenly I realize that he's not joking. I
mean, he doesn't know a thing about it. He's sitting in the room with
the guys who did Lufthansa and he doesn't even know it. His own
brother, Paulie, has just salted away one third of the loot in Florida,
and Lenny's totally in the dark. Paulie had had his son Petey fly the
money down in a garbage bag inside a hang-up travel bag the morning
of the robbery. Petey went first-class and watched his bag all the way.

"As Stacks and Lenny carried on, I looked at Paulie. He didn't
look happy. Jimmy was watching Paulie's every move. I knew that
Stacks had signed his death warrant that day. Jimmy gave the order,

but it was Paulie who gave Jimmy the look. That weekend Tommy DeSimone and Angelo Sepe went to see Stacks. It was easy. The guy was still in bed. They did it fast. Six in the head.

"When Marty Krugman heard about Stacks, he thought Stacks got whacked in some drug deal or over some plastic. And that's the way everybody played it. Jimmy sent me over to Stacks's family. We paid for everything. I spent Christmas Eve in the funeral parlor with Stacks's family. I told the family Jimmy and Tommy couldn't come because they had to be in the halfway house.

"Marty was bound to be next. He was breaking Jimmy's balls. He was breaking my balls. He was crying that he needed his money to pay the loan sharks. He owed about forty thousand dollars, and he kept saying that he needed it now. He wanted to know why he had to pay the interest every week.

"I told him to take it easy. I told him he'd get the money. But Marty didn't want to pay the interest. By this time it was already January, and he was hanging around Robert's every day. You couldn't get rid of the guy. He was getting worse and worse. He was where he wasn't supposed to be.

"And by now there was constant surveillance on everybody. There were cars parked around the clock outside the bar. The feds were down the block. The heat was getting worse and worse. And still Marty kept coming around.

"I wanted no part of it. I kept telling him to smarten up. I'd tell him he'd get his end, but he just wouldn't stop. He told me that Jimmy had given him fifty thousand dollars right before Christmas but that he had given forty thousand of it to Lou Werner because Werner was busting his chops for his share. I knew what was happening and I never asked for a nickel.

"I didn't even ask Jimmy for the money he gave me before the holidays. He said come over to the house. When I got there, Jimmy went into the kitchen and opened the breadbox. There were stacks of money inside. There had to be a hundred thousand in there. He gave me ten grand. I gave Karen three grand to go Christmas shopping. I put seven in my own kick, and that night I dropped by Harold's Pools and bought a three-hundred-dollar permanent Christmas tree. The kids had a great time. It was the most expensive tree Harold had. It was a white plastic tree with purple balls.

"The week after Christmas, Jimmy has me drive some bad coke down to Florida for him. Jimmy had paid a quarter of a million for it, and he wanted me to bring it down there, and he wanted to kill the guy who sold it to him. He was going to make the guy give back the money and then he was going to murder him right there in the Green Lantern Lounge in Fort Lauderdale.

"Tommy would have gone down there with Jimmy that weekend, except Tommy was going to be made. He was finally getting his button. For Tommy it was a dream come true. If you wanted to be a wiseguy, you had to be made. It was like being baptized.

"We had heard that Bruno Facciolo and Petey Vario were going to vouch for him. They were supposed to pick him up and drive him to where they were having the little ceremony, but when Jimmy called and asked if he had seen his godmother yet, Tommy's mother said it was snowing so much it had been called off. The next day Jimmy called again. I saw him in the booth. He listened, and then I saw him raise his hand and jam the phone down on the hook with all his strength. The whole phone booth shook. I never saw him like that. I never saw such anger. I was scared.

"He came out of the booth and I saw he had tears in his eyes. I don't know what's going on, and he says that they just whacked Tommy. Jimmy's crying. He said they whacked Tommy. The Gotti crew. They whacked Tommy. It was over Tommy having killed Billy Batts and a guy named Foxy. They were made guys with the Gambinos, and Tommy had killed them without an okay. Nobody knew Tommy had done it but the Gambino people had somehow gotten the proof. They had a sit-down with Paulie and they got Paulie's okay to kill Tommy.

"The way they did it was to have Tommy think he was going to get made. He thought he was going to his christening. He got all slicked up. He wanted to look good. Two of his own crew came to pick him up. He was smiling. He was going to be made. Nobody ever saw him again.

"We came right back to New York. The guy who sold Jimmy the bad coke got a reprieve. There was nothing to do. Even Jimmy couldn't revenge Tommy. It was between the Italians, and on that level Jimmy didn't belong, any more than I did, because my father was Irish.

"Right after New Year's the Lufthansa heat got to be too much at Robert's, so everyone moved to a new place Vinnie Asaro opened on Rockaway Boulevard. Vinnie was spending a fortune fixing up the place, which was right next door to his fence company. I remember when I got back from Florida, Marty was all over me. He was hanging around Vinnie's new joint now, and he wanted to know about Tommy. He wanted to know about Stacks. What was going on? He knew Tommy had had trouble with the Gotti crew and that Stacks was probably hit over a business deal that went bad, but he was nervous. I think he sensed something was wrong. He used to hang around Vinnie's bar waiting for war news.

"And that's where they whacked him out. At the bar. On January 6. Fran called at seven o'clock the next morning and said Marty hadn't come home that night. I knew right away. I couldn't get back to sleep. She called back at nine. I told her that I'd go out and look for him later that morning.

"I drove over to Vinnie's fence company, and I saw Jimmy's car parked outside. I walked in and said that Fran had just called me. Jimmy was sitting there. Vinnie was sitting next to him. Jimmy said, 'He's gone.' Just like that. I looked at him. I shook my head. He said, 'Go pick up your wife and go over there. Tell her that he's probably with a girlfriend. Give her a story.'

"When Karen and I got to Fran's she was hysterical. She knew like I knew that he was dead. She said that he had called her at nine-thirty the night before and said he was going to be late. He told her that everything was fine. She said that he was supposed to get some money.

"I'm sitting there holding her hand and I'm thinking about Jimmy. Murders never bothered Jimmy. He started doing them as a kid in jail for old Mafiosi. In prison you don't have nice little fights. You have to kill the guy you fight. That's where Jimmy learned. Over the years he had killed strangers and he had killed his closest friends. It didn't matter. Business was business, and if he got it into his head that you were dangerous to him, or that you were going to cost him money, or that you were getting cute, he'd kill you. It was that simple. We might have been close. Our families were close. We exchanged Christmas presents. We went on vacations together. Still, I knew he could blow me away right there and get Mickey, his wife, to call Karen and ask where I was. 'We're real worried,' Mickey would say. 'We've been waiting for him. Did he leave yet? What could be holding him up? Do you think he's okay?' Meanwhile Jimmy's planting me with a boxful of lime in the Jamaica Marshes, across the street from where he lives.

"Fran was blabbering away about the money. She was worried she'd have to pay the loan sharks. I told her not to worry about them. She said she didn't have any money. Karen told her not to worry about it. Marty would turn up. Then Fran broke down about the robbery. She said that Marty was going to give me $150,000 and that he was going to give Frank Menna $50,000. I was trying to console her and at the same time deny that I knew anything about any robbery. But she kept saying that she knew that I knew. She wouldn't stop. I wanted to get away from there as fast as I could. It was just beginning."

Eighteen

For the media, caught in the usual preholiday news doldrums, the Lufthansa robbery was the greatest Christmas present of all. Newspapers and television stations presented it as a six-million-dollar entertainment crime, a show-biz caper in which there hadn't been a shot fired and the only discernible victim was a German airline, for which much of the city's population had very little historic sympathy.

The ballyhoo in the press was taken by various enforcement agencies as a personal affront. The FBI, with jurisdiction over all interstate crimes and unlimited overtime policies, assigned over a hundred agents to the case in the first forty-eight hours. Custom agents, the Port Authority police, the New York City Police Department, insurance company investigators, Brink's armored truck company, and Lufthansa's own security men swarmed over the scene of the crime, devouring clues and questioning witnesses.

Edward A. McDonald, the assistant U.S. attorney who was put in charge of the case, was a thirty-two-year-old, six-foot-five-inch former college basketball player who lived with his wife and his three sons in the same tough Brooklyn neighborhood in which he had grown up. McDonald's father and grandfather had both worked on the docks, and he was no stranger to wiseguys. He saw his first gangland killing from the social studies classroom window at Xavierian

High School, in Bay Ridge; five days later, when he went over to Bliss Park to practice his jump shot, he found that the mob had dumped a corpse on the basketball court.

According to McDonald, there was never any mystery about who robbed Lufthansa. Within the first couple of hours at least a half dozen police and FBI informants—many of them part-time hijackers and petty cargo thieves—called to report that Lufthansa had been the work of Jimmy Burke and the crew from Robert's Lounge. At about the same time the Lufthansa cargo workers who had caught a glimpse of the gunman who took his ski mask off during the robbery picked a photograph out of the police lineup book which they said resembled the robber. It turned out to be a mug shot of Tommy DeSimone. A top mobster, who was a member of the Joe Colombo crime family and also happened to be a confidential FBI informant, called his contact agent and identified Jimmy Burke as the man behind Lufthansa and said that Angelo Sepe, Sepe's ex-brother-in-law Anthony Rodriquez, Tommy DeSimone, and Jimmy Burke's twenty-year-old son Frankie were four of the gunmen involved in the robbery. When photographs of these four suspects were shown to cargo workers who had been working the night of the robbery, Kerry Whalen, the night guard who had been hit across the forehead when he first encountered the gunmen, picked out one that he said resembled the man who hit him. It was a mug shot of Angelo Sepe.

Eyewitness identification of suspects who "resemble" gunmen and the word of mob informants who cannot come forward and testify in court are not enough to charge anyone with a crime. But they are more than enough to put suspects under surveillance. By the end of the first week dozens of FBI men and city cops, using cars, trucks, vans spotter planes, and helicopters, began a round-the-clock surveillance of Jimmy Burke, Angelo Sepe, Tommy DeSimone, and Anthony Rodriquez. Undercover cops dressed as cargo workers and truckers started hanging around Robert's Lounge and the Owl Tavern. McDonald got the court's approval to install electronic bugs and homing devices in Jimmy's Olds, Tommy's Lincoln, and the new, white Thunderbird sedan that Sepe had bought shortly after the robbery for nine thousand dollars cash in fifty- and hundred-dollar bills. McDonald even leaked stories to the press about the robbery, hoping that they would help stimulate conversations in the bugged cars.

For the next eight weeks the investigation became a game of nerves. Jimmy and the crew knew they were the prime suspects for the Lufthansa robbery—they could even read about themselves in the newspapers—but they continued to live their normal wiseguy lives, hanging around their same haunts and effortlessly slipping their tails whenever they wished by making unexpected U-turns on busy streets, jumping red lights, or backing up the entry ramps of the city's highways. They managed to lose the FBI spotter planes and helicopters by driving into the FAA's restricted flight zone at JFK, where all nonscheduled plane traffic, including FBI surveillance planes, is prohibited. Even the state-of-the-art car bugs turned out to be less effective than McDonald had hoped: whenever Jimmy, Angelo, and Tommy stepped into their cars, they turned up the volume of their car radios full blast.

There were a few bits of tantalizing chatter that the FBI managed to record in spite of the obliterating wall of rock and disco music, such as Sepe telling an unidentified man about ". . . a brown case and a bag from Lufthansa . . ." or his telling his girlfriend, Hope Barron, ". . . I want to see . . . look where the money's at . . . dig a hole in the cellar [inaudible] rear lawn . . ." But this was still not enough to connect Sepe and his pals to the theft.

After a while the crew became so adept at slipping tails that sometimes one or more members of the gang would disappear for days at a time. McDonald received reports that his suspects had been spotted as far away as Fort Lauderdale and Miami Beach. Of course, he could have revoked their paroles and sent Jimmy, DeSimone, and Sepe right back to jail for consorting with each other, but that was not going to solve the Lufthansa robbery, nor was it going to get any of the money back.

McDonald knew from the start that Lufthansa had been an inside job. How else would the six gunmen have known which of the twenty-two giant cargo warehouses in the 348-acre Kennedy freight-terminal area just happened to have six million dollars in cash and jewels sitting around over the weekend? Such large sums are usually picked up by armored truck shortly after they arrive and are immediately deposited in banks. The gunmen also knew the names and the locations of all the employees working that night; they knew about the perimeter alarms that required a special magnetic key, and they knew where to find the key and how to disconnect the automatic security cameras without sounding the silent alarm. McDonald was convinced that if the surveillance and electronic techniques failed to catch the pros, the amateur inside man would eventually lead to Burke and the men who actually carried out the robbery.

Lufthansa's own security men gave McDonald Lou Werner's name within hours of the robbery. Werner had already been the suspect in an earlier theft of twenty-two thousand dollars in foreign currency, but there had not been enough evidence at the time to arrest him or have him fired. This occasion was different. It turned out that Lou Werner had prevented the Brink's armored-truck guards from making their routine pickup of the six million in cash and jewels on the Friday before the robbery. Werner had claimed that he had to get the approval of a cargo executive to sign the release. One of the Brink's guards had complained that this was not the procedure, but nevertheless, Werner had disappeared for the next hour and a half and had not reappeared in the cargo area until after the guards had been ordered to continue their rounds without the Lufthansa money. So Lou Werner was not only responsible for the money and jewels being left at the airport over the weekend but he was one of the few Lufthansa employees who knew it was still there.

Such pros as Jimmy Burke never seemed to talk about anything indictable, even in what they had to assume was the privacy and safety of their own cars, but an amateur such as Lou Werner couldn't shut up. He seemed compelled to drop hints about the robbery to everyone he knew. He boasted about coming into some money. He told his barroom pals that he had paid off his bookies and loan sharks. He announced that he was heading for Miami to spend Christmas week.

To the agents involved, following up on Werner's domestic intricacies was more like plodding through a comic soap opera than investigating a robbery. They found, for instance, that just before the robbery Werner had told his estranged wife, Beverly, that he would be coming into a great score and that she would most assuredly regret having left him after twenty-three years. He told his best friend, William Fischetti, about the robbery at least a month before it took place and agreed to invest thirty-thousand dollars of the loot in Fischetti's taxicab business. Then, two weeks later, Werner found out that Fischetti, who was married, was having an affair with his estranged wife, Beverly; he got so angry he called his old pal and withdrew from the business proposition. On the morning of the robbery, with the radio and newspapers announcing the spectacular heist, Werner was apparently still so incensed at his ex-pal that he called Fischetti at home and shouted, "See, big mouth!" and hung up. A couple of days after the robbery, when the newspapers were filled with headlines about the multimillion-dollar score, Werner proudly boasted all to his girlfriend, Janet Barbieri, a thirty-six-year-old divorced mother of three. Barbieri promptly burst into tears and screamed hysterically that he would wind up in jail. Werner was so depressed by his girlfriend's reaction that he went to his local bar and proceeded to tell the whole story to his favorite bartender—but only after swearing him to secrecy.

The FBI, of course, talked to everyone who knew Werner, and just about everyone who knew Werner talked to the FBI. Fischetti, for instance, was so worried that his wife would find out about his affair with Beverly Werner that he agreed to cooperate fully as long as he wasn't interviewed in his own home. For weeks FBI agents met Fischetti in coffee shops and taxicabs, and he told them everything he knew—which was a lot.

Fischetti had known Werner for years and said that Werner and another Lufthansa cargo worker, Peter Gruenewald, had concocted the plan to rob the airline months before the robbery. Fischetti said the pair had hit upon the scheme after being involved in the theft of twenty-two thousand dollars in foreign currency and deciding that it was foolish to chance getting caught or fired for stealing such a paltry sum. If they were going to take any money from the vault and run the risk of getting caught, it might as well be for at least a million dollars.

Fischetti said that Werner and Gruenewald then worked for months on their heist, and when their step-by-step blueprint was finished, Gruenewald had the job of shopping it around the airport bars looking for the right men to carry it out. Gruenewald spent months testing one prospective holdup man, a notorious barroom rowdy, but decided against using him when he realized the man wasn't serious enough. When Gruenewald turned out to be much too slow in finding the robbers, Fischetti said, Werner took matters into his own hands and asked his bookmaker, Frank Menna, if he knew of anyone who could carry out the undertaking.

When the FBI first approached Gruenewald he denied any knowledge of the plan, but agents soon lined up the barroom rowdy Gruenewald had approached for the robbery, as well as Fischetti, as a witness against him. On Friday, February 16, nine weeks after the robbery, agents found that Gruenewald had applied for a standby ticket from New York to Bogotá, Colombia, and then on to Taiwan and Japan. Gruenewald said he was on his way to see his estranged wife in Taiwan, where she lived with her family. Gruenewald was arrested and held as a material witness in the Lufthansa case. He decided to cooperate with McDonald in assembling the case against Werner.

McDonald knew that with the testimony of Gruenewald, Fischetti, Beverly Werner, Janet Barbieri, and Frank Menna he had enough evidence to charge Lou Werner as a participant in the Lufthansa robbery. McDonald had also compiled enough evidence against Angelo Sepe to charge him with the robbery and, more important, to get a warrant to search Sepe's girlfriend's Mattituck, Long Island, house and yard for the money. The agents who had been following Sepe for weeks and had been listening to hours of rock music and snippets of conversation were convinced that the money was buried somewhere at Hope Barren's house.

McDonald's objective was not just to convict Werner but to convince him to cooperate with the feds. Werner had to roll over on the men he hired to do the robbery. But the day Werner was arrested he proved to be tougher than McDonald or any of the agents had thought. He had talked incessantly before his arrest, but he stopped talking once he was in custody. On the night of his arrest, after hours of questioning, Werner continued to insist that he had had nothing whatsoever to do with the robbery. He claimed he had boasted and lied about his role in the heist only because it boosted his ego.

McDonald decided to confront Werner with his conspirator right there in the Strike Force office. Werner was sitting in a large conference room when Gruenewald and McDonald walked in together. Werner hadn't seen Gruenewald for over a week and he might have assumed that his friend had taken the plane to Bogotá and the Orient as planned. Now Werner saw Gruenewald walk in with the prosecutor, and he knew that Gruenewald was cooperating.

Werner began to tremble. His chest began to heave. McDonald said later that he was afraid that Werner might have a heart attack right there in the office. Gruenewald began methodically to urge his friend to cooperate. "They know everything," Gruenewald said. "Why should you be the only one punished?" If Werner helped with the investigation, he could be guaranteed a walk or probation, especially if he helped McDonald nail the robbers and recover the money. Gruenewald tried. He was very persistent. But Werner insisted that he didn't know what Gruenewald was talking about. He claimed that he was getting a raw deal. He said that if McDonald thought he was guilty, he would have to prove it in court.

The case against Werner was all that McDonald had. The months of surveillance and eavesdropping had only confirmed his suspicions about Burke and the crew, but they had not provided much evidence. The search of Sepe's girlfriend's house and the surrounding property had not turned up the money the FBI had been certain it would find. On May 23, thirty-five days after McDonald had arrested Sepe, he had to drop the charges against him because there was not enough evidence for an indictment. Jimmy and the crew could still be put away for violating parole, but then there would be no way that they might accidentally stumble and either implicate themselves or reveal the whereabouts of the money.

But far more disturbing, as far as McDonald was concerned, were the reports of murders and disappearances connected with Lufthansa. As McDonald went about assembling the case against Werner, key witnesses began to disappear. On December 18, for instance, just one week after the robbery, Queens police found the body of a small-time black crook named Parnell Steven "Stacks" Edwards, thirty-one, lying under the covers of a bed in his Ozone Park apartment with six .38s in his chest and head. The door to his apartment had not been forced and there were no signs of struggle. The apartment had also been wiped clean of fingerprints. There was money and jewelry strewn around, so the police discounted robbery as a motive. From the casual position of the body it also looked as though the victim knew his killers and had had no reason to think he was in danger.

On January 14 Tommy DeSimone's wife, Cookie, reported to the police that her husband had disappeared. She said that Tommy had borrowed sixty dollars from her a few weeks earlier, and she hadn't heard from or seen him since. At first the police suspected that Tommy had decided to get lost after he found out that two of the Lufthansa cargo workers had identified him from mug shots as the gunman who had removed his mask during the robbery. But then the word began to come back that Tommy DeSimone was gone forever.

Three days later, on January 17, the body of a forty-two-year-old hustler and con man named Richard Eaton was discovered in a refrigeration truck that had been abandoned in Gravesend Bay, Brooklyn. The body had been found by children playing inside the abandoned trailers. The hands and legs were tied with wire and the neck was broken. There was some delay in identifying the body since it had been frozen so stiff that it took more than two days to thaw. It was only then, while going through the man's pockets, that police found Jimmy Burke's name and phone number. When a preliminary police investigation revealed that Eaton had occasionally worked as a courier and front man for Jimmy Burke, the city cops took their dossier and went over to see Ed McDonald.

The police said they had learned that Eaton had just returned from a trip to Florida, where he was supposed to have laundered huge amounts of money. On one of the Sepe tapes, amid static and rock music, Sepe was heard to complain that someone was trying to cheat him while counting the money. There was also some discussion about a trip to Florida and money. McDonald had FBI men and city cops retrace Eaton's steps and even opened the safe deposit box in which they were told Eaton had placed millions of dollars. The box was empty.

About this time a Long Island housewife named Fran Krugman reported that her husband, Marty, had disappeared. She told the local police that she had last heard from him on January 6, when he called to say that he wouldn't be home for a while. By the time McDonald found out that Marty Krugman had been the man to whom Frank Menna had sent Lou Werner, it was too late. McDonald would have given anything to find out about the men to whom Marty Krugman had passed on Werner's plan. Frank Menna had told McDonald that all he had done was transmit Werner's request to his bookmaker boss, Krugman. Menna said that Krugman took over from there. Krugman was one of the only links McDonald knew of directly connected to the robbery. Krugman had been an airport bookmaker, and he had also been known to be under the mob's protection. He had been associated with the Burke crew and had been seen frequenting Robert's Lounge. As it worked out, Krugman disappeared just before McDonald and the FBI had started to look for him. By then he was presumed dead.

Two weeks later, on February 10, Theresa Ferrara, a stunning, twenty-seven-year-old beautician, got an emergency call from a friend and ran out of her beauty shop in Bellmore, Long Island, to meet someone in a nearby diner. Ferrara had apparently been concerned enough about the meeting to have asked her nineteen-year-old niece, Maria Sanacore, to come looking for her at the diner if she had not returned in fifteen minutes. Ferrara left her bag, keys, and coat behind. "I have a chance to make ten thousand dollars," she told her cousin as she raced out of the door. She was never seen again.

The Nassau police began a routine missing-persons investigation. They discovered that Ferrara had recently moved to a thousand-dollar-a-month apartment; when the rental agent gave them her previous address, it turned out that she and Tommy DeSimone had lived in the same two-family house in Ozone Park. On May 18 a female torso was found in the waters off Barnegat Inlet, near Toms River, New Jersey. An autopsy was performed at the Toms River Community Hospital, where comparison X-rays were used to positively identify the body as that of Theresa Ferrara.

By the time Lou Werner went to trial in April, five possible witnesses had either been murdered or had disappeared, and McDonald had assigned round-the-clock protection to all of the survivors he planned to use in court. Gruenewald testified that he and Werner had concocted the plan together and that Werner had recruited the robbers behind his back. The barroom rowdy whom Gruenewald had first approached to do the robbery testified that Gruenewald had gone over the plans and told him that he would have to get the information about bypassing the alarms from Lou Werner. Even Janet Barbieri, Werner's girlfriend, wound up reluctantly testifying that Werner had boasted to her that he had been responsible for the robbery.

On May 16, after a ten-day trial, Lou Werner was found guilty of helping to plan and carry out the Lufthansa robbery. He was the only person charged with the robbery and was facing twenty-five years' imprisonment. If there was any possibility of finally getting Lou Werner to talk, it was now. Werner had refused to talk in order to take his chances at trial. If he had been acquitted he would have gone free and would have been able to keep whatever money he had earned from the robbery. But Werner was convicted, and unless he wanted to spend the next twenty-five years in prison, he was going to have to cooperate.

Although McDonald did not know it at the time, Werner had met with only one member of Jimmy Burke's gang—Joe Buddha Manri. Manri had been sent by Jimmy to check out Werner's plan and had huddled over it in the parking lot of the Kennedy Airport Diner. Manri had left eighty-five thousand dollars in two packages at the airport motel for Werner. Had Werner chosen to cooperate, he could have implicated Manri, and only Manri.

The afternoon he was convicted, Lou Werner was taken back to the federal prison to await sentencing. He was held on the third floor, the detention area reserved for prisoners whose lives were in danger or who had decided to talk. Jimmy Burke, who had finally been picked up on April 13 for parole violation, was being held in the same prison. He was visited after the trial by one of his lawyers, who said that Werner had been convicted, was facing heavy time, and was in protective custody.

Later that night a radio car from the 63rd Precinct in Brooklyn found the bodies of Joseph "Joe Buddha" Manri, forty-seven, of Ozone Park, and Robert "Frenchy" McMahon, forty-two, of Wantagh, Long Island, slumped in the front seat of a two-door 1973 blue Buick parked at the corner of Schenectady Avenue and Avenue M, in the Mill Basin section of Brooklyn. Each man had been killed with a single shot from a .44-caliber gun in the back of the head. Now Manri was dead and Lou Werner's only possible ticket out of jail was gone.

Nineteen

On the day I finally got arrested my friends and family were driving me crazy. I was working such long hours that I was snorting about a gram of coke a day just to keep all the insanity together. My partner, Bobby Germaine, and I were getting our stuff from Charlie the Jap, who's been a junk guy all his life, and we were going crazy trying to keep it a secret from Paulie Vario. Paulie had been yelling about me getting involved with junk ever since I got out of the can, but meanwhile he's not coming up with too much for me to live on.

"Jimmy Burke was laying low ever since Lufthansa, and I couldn't earn like before with him. Anyway, I'm getting too old for sticking up trucks. Bill Arico had been caught on a jewelry heist, and I had been supporting his wife, Joan, and his two kids until he was able to escape from Riker's with a jeweler's saw I got for Joan to give him. Two of the Boston College basketball players I was paying screwed up on another game and there was hell to pay.

"Meanwhile the FBI had been to the house looking for some guns. They had a warrant and they were gentlemen. They waited until the kids went to school. They went through everything, but I had managed to get most of the pieces out just the week before. There was one nine-millimeter pistol in the bedroom bureau, and Karen knew enough to ask if she could get dressed. They said okay, and she went upstairs and shoved the gun into her panties. Later she complained because the thing was so goddamn cold.

"On top of all this there's my girlfriend, Robin. The truth is I should have gotten rid of Robin, but she was working with me on the dope. I used her place to store and cut the stuff. She sold a little too, but mostly she was her own best customer. And every time I went over there she wanted to have a talk about the relationship.

"I was under so much pressure that the day I got pinched almost came as a relief. I must have left the house about seven in the morning. I was going to pick up my brother Michael at New York Hospital. He was being treated for his spina bifida. On the way to the hospital I planned to drop by Jimmy's house. Jimmy had ordered some guns from a guy I had been doing business with in a Connecticut armory. The guy had dropped off Jimmy's guns at my house the night before. Jimmy had some thirty-two-caliber silencers, and he wanted guns to go along with his silencers. Here's Jimmy, heat all over him from Lufthansa, on parole, just like me, and he's looking to buy guns for himself. Bobby Germaine wanted some guns too. He said he'd take whatever Jimmy didn't take. Germaine, you must understand, was on the lam in six different jurisdictions, was pretending to be a freelance writer—he even had a typewriter all set up with paper—and already had an arsenal of guns and shotguns stashed all over his place. He didn't need those guns any more than Jimmy did, but those are the kinds of gun nuts I'm dealing with at the time.

"I figured I'd stop off at Jimmy's house, drop off the guns, then drive into the city and pick up my brother at the hospital and drive him back to my house. I threw the guns in the trunk of the car, and I heard this helicopter. I looked up and saw it. It was hovering right over my head and it was red. You notice a red helicopter over your house at seven o'clock Sunday morning. I got in the car and drove toward Jimmy's house in Howard Beach. For a while I noticed that the copter seemed to be following me, but by the time I got near his house on Cross Bay Boulevard it was gone.

"Jimmy was already awake. He was waiting in the doorway like a kid at Christmas. He came out, and he started to look at the guns before we got into his foyer. I reminded him about the heat. I told him about the helicopter. He looked at me like I was nuts. There he was taking guns out on the sidewalk and looking at me like I'm nuts. But I saw that he was impatient. He wanted to see the guns. When we got into the foyer he ripped open the paper bag, took one look at the guns and screamed, 'Fuck! These are no good! My silencers won't fit these things. I don't want these things.' All of a sudden I knew he didn't want to pay me for the guns. All of a sudden I knew I was stuck a few hundred. I'd bought the damn things for him. *He* had wanted them, not me. And now I was stuck. I didn't say anything.

"I'd known Jimmy for over twenty years, but I had never seen him crazier than he had been since Lufthansa. Ever since the stickup he had been getting progressively worse, and I knew better than to argue with him in the morning. I knew that at least eight of the guys who'd done the Lufthansa job were dead, and I knew the only reason they were gone was because they'd started bothering Jimmy about the money. Jimmy had gone crazy with the money. And sometimes I think even he knew it. I remember we were driving around one day on this or that, and he's sort of half talking, and he blurts out that sometimes he thinks that the money is cursed. That's the word he used—'cursed.'

"The way Jimmy saw it, Marty, or Stacks, or Frenchy McMahon, or Joe Buddha, or whoever wanted his share of the Lufthansa money was taking the dough out of Jimmy's pocket. That was Jimmy's money. Anyone trying to take some of that money made Jimmy feel like they were trying to rob him. For Jimmy, if it was a matter of giving a guy a quarter of a million bucks or two behind the ear, it was no contest. It was a time when you didn't argue with Jimmy. You never knew what he'd do. So I just repacked the guns in the ripped bag and turned around and left. He was so disappointed and pissed he didn't even say good-bye.

"Now I was on the way to the hospital. I still had the guns in the trunk of the car, and I was late for picking up my brother. I must have been doing eighty miles an hour. I looked up from the Long Island Expressway and I saw the helicopter. I couldn't believe it'd picked me up again. I was driving along and looking for the plane, and as I sailed over the rise before heading toward the Midtown Tunnel entrance I saw a pile of cars stacked up every which way on the road. It's curb to curb, and I couldn't stop. I had a helicopter on my head, a trunk full of guns, and I was sailing along into a twenty-car pileup.

"I started to stand on the brakes. I pulled the emergency. And I still wasn't stopping. I cut the wheel into the curb and began scraping my way to a halt. I could smell the burning. I began to slow down and finally stopped just inches from the pileup. I was shaking. Finally they cleared the mess away, and when I got to the hospital, my brother's doctor took one look at me and wanted me to get in bed. I explained that I had almost gotten into an accident and that I had been partying all night, and he took mercy and gave me ten milligrams of Valium. I put my brother in the car and we headed home. My plan was to drop off my brother at the house and pick up Karen. Michael was having dinner with us.

"On our way back to my house I looked out the car window, and what do I see but the red helicopter. I watched it for a while and then I asked my brother, 'Is that helicopter following us?' He looked at me as though I'm on acid. But there it was, hanging in the air. As we drove toward the house the helicopter stayed with us, but even then my brother didn't seem to think that much about it. If it's anybody, I thought, it's got to be the feds. The treasury guys must still be looking for the guns. It has to be the feds. Only the feds have money to burn on helicopters.

"I was cooking dinner that night. I had to start braising the beef, pork butt, and veal shanks for the ragu tomato sauce. It's Michael's favorite. I was making ziti with meat gravy, and I'm planning to roast some peppers over the flames, and I was putting on some string beans with olive oil and garlic, and I had got some beautiful milk-white veal cutlets, cut just right, that I was going to fry up before dinner as an appetizer.

"Karen and I were going over to Bobby Germaine's to give him the guns Jimmy didn't want and to pick up some money he had for me. I also had to get some heroin from him so that Judy Wicks, one of my couriers, would be able to fly out to Pittsburgh later that night with a half a kilo. Judy, who was a friend of the family, was already at my house when my brother and I got there. She looked like a Kansas preacher's daughter. That, of course, was what made her such a good courier. Skinny, dirty-blond hair, dumb pink-and-blue hat and crummy Dacron clothes out of the Sears catalogue. Sometimes, with heavy loads, she'd borrow a baby for the trip. She looked so pathetic that the only people who ever stopped her were Travelers Aid social workers looking to stir up business. Judy was going to hang around the house until I got back with the stuff. Then, after we had all had dinner, I was going to drive her to the airport for her flight to Pittsburgh.

"I was home for about an hour. I braised the meat. I squeezed the tomatoes through the colander—I don't like the seeds. I kept looking out the window. The helicopter was gone. I waited a while and listened for the noise. It seemed to have stopped. I asked Michael to watch the sauce, and Karen and I started for Germaine's. We were halfway there when I noticed the red helicopter again. But now it was really close. I could almost see the guy sticking his head out the window. I didn't want to take the copter to Germaine's hideout. And I sure didn't like driving around with Jimmy's guns in the trunk of the car. Karen and I weren't very far from my mother's, so I decided to drop by for a minute. Karen didn't ask any questions. I knew there was some overhead cover in my mother's carport, so I could unload the guns without being seen from above. When we got to my mother's house I took the guns out of the trunk and put them in her garbage cans. I sent Karen inside to tell her not to touch anything outside the house or around the garbage cans, no matter what. The minute I got rid of the guns I felt better. So I decided to shake the helicopter and go over to Germaine's and get the money and dope.

"I told Karen, 'Let's go shopping.' We drove to a giant shopping mall, parked the car, and went inside. I was ready to spend a couple of hours walking around. Also, I wanted to call Bobby Germaine and tell him about the heat. I went to a phone booth in the mall and called him. I told him I wasn't coming with the guns. I said, 'I'm being followed, for Chrissake. I've had a helicopter following me all day.' He said I was crazy, I was paranoid. By four o'clock, when we left the shopping mall, the helicopter was gone. It must have run out of gas. Karen and I got in the car and drove back to my mother's. Still no helicopter. I looked for a land tail. Nothing.

"I got the guns from my mother's garbage. I told Karen we were going to Bobby Germaine's but we were taking the long way. She started to drive and drive and drive. We went from town to town. Up streets. Into cul-de-sacs. We made U-turns. We speeded up and then suddenly pulled over to the curb and stopped. Went through lights. The whole bit. I was checking cars and watching license plates from the rear seat. Nothing.

"Finally we got to Germaine's. He had the garden apartment in a house in Commack. When I got there I began to feel better. 'You see? Didn't I tell you you're paranoid?' Germaine said. We all laughed. I snorted some more coke, and soon it got me back together. Then Germaine gave me the package of heroin I was going to give to Judy.

"Now I've got to get home to get the package ready to give to Judy for the trip. I also had to get over to my girlfriend Robin's house and give the package a whack with some quinine. I hadn't seen Robin in a few days, and I knew she was going to want me to hang around longer than I wanted to. I had the cooking to finish, and I had to get Judy ready for her trip, and I knew Robin was going to get on my ass. It was going to be awful. The phone rang. It was Robin. Germaine gave me a signal so Karen didn't know who was calling. Robin wanted to know when I'd be getting to her place. I said in about an hour. Could I stay for dinner? We'll talk about it later, I said. Now I know it's not going to be awful, it's going to be worse than awful. Then I called Judy at my house. I wanted her to know I had the stuff and that she would be making the trip to Pittsburgh. I said, 'You know what you've got to do?' She says, 'Yeah.' Judy had to make plane reservations to go to Pittsburgh that night with the dope. I said, 'You know where to go?' 'Yeah, yeah,' she said. 'You know who to call?' I asked her. 'Yeah, yeah, yeah,' she said.

"Then I told her to leave my house and go to a phone booth and make all the calls. She made a noise like I was some kind of idiot picking on her about things she already knew. 'Just make sure you leave the house,' I said. 'Don't use the house phone,' I said. So I hung up and what did she do? She used the phone in my house. She used the phone to make the reservations for Pittsburgh and to call Paul Mazzei and tell him when she'll be arriving. Now the cops know everything. They know that a package is leaving from my house for the airport, and they even have the time and the flight number. I'm a pig on the way to slaughter and I don't know it.

"As soon as I got back home I started cooking. I had a few hours until Judy's flight, and I had told my brother to keep an eye on the *ragu*. All day long the guy had been watching helicopters and tomato sauce. I asked Judy if she had called from the outside. There had been enough heat around for me not to trust my phones at all. If she had told me the truth I might have changed everything. I could have canceled the trip. I could have hidden the junk. But instead she got real annoyed at my question. 'Of course,' she said with a humph. I left everything at my house, with Karen in charge, and I drove over to Robin's with the dope. I wanted to mix it once and get back to the meat gravy, but now Robin was pissed. She wanted a conversation about why we're not seeing enough of each other. We started arguing and she's screaming, and I'm mixing heroin, and she's slamming things, and I got out of the house minutes before she started throwing things.

"By eight-thirty we had all finished eating. Judy had an eleven o'clock flight. At nine-thirty she said she had to go home. What for? I said. She said she wanted to go home to get her hat. I'd been carrying a pound of heroin around in my jacket all day and I wanted Judy to start taping it to her leg. No, she said, she had to go home to get her hat. I couldn't believe it. I told her to forget it. I was exhausted. I didn't need a trip to Rockaway just because she wanted her hat. She got mad. I mean, she's insisting. It's her lucky hat. She needs it. She's afraid to fly without it. She always wears it. It was a blue-and-pink thing that sat on top of her head. It was the most Middle-Western, rube thing you ever saw. The point is, if she insisted, I had to drive her home for her damn hat.

"When I got into the car I suddenly realized that I was still carrying half a kilo of heroin in my pocket. I remember saying to myself, 'What do I have to drive around with this stuff for?' So while the engine was still idling I got out of the car and went back inside the house and stuck the packages in a recessed light near the entry steps. I then got back in the car and started to drive Judy home. I wasn't fifty feet out of the driveway when my car was blocked. There were cars all over the place. I thought maybe there'd been an accident in front of my house. Then I thought, It's my turn to get whacked for Lufthansa. I saw this guy in a windbreaker who popped up alongside the car and jammed a gun against the side of my head. For a second I thought it was over. Then he screamed, 'Make one move, motherfucker, and I'll blow you away!' That's when I began to relax. That's when I knew they were cops. Only cops talk that way. If it had been wiseguys, I wouldn't have heard a thing. I would have been dead."

Twenty

When Nassau County Narcotics Detective Daniel Mann first heard about Henry Hill, he had no idea Hill was going to be any different from the thirty or forty other suburban drug dealers he arrested every year. Even when some of the first intelligence reports, surveillances, and wiretap information began coming in, he was still doubtful. Danny Mann had been a cop too long to get himself excited before getting kissed.

The Hill case had started just like all the others. There was an informant. In the Hill case it was a nineteen-year-old Commack, Long Island, youngster, who had been arrested for selling twelve hundred dollars' worth of Quaaludes to Nassau County undercover cops on three different occasions. Undercovers always like to string together more than one or two sales before making their arrests. Multiple sales tend to solidify a case and give the prosecutor more clout at the inevitable plea-bargaining table. An airtight case also means those arrested are more likely to cooperate and be coaxed into giving up their friends and partners in return for leniency. In this case the youngster needed no coaxing. Within minutes of being brought to the Mineola precinct for booking he was looking for a deal. The kid—a beefy, long-haired, ex-high school lineman—had been arrested before. In fact, it turned out that he was already an informant, giving up the people from whom he was buying his drugs. He even had his C.I., or "confidential informant" number, and he suggested that Danny Mann check him out with Bruce Walter, his case agent, with the Brooklyn district attorney's office. In return for leniency, the young man said, he would be willing to work as an informant for Mann and the Nassau cops.

Mann remembers looking at the kid and doubting that any bargain could be struck. What could the kid offer that would be worth his while? Danny Mann was not interested in pursuing druggie kids. No, no, the kid said. He could give up more than college kids. He knew about wiseguys. He could give up a wiseguy drug ring operating right under Mann's nose. It was an organized-crime heroin and cocaine ring, and they were operating out of Rockville Centre and distributing drugs all over the country. The kid said he had even been invited to work as a courier by one of the bosses.

Danny Mann left the room. He called his old pal Bruce Walter, the New York City police detective assigned to the youngster's case in Brooklyn. Was the kid for real? "You got a winner," Walters said. "Have fun."

The youngster was a small-time punk. He had quit high school before graduation and got most of his money as a chemistry salesman, selling pharmaceutical concoctions such as Quaaludes, amphetamines, LSD, and angel dust rather than heroin and cocaine. His father, an ex-con, was a fugitive in connection with a bank robbery and other cases. The young man lived at home with his mother, a part-time shopping-mall hair stylist.

A deal was struck. If the youngster could really "give up" an organized-crime drug ring, the charges against him would be reduced, if not dropped, and his cooperation would be conveyed by both police and prosecutor to the sentencing judge. If he was helpful, in other words, he might be able to get a walk. The drug business, of course, is just filled with people like this youngster. There are literally thousands of them, all leaking bits of information about each other, the smart ones holding something back for a rainy day, all of them with confidential-informant numbers and case agents and prosecutors whom they keep apprised of everything going on in the street. In addition to youngsters and petty dealers, however, many of the biggest and most successful narcotics importers and distributors, some of them top organized-crime figures, are also confidential informants to one set of cops or another. The drug business is simply a business of informants. Partners, friends, brothers—there are no stand-up guys in the drug trade. It is a multibillion-dollar business in which it is understood that everyone is ratting out everyone else.

While Detective Mann and William Broder, the Nassau County assistant district attorney, began taking notes, the youngster started giving them details about the ring. He said it was run by members of the Lucchese crime family and that it was connected with Paul Vario. The ring's leader, as far as the informant knew, was Henry Hill, an ex-con whom he knew to be very closely associated with Paul Vario of the Lucchese family. Mann and Broder were impressed. They had not come across many people close to Paul Vario before, let alone any who might be able to implicate the elusive mob boss in anything as serious as drugs. Most of the people who could have done Paul Vario any damage wound up dead long before Mann or anyone else from law enforcement got around to seeing them.

The youngster said he had known Hill for many years. He had visited Hill's house numerous times and knew Hill's wife and children. The youngster said he gained access to the house because he had relatives and friends who were very friendly with the Hills and so he had never really been considered a stranger. He insisted to Mann, however, that he would not talk about any of these relatives or friends, since they were not related to the case at hand. He said he knew the Hill operation had to be a large one because of the kinds of people with whom Hill was connected. Hill, he said, was close to Jimmy Burke, had been a part of the Kennedy Airport truck-hijacking gang, and had probably been in on the Lufthansa robbery.

The youngster told Mann that the first time he knew that Hill was in the drug business was back in 1979. Hill had just been released from prison. The youngster said he had been doing some landscape work at Hill's house, and while he was waiting for a friend, who was also a friend of Hill's, to pick him up, Hill had suggested that he start earning extra money as a "mule," or drug courier, for the operation. Hill had then taken him into the first-floor bedroom to show him the drugs. The bedroom could be entered only through an electronically operated door. Once inside, Hill showed him five kilos of cocaine, stored in a walk-in closet. He said that Hill took out one of the kilos so that he could examine it more carefully. Hill said he was handling eight kilos of cocaine a week and needed help in distributing the drugs. According to the youngster, Hill offered him five thousand dollars a trip for transporting cocaine to various spots around the country.

Using the youngster's information and an accompanying affidavit from the Brooklyn district attorney that verified the youngster's reliability as an informant, Mann applied for a wiretap order to be signed by a Nassau County judge. In his affidavit to the court Mann said he needed the wiretap authorization because the usual methods of investigation would not be successful in the Hill case. For instance, the informant, who knew Hill personally, was much too frightened to introduce an undercover agent into the operation because he feared for his life. Mann also said that preliminary surveillances of Hill revealed that he was extremely wary, rendering the usual surveillance techniques inadequate. Mann said that Hill would purposely drive more than sixty miles an hour along back streets, go through red lights, and make unauthorized U-turns routinely, just to see if he was possibly being followed. Hill was careful about whom he spoke to and never put himself in the position of being overheard in a restaurant or other public place. In fact, in public Hill often used the old prison trick to guard against lip-readers: he covered his mouth when he spoke. Mann was granted a thirty-day wiretap order authorizing him to monitor Hill's telephone at 19 St. Marks Avenue, Rockville Centre, Long Island, and also a phone in a nearby basement apartment, where, according to the informant, most of the drugs were delivered, cut, and packaged. The basement apartment, at 250 Lakeview Avenue, also Rockville Centre, was occupied by Robin Cooperman.

Tapes were made daily. Each reel ran twenty-four hundred feet. By the time Mann had finished his investigation of Henry and the drug operation, he had acquired thirty-five reels of tape. Each had been signed by the detectives who monitored the calls and sealed by the court. Mann had also set up his men across the street from Henry's house for surveillance pictures. Mann used a small garage that belonged to a retired civil servant.

It was not long before Mann and the rest of the men in the unit realized that they had inadvertently come across a thirty-seven-year-old ex-con whose life ran like a thread through much of the city's organized-crime fabric. Henry Hill was providing Danny Mann and the squad with a fascinating once-in-a-lifetime peek into the day-to-day workings of a wiseguy. It wasn't that Henry was a boss. And it had nothing to do with his lofty rank within a crime family or the easy viciousness with which hoods from Henry's world are identified. Henry, in fact, was neither of high rank nor particularly vicious; he wasn't even tough as far as the cops could determine. What distinguished Henry from most of the other wiseguys who were under surveillance was the fact that he seemed to have total access to all levels of the mob world.

Most of the hoods the police had been able to watch over the years were relegated to one or perhaps two very narrowly delineated areas of mob business. Narcotics cops followed junk dealers, their suppliers, their couriers, and even a few distributors. Gambling-suppression squads kept tabs on bookmakers and policy bankers, who never seemed to talk to anyone who wasn't either another bookmaker or a customer. There were loan sharks, hijackers, labor racketeers, and extortionists of all kinds almost constantly under police surveillance, but never before had Danny Mann and the Nassau narcotics squad come up with a drug dealer who appeared to be involved with so much else. In addition, Henry did not appear to be limited by any rank or status within the mob. Most wiseguys the narks had followed always remained within their own ranks at all times. If they were street-level junk dealers or bookies or loan sharks, they remained such and never, under any circumstances, approached a mobster of higher rank. The protocol was strictly enforced, and it was considered necessary in order to protect the mob's executive hierarchy from being compromised by their own men. The insulation between the men who actually committed the crimes and the men who directed them and profited most from the crooked schemes was scrupulously maintained.

Henry Hill was different. Somehow he was able to move effortlessly through all levels of the mob's hierarchy. At first it thoroughly baffled Mann and his squad. Henry was not listed as an organized-crime member or associate on any of the department's intelligence books. Nor did his name pop up on any of the wiretap indexes maintained by the department. And yet he was obviously involved with large-scale bookmakers, jewelry fences, loan sharks, and union racketeers and, in fact, seemed to be arranging for top hoods to buy up nonunion garment factories in Brooklyn and Queens at the same time Danny Mann was looking into his junk deals.

When Dennis Dillon, the Nassau district attorney, realized whom his narcotics unit was listening in on, he was delighted. Detectives began collecting Hill's garbage during the early morning hours and came up with discarded bits of notepaper and the backs of envelopes covered with the incriminating arrival and departure times of airline flights they soon connected to the comings and goings of known couriers. There were also sheets of paper that contained doodles and mathematical calculations pertaining to kilos and half kilos of flea powder and dog food. Hill's Pittsburgh distributor, Paul Mazzei, turned out to run a dog-grooming salon as a front. Using everything from bakery trucks to helicopters, narcotics detectives tailed Henry Hill for over two months, following him from one hangout to another, noting his conversations and meetings and listing his apparent dealings and friendships with some of the best-known racketeers in the city. They followed his seemingly endless peregrinations through so many layers of the underworld that their original pocket-size notebooks soon gave way to wall-size charts.

But most of the case against Henry Hill was based on the wiretap reports. Mann had accumulated two months' worth of authorized wiretaps, and all of it implicated Henry and his gang far beyond the pleadings and doubt-casting of even the most eloquent lawyer.

"I've sat on hundreds upon hundreds of wires," Mann said. "At the time of the Hill investigation I'd been a narcotics detective for five or six years, and I knew that eventually everybody gives themselves up over their phones. The real wiseguys, the Paul Varios and the Carlo Gambinos, don't even have phones. Vario wouldn't have one in his house. He used to get all his calls through an intermediary who lived nearby and would have to run through the rain to Paulie's house and give him the message.

"The danger with the phone, even for wiseguys, is that it's so easy. You talk on it all day long and all night long saying nothing. Your wife orders groceries. You find out the correct time. You call Grandma about dinner Sunday. You begin to forget that it's live. That it can hang you.

"One of the most common errors made by those being tapped, especially in drug cases where the subjects might even suspect they are being overheard, is to employ a 'code' language. In court we get experienced narcotics agents and other experts who can always interpret the code in such a way that even the most sympathetic juries will vote to convict. In the Hill case, for instance, they used gems, such as opals, as a code for drugs. They talked about the amount of money opals should be bought and sold for. In these cases a prosecutor would simply call in a professional jeweler to testify that the amounts of money being attributed to the gems had no basis in reality."

Detective Mann and the Nassau narcotics squad began recording Henry Hill's Rockville Centre telephone in March of 1980, and within days had prepared the following report for the court in order to extend the wiretap order:

Thus far monitoring has generally revealed that Henry Hill is in the upper echelon—perhaps the head—of a large-scale, organized, interstate drug trafficking and distribution operation which he runs from at least two known locations in Nassau County: (1) his residence at 19 St. Marks Avenue, Rockville Centre, and (2) the residence of Robin Cooperman, 250 Lakeview Avenue, Rockville Centre (referred to during intercepted telephone conversations as "the bat cave").

Still unknown are the full scope of Hill's illegal operation, the identity of the conspirators, and the precise type of controlled substances involved. Monitoring has revealed that at the local level the ring appears to center around Henry Hill, Robin Cooperman, and Judy Wicks; however, many others still as yet unidentified are involved and the nature and scope of their involvement remains unknown at the present time.

Over the course of monitoring, Henry Hill, or others associated with Henry Hill, have conversed, in coded terms or in a manner clearly indicative of drug transactions, with Paul Mazzei, Judy Wicks, Robin Cooperman, Mel Telsey, Steven Fish, Tony Asta, Bob Albert, Bob Breener, Marvin Koch, and individuals referred to as "Bob," "Linda," "Ann," "Mac," and "Kareem," whose last names remain unknown, as well as others whose identity remains unknown.

Uncertainty surrounds the identity of the controlled substances in which Henry Hill and his coconspirators are trafficking because Hill's conversations with his contacts are uniformly guarded, vague and replete with obviously coded language. Terms such as "opals," "stones," "buds," "karats," "OZ," "whole," "quarter," "half," and "one-for-two," have been employed in an obvious reference to things other than what they commonly connote. However, details surrounding the code terms, such as prices, and the inappropriate use of the terms themselves, make clear that drug transactions are being discussed. Some of the individuals listed in the heading of this affidavit have conferred with Henry Hill or his associates in the above-mentioned coded terms; others, particularly the local callers, have used abbreviated language and have exhibited a general hesitancy to discuss the subject matter of the telephone call thereby indicating their participation to one degree or another in the drug-related conspiracy.

In monitoring Hill's phone on March 29, Mann picked up a conversation between Hill and Paul Mazzei, who later turned out to be his Pittsburgh distributor, of such bizarre syntax that any jury would convict.

MAZZEI: You know the golf club and the dogs you gave me in return?

HILL: Yeah.

MAZZEI: Can you still do that?

HILL: Same kind of golf clubs?

MAZZEI: No. No golf clubs. Can you still give me the dogs if I can pay for the golf clubs?

HILL: Yeah. Sure.

[portion of conversation omitted]

MAZZEI: You front me the shampoo and I'll front you the dog pills. . . . What time tomorrow?

HILL: Anytime after twelve.

MAZZEI: You won't hold my lady friend up?

HILL: No.

MAZZEI: Somebody will just exchange dogs.

By the time Danny Mann and the Nassau prosecutors were ready to make their arrests they had amassed so much information that in addition to arresting Henry, they also brought in thirteen other members of the ring, including Robert Ginova, a porno film producer who drove a chocolate-colored Rolls; Paul Mazzei, who was picked up in Pittsburgh on a warrant and held for Nassau County; Frank Basile, the twenty-year-old son of Philly Basile, the disco king whom Vario had forced to give Henry his no-show job for parole; and Bobby Germaine, not only Henry's partner in the drug ring but a fugitive in connection with a botched multimillion-dollar wholesale jewelry robbery on East Fifty-seventh Street.

When Mann went to arrest Germaine, the unit had shotguns, bullet-proof vests, and search warrants for the Commack, Long Island, house that Germaine had been renting under an assumed name. When the cops walked in, Germaine insisted they had the wrong man. He showed them his identification. He insisted he was a freelance writer. He showed them the book he was writing. In the precinct, of course, his fingerprints proved otherwise. When Bobby's true identification was tossed over to Mann's desk, it was a minute or two before the detective had a chance to read the badly Thermofaxed record sent down from Albany. When he saw that "Bobby" from the Hill wiretaps was Robert Germaine Sr., he thought that he had somehow mixed up the papers on his desk. But he hadn't. Robert Germaine Sr. was none other than the father of the nineteen-year-old confidential informant whose information had started the entire investigation in the first place. The youngster had started by giving up Henry Hill but had ended up turning in his own father.

It was then that the three burly detectives came into Mann's office, all of them smiling. They were carrying large cardboard boxes

marked "Evidence" in big red letters. The boxes were filled with
Robin's kitchen. There were spoons, sieves, mixing bowls, scales,
and strainers. The cops gathered around and began wiping their fingers around the insides of the mixing bowls like children swabbing
up batter and then rolled their eyes into their heads. It was their
way of telling Mann that Robin's kitchen utensils were covered with
traces of drugs. Danny Mann had suspected the kitchen would be
covered with a thin layer of dope. He had listened to too many hours
of Henry and Robin's conversations about cleaning up the residue of
evidence after mixing and cutting a batch of stuff. Robin had always
hated to do dishes. No matter how many times Henry had warned
her to wash the bowls and strainers after mixing, she just wouldn't
do it. Henry had even bought her a dishwasher. But it had done
no good. Danny Mann found it amusing that Henry was facing a
sentence of twenty-five years to life because his girlfriend hated to
wash dishes.

Twenty-one

For Assistant U.S. Attorney McDonald and the Strike Force prosecutors Henry Hill was a bonanza. He was not a mob boss or even a noncommissioned officer in the mob, but he was an earner, the kind of sidewalk mechanic who knew something about everything. He could have written the handbook on street-level mob operations. Ever since the first day he walked into the Euclid Avenue Taxicab Company, back in 1954, Henry had been fascinated by the world he had longed to join, and there was little he hadn't learned and even less that he had forgotten.

Within twenty-four hours McDonald began making arrangements with the Nassau prosecutors to turn their routine drug pinch over to the feds in order to snare bigger fish. Henry was about to become a prize catch, a player in a larger game, even though at first he did not know it.

When the feds first arrived at his jail cell, Henry thought he could use them to help con his way out. Residues of coke and optimism were still in his system. One day he would tell his parole officer he might be willing to talk if he could get back on the street, and the next day he would deny having made the suggestion. He stirred the interest of the FBI by giving them tips on hijackings, murders, and Lufthansa, but he never delivered a punchline.

Henry continued to scramble, hustle, and con for days after his arrest, but these were the last spastic jerks of a hood whose time had expired, the final reflex actions of a wiseguy who did not yet know that he was already dead.

KAREN: On the night he got arrested, two detectives rang the bell. They had a search warrant. I didn't know that they had just arrested Henry and everybody. I didn't know what was going on. So even though I was surprised by the cops, I felt safe. I felt that I had nothing to hide.

I asked them if they wanted coffee. I had just put on a new pot. Some of the wives, like Mickey Burke, used to curse at the cops and make nasty remarks and spit on the floor. That never made any sense to me. It was better to be polite and call the lawyer.

First the detectives wanted to know where everyone in the house was, and they wanted us all to go into one room while they searched. They never said what they were looking for. The kids, who had been through it all before, just kept watching television.

The detectives were very polite. They asked us to be calm and said they would try to get finished as quickly as possible. They went through everything. Closets. Bureau drawers. Kitchen cabinets. Suitcases. Even the pockets of our clothes hanging in the closets.

I figured out what was going on after some other detectives came over from searching Robin's house. Our lawyer, Richie Oddo, called and said Henry had been arrested for drugs and would be arraigned in the morning.

I didn't think it was such a big deal at first. They found some traces of drugs at Robin's house but nothing on Henry or at our place. I thought maybe we could beat the case. Especially after Henry gave me a signal in court the next morning. He just arched his hand a little bit, and I knew immediately where the drugs were hidden. That's what comes from seventeen years of being married. I knew that that motion meant that the drugs were on a small ledge behind some recessed lights we had installed inside a wall bench at the entrance to the bedroom. The cops had searched there, but you would have to know that you had to reach down and then up to find the ledge. Right after court I ran home, got the stuff—it must have been about a pound of heroin—and flushed it down the toilet. Now they had no proof.

They were holding Henry in $150,000 bail, and he said that he wanted to stay inside for a couple of weeks or so to clean out his system. He had been taking so many pills and snorting so much stuff that he couldn't think straight. I thought that sounded like a good idea. And I also thought that with no evidence, we had a good chance of beating the case.

That's why I couldn't figure out why Henry was so nervous when I went to visit him and why Jimmy and Mickey were acting so strange. Everyone was edgy. Then I went to see Richie Oddo, the lawyer. Lenny Vario was there. The Oddos and the Varios are related. Richie said he had not been able to see Henry for a couple of days. He was Henry's lawyer. What was wrong? Was Henry hiding from his own lawyer? Richie didn't understand. I could see it was making him suspicious.

Lenny Vario said he had known Henry all his life. He said that Henry was a stand-up guy. It was as though he was reassuring the lawyer, but he was really sending a message through me. Lenny said that Henry would never talk against certain people, that he'd commit suicide first.

Mickey Burke called me every day. She kept asking when Henry was coming home. I knew she was calling for Jimmy. I told her what Henry had told me to say—that he was drying out and trying to get the bail reduced.

One day during the first week, Jimmy called and said he had some material for the T-shirt factory we had in the garage. He said I should pick it up at his shop on Liberty Avenue. I said I couldn't, I was in a hurry, I wanted to get to court, Henry was making one of his appearances. He said for me to come by anyway, it wasn't out of my way.

When I got to the shop, Jimmy asked about things. He was smiling and asked if I needed anything. I said I was in a hurry, and he said the material was in one of the stores down the block.

Jimmy walked outside with me and stood on the street as I started walking down the block toward the store. I noticed that all of the stores along the block had their windows painted out. It gave me a funny feeling. I kept walking, and when I looked back I could see Jimmy standing there pointing for me to go inside one of the stores.

Inside I could see this guy who was always around Jimmy. Once I had seen him on a ladder painting Jimmy's house. He was very creepy. I always suspected that he did Jimmy's dirty work. He was just standing around inside. He wasn't completely facing the door, so I could get a look at him without him seeing me. He looked like he might have been doing some work inside. Who knows? I don't know why, but something struck me as being wrong.

So instead of going inside, I waved back at Jimmy and said that I was late for court and that I'd pick the stuff up later. Jimmy kept pointing me to the store, but I kept going. I jumped in the car and took off. It was not a big thing. I was in a hurry, and I didn't like the look of the store and that guy. I didn't think of it again until much later.

The next day I went to see Paulie. He was very upset with Henry. He was scowling. He was at Geffkens Bar, on Flatlands Avenue. There were the usual bunch of guys lined up to see him. The minute he saw me, he took me to the side. I told him about Henry's arrest. He said he wasn't going to help Henry get out of this. He said he had warned Henry about being in drugs a month earlier at his niece's wedding—he'd told Henry he would not help if Henry got jammed up. That meant Paulie wouldn't use any of his influence with the cops or the courts or the lawyers or the bondsmen to help. On any other case Henry would have been out on bail already just because Paulie nodded to the bondsman. This time, because of drugs, Henry was still inside.

Then Paulie looked at me. He said that he was going to have to turn his back on Henry. He reached in his pocket and gave me three thousand dollars. He just put it in my hand and covered my hand with his for a second. He didn't even count it. When he turned away I could see that he was crying.

MCDONALD: Henry Hill's arrest was the first real break we'd had in the Lufthansa case in over a year. Ever since Lou Werner's conviction the case had stagnated. Most of the witnesses and participants had either been murdered or disappeared. For instance, on the same night we convicted Lou Werner, Joe Manri and Frenchy McMahon were murdered. A month later Paolo LiCastri's body turned up on top of a smoldering garbage heap in a lot off Flatlands Avenue, Brooklyn. Then Louis Cafora and his new wife, Joanna, disappeared. They were last seen happily driving away from some relative's house in Queens in a new Cadillac Fat Louis had bought his bride.

Henry was one of the crew's only survivors, and he was finally caught in a position where he might be persuaded to talk. He was facing twenty-five years to life on the Nassau County narcotics conspiracy. His girlfriend and even his wife could also be tied into the drug conspiracy, and life could be made very unpleasant for them. He knew this. He also knew that we could send him back to prison to serve out the last four years on the extortion case for violating his parole and that there was a very good chance that he was going to be killed by his best friends.

Henry was too vulnerable. He was facing too much time for a guy like Jimmy to take any chances with him. We suspected that Jimmy was just biding his time for the most opportune moment. We had very good information from informants that Henry was the next on the hit parade. Paul Vario had pretty much turned his back on him, which meant whatever happened happened.

If there was ever a time to flip him against his old crew it was at that moment. From the first day Henry was held in the Nassau jail on the drug charges, we had federal agents talking to him about turning. Jimmy Fox, his parole officer, kept warning him about the danger of going back on the street. Steven Carbone and Tom Sweeney, the FBI men who had stayed with the Lufthansa case, showed him pictures of the bodies.

Also, Henry wasn't totally against working out some kind of a deal. On the first morning after his arrest he had asked his parole officer whether there was some kind of an arrangement that could be made. He said that he knew about Lufthansa and would be willing to tell us something, as long as he didn't have to testify or surface as an informant. He told his parole officer that he could be our "man on the street."

That was not what we had in mind, so we kept up the pressure and he kept on dangling the bait. It was a game of feeling each other out, except that we knew and he knew that he really had no place to go. The pressure on him was intensified every time the agents showed up at the jail to talk to him. The word inside spreads quickly when someone is repeatedly interviewed by the police or feds. The supposition is that the prisoner must be talking. Otherwise why would the agents come back day after day?

As far as we were concerned, it was just a matter of time. We considered him important enough so that we went back to talk with him even though he screamed in front of the other prisoners and guards that he wouldn't talk to us and that we were trying to get him killed. The minute the door closed he changed his attitude completely. He wasn't telling us anything yet, but he wasn't screaming either, and he'd give us a tidbit here and there about nonrelated matters.

Also, when we issued a writ and had him brought from the Nassau jail to the Strike Force offices, he was the one who suggested that we do the same thing with Bobby Germaine, so that it wouldn't look like he was the only defendant being questioned. I thought we were doing very well considering the kind of wiseguy we had snared, and that's why I went through the roof when I found out that after three weeks in jail, where we'd had complete access to him, he had somehow managed to bail himself out and had disappeared.

HENRY: My scheme was to play them along until I got my own head clear, got my bail reduced, and got back on the street. I knew I was vulnerable. I knew that you were vulnerable when you were worth more dead than alive. It was that simple. But I still couldn't really believe it, and I didn't really know what I was going to do. Sometimes I thought I'd just get some money and go on the lam for a while. Then I thought I might get my head clear and straighten it all out with Paulie. I kept thinking that if I watched my step, if I kept the thought of my getting whacked in the middle of my mind, I might have a chance of surviving.

In my case I knew that getting caught in the drug thing really put me in the box. Paulie had put the taboo on drugs. It was outlawed. None of us were supposed to be in drugs. It wasn't that Paulie wanted to take some moral position. That wasn't it. What Paulie didn't want to have happen is what happened to one of his best friends, Carmine Tramunti, who went away for fifteen years just because he nodded hello to Fat Gigi Inglese in a restaurant. The jury decided to believe the prosecutor that Tramunti was nodding his agreement to a drug deal. That was it. Bang. Fifteen years at the age of fifty-seven. The guy never got out. Just at a time in his life when he was going to enjoy, when it was supposed to begin to pay off, he gets sent away forever and then dies in the can. Paulie was not going to let that happen to him. He'd kill you first.

So I knew that arrest on the drug charge made me vulnerable. Maybe too vulnerable to live. There wouldn't have been any hard feelings. I was just facing too much time. The crew also knew I was snorting a lot of coke and eating ludes. Jimmy once said my brain had turned to candy. I wasn't the only guy in the crew taking drugs. Sepe and Stabile had bigger noses than mine. But I was the one who was caught and I was the one who they felt might make a deal.

The fact that I had never made a deal before, the fact that I had always been stand-up, the fact that I had done two years in Nassau and four years in Lewisburg standing on my head and never gave up a mouse counted for nothing. What you did yesterday doesn't count. It's what you're doing today and could do tomorrow that counts. From where my friends stood, from where Jimmy was standing, I was a liability. I was no longer safe. I didn't need pictures.

In fact, I knew it was going to be Jimmy even before the feds played me the tape of Sepe and Stabile talking about getting rid of me. I could hear them. Sepe sounded anxious to get it over with. He said that I was no good, that I was a junkie. But Jimmy was calm. He told them not to worry about it. And that was all I heard.

Sitting in my cell, I knew I was up for grabs. In the old days Jimmy would have torn Sepe's heart out for even suggesting that I get whacked. That was the main reason why I stayed inside. I had to sort it all out. And every day I was inside, Jimmy or Mickey called my wife and asked when I was getting out, and every day that she could, Karen came to the jail and told me everything they said.

If you're a part of a crew, nobody ever tells you that they're going to kill you. It doesn't happen that way. There aren't any great arguments or finger-biting curses like in Mafia movies. Your murderers come with smiles. They come as friends, people who have cared deeply about you all your life, and they always come at a time when you are at your weakest and most in need of their help and support.

But still I wasn't sure. I grew up with Jimmy. He brought me along. Paulie and Tuddy put me in his hands. He was supposed to watch out for me, and he did. He was the best teacher a guy could want. It was Jimmy who got me into cigarette bootlegging and hi-jackings. We buried bodies. We did Air France and Lufthansa. We got sentenced to ten years for putting the arm on the guy in Florida. He was at the hospital when Karen had the kids, and we went to birthday parties and holidays at each other's houses. We did it all, and now maybe he's going to kill me. Two weeks before my arrest I got so paranoid and stoned that Karen got me to go see a shrink. It was nuts. I couldn't tell him anything, but she insisted. I talked to him in general terms. I told him that I was trying to get away from drug people. I said I was afraid I was going to be killed. He told me to get a phone machine.

If I was going to survive, I was going to have to turn on everything I knew. The decision was almost made for me. In jail I didn't think so much about whether or not to turn as I did about exactly how I could manage to do it and still get out of jail long enough to collect the money and dope I had out on the street. I had about $18,000 in heroin stashed in the house that the cops hadn't found. I had $20,000 owed to me by Mazzei. I'd probably have to kiss that good-bye. I had about $40,000 in loan-shark money out on the street. I wanted to recoup some of that. There was money owed me by fences on some of the jewel robberies and I had money owed me from some gun deals. Added up, there was enough to risk my neck before getting arrested by the cops or killed by my friends. It was going to have to be a con, a hustle, just like everything else.

So every day when the feds would come to my cell to ask about Lufthansa or some murder, I would curse at them and yell that they should go away. Once I even refused to leave my cell. There were two FBI men downstairs waiting to take me to McDonald's office. "Fuck you and McDonald," I yelled. I kept yelling they'd have to carry me out. Finally four prison hacks came to my cell and said if I didn't go quietly I'd go unconsciously. Without overdoing anything, I put up enough of a racket most of the time to at least give the other prisoners the impression that I wasn't cooperating.

It was a scary time. There were guys from Jimmy's crew, like John Savino, who were on work-release, and they'd leave every morning with all the news about who was cooperating and who was not. I was being as cautious as I could—I hadn't told anybody anything yet, but I remember shaking myself to sleep with fear every night I stayed in jail. I was afraid Jimmy would find out what I was planning and have me killed right there in my cell.

McDonald used to say that I was safe as long as I stayed in jail. I had to laugh at him. I told him that if Jimmy wanted to whack me out, he could walk right in the front door, borrow a gun from one of the guards, blow me away in my cell, and walk out without being stopped.

I had to figure that Paulie and Jimmy would know everything that went on in the jail, and if they knew I was going to McDonald's office every day, they'd know I was talking or at least thinking about talking. So I told McDonald that every time I was brought over to his office, he had to bring Germaine over too. This gave me the chance to scream and yell at Richie Oddo, my lawyer, that I was being harassed, that he was a shitty lawyer. To calm me down, Oddo used to say they were harassing Germaine too. Then I'd yell some more that I didn't care what they were doing with Bobby, I wanted to be left alone.

I wanted all of my screaming and yelling about being harassed to get back to Jimmy and Paulie. Then, as soon as Oddo would leave, I'd spend the rest of the afternoon in McDonald's office drinking coffee and listening to them try to con me. During those sessions I never said I'd help and I never said I wouldn't. I just kept them hanging, but I knew they knew that I would eventually have to cooperate. They knew I had nowhere to go.

And still, the idea of trusting myself to the feds was almost as scary as having to face Jimmy. It wasn't that the feds were crooked and would sell me out. It was that they were so dumb. They were always making mistakes. In my own drug case, for instance, I knew that the informant was Bobby Germaine's son, because the cops had accidentally left his name in the court papers. They were always fucking up like that, and I didn't want them fucking up with my life.

On May 16, after eighteen days in jail, I felt the time was right to make my move. I had Karen and my mother-in-law come to the jail at one o'clock Saturday morning with ten thousand dollars in cash bail. I knew the agents and my parole officer would be off for the weekend. I would have a couple of days to pick up some cash and also a couple of days to see whether the feds were right, whether Jimmy was really planning to kill me. Scared as I was of Jimmy, it was still hard for me to accept.

I knew that Jimmy had Mickey calling Karen twice a day from the first day I got pinched. They wanted to know if I was okay. Did I need anything? When was I coming home? The same kinds of questions they would have asked any other time I got pinched, except now everything was suspect. I was feeling paranoid, but I also knew that sometimes you were either paranoid or dead.

I remember walking out of the jail and getting into the car very quickly. I had this feeling I was going to get killed right outside the jail. I didn't feel safe until I got home. That's when Karen told me she'd flushed the junk. Eighteen thousand dollars she flushed. How could she do that? Why did I give her the signal? she asked. I hadn't given her the signal to flush it, just to hide it if the cops came back to search with dogs. She started screaming and crying. I started screaming and yelling at her. We screamed until we were hoarse. I slept with a gun all night.

When Mickey called on Saturday morning to find out how things were, Karen said they were fine, I was home. Mickey almost dropped the phone. She wanted to know why Karen hadn't told her. They could have helped with the bail money. That was exactly why I hadn't told anyone. That's why I had Karen's mother show up with cash. That's why I had my bedroll all tucked up and was ready to check out immediately. I didn't want any guard calling up on me. I didn't want to be greeted by anybody other than Karen and her mother when I walked out of the jail.

Mickey said Jimmy wanted to meet me as soon as I woke up. I had told Karen to say there was a lot of heat all around and that we were going to go to a bar mitzvah that night and that I'd meet Jimmy

Sunday morning. I wanted to use Saturday to raise money and I also wanted to see if I could detect any signs of trouble.

Sunday morning I met Jimmy at the Sherwood Diner, on Rockaway Boulevard. It was a crowded place where we were known. I got there about fifteen minutes early and I saw that Jimmy was already there. He had taken the booth at the end of the restaurant, where he could see everyone who came into the place and anyone who pulled into the parking lot. He wanted to see if I had been tailed.

He hadn't touched his honeydew melon or coffee. In the old days Jimmy would have eaten the melon, three or four eggs, sausages, home fries, some crullers, toasted English muffins, and smeared lots of catsup all over everything. Jimmy loved catsup. He put it on everything, even his steaks. Jimmy was also fidgeting around. He was jumpy. He had started wearing glasses, and he was taking them off and putting them on.

I felt drained, and nothing had helped—not the shower, not the fresh shirt Karen had ironed, not the cologne. Nothing could get the smell of the jail and fear out of my nose. Jimmy stood up. He was smiling. He opened his arms to give me a bear hug. My court papers were all over the table. Jimmy had gotten them from the lawyers. When I sat down with him, it almost felt like it was the old days.

On the surface, of course, everything was supposed to be fine. We were supposed to be discussing my drug case, just like the dozens of other cases of mine we had discussed together, but this time I knew that the thing we were really discussing was me. I knew I was hot. I was dangerous. I knew that I could give Jimmy up and cut myself a deal with the government. I could give up Lufthansa and I could give up Paulie. I could put Jimmy and Paulie behind bars for the rest of their lives. And I knew Jimmy knew it.

None of this was said, of course. In fact, almost nothing was ever really said. Even if the feds had somehow wired our table, and then played back the tape, they wouldn't have been able to make much sense out of our conversation. It was in half words. Shrugs. We talked about this guy and the other guy and the guy from over here and the guy from over there and the guy with the hair and the guy from downtown. At the end of the conversation I would know what we talked about and Jimmy would know what we talked about, but nobody else would know.

Jimmy had been through the papers, and he said that there had been a rat in the case. I knew he meant Bobby Germaine's kid, but I tried to slough it off. I said that they hadn't found any drugs on me or in my house. I kept saying that they didn't have a strong case, but I could see Jimmy was very nervous anyway.

He wanted to know about all the people I had working for me. He wanted to know whether Robin and Judy and the rest of the people arrested knew about him. I told him they knew nothing, but I could see he didn't believe me. He wanted to know if I had talked to Paulie yet. I said no.

Jimmy was trying to look confident. He said he had some ideas about my case. I could see what he was doing. As long as I thought he was trying to help me, he knew that I'd stay close. Then, when he felt the time was right, when I was no longer dangerous to hit, he would whack me. Jimmy was biding time to make sure he could kill me without getting Paulie upset and putting his own neck on the line.

As long as Jimmy thought I didn't know what he had planned, I had a chance of copping time on the street and scooping up some money. I had to pretend to Jimmy I didn't know what he might have had planned, and he had to pretend that he had nothing but my best interests at heart.

Then he said that he wanted me to go down to Florida in a few days. He said there was some money to be made. He said he had to meet me again soon about the case. He said we should meet on Wednesday in a bar owned by Charlie the Jap, on Queens Boulevard, in Sunnyside.

I'd never heard of the place. I've been operating with Jimmy for twenty-five years. We've been in a thousand bars together in Queens, and we've spent six years in the can together, and suddenly he wants to meet me in a bar I've never seen before.

I nod yeah, sure, but I already know there's no way in the world I'm going into that bar. As soon as breakfast is over, I drive past the place. I'm not waiting till Wednesday.

It was just the kind of place Jimmy has used in the past for hits. The place was controlled by one of the crew. It had a back entrance, and there was a parking area in the rear where you could take out a body bag in a rug without anyone seeing. Forget it. If Jimmy thought I was meeting him in that place on Wednesday he was nuts.

Instead, I showed up at Jimmy's sweatshop on Liberty Avenue on Monday. I had been out all morning trying to raise money. In the afternoon I had Karen drive me over to his shop. While I waited in a bar across the street, she went inside and told him I wanted to see him.

He came right over with Karen. I could see that he was nervous and surprised. He wasn't sure what I was going to do. Then he said if he gave me the name and address of Bobby Germaine's kid in Florida, would I go down there with Anthony Stabile and whack him. This was crazy, but I wasn't going to argue. Jimmy had never asked me to do anything like that before. And he'd never asked me to do something like that in front of Karen. Never.

I went along with him, but I reminded him that the kid was Germaine's son. I mean we were going to whack the guy's kid. Jimmy shook his head and said it was okay. He said that one of the lawyers had gone to see Germaine in the can and had told him that his kid was the informant and that Germaine had told the lawyer to "hit the rat." This was where we were. We were putting hits on our own kids.

Meanwhile Jimmy's at the bar waving around the piece of paper with the kid's alias and address on it. He wants me to go to Florida and whack the kid with Stabile. But I know that Stabile and Sepe were the two the feds had mentioned who were pushing Jimmy to whack me. If I go to Florida with Stabile, I know I'm not coming back.

I dropped Karen at the house and went out looking for more money. I gave her the gun that I had been sleeping with ever since I got out on bail. I had a small rented car that could not be traced to me, and I even got her a rental so that we wouldn't be driving around in cars that were known. The Nassau DA had confiscated my Volvo.

My plan was to stay on the street as long as I could and to make as much money as I could. I felt I was pretty safe because Jimmy was expecting me to go to Florida. But my plan didn't work. When I pulled up to the house later that afternoon I was surrounded by eight agents. They had found out I was loose. McDonald wasn't taking any chances. They arrested me as a material witness in Lufthansa. I was going to cut a deal or I was going to sink.

Twenty-two

Karen: As soon as they picked him up, the kids and I went to the FBI office in Queens. We had FBI men and federal marshals all around us. My mother, who was going crazy by now, came along. I went into Ed McDonald's office, and he said that we all had to go into the witness program. He explained that we were all in danger. Henry. Me. The kids. He said that the only chance we had was for Henry to cooperate. We had to start a new life. I asked, what if I let Henry go into the witness program and the kids and I stayed at home? McDonald said we would still be in danger, because they might try to get to Henry through me and the kids.

McDonald made it plain. He had federal marshals with him. They all explained. They said that when Henry appeared in court, the people he was testifying against would be looking for us. Henry was the only thing that stood between those people being free and spending the rest of their lives in jail. If they thought my parents or my sisters knew where we were, their lives wouldn't be worth two cents. They would make them tell where we were, and then we would be killed.

Then McDonald started his little blackmail. He said that there was enough evidence to indict me in the narcotics case. He said that we would all be on trial, and he asked what I thought the effect of that might have on the kids.

I was pretty much in a daze, but when I walked out of his office I knew I was going into the program. Henry had told McDonald he would cooperate if I agreed to go into the program with him. He said he wasn't going in alone.

I had no choice. They're going to prosecute my husband and me. "How could you look after the kids?" McDonald asked me. They made it impossible for me to make any other decision.

The minute I walked out of McDonald's office Henry grabbed me and said I had to stay with him. He didn't want to go into the program alone. He wasn't going to go without me.

My mother had been waiting outside McDonald's office with the kids. She was very upset. She wanted Henry to go into the program alone. I said what other choice did I have if my life was in jeopardy? They could kidnap me and the kids just to get to Henry. She started yelling about Henry, how he had never been any good, how he had brought all this upon us.

McDonald had said that they would pack me and the kids right then. They'd take me home under guard and pack me. We would be gone. It meant leaving everything immediately. My mother. My father. My sisters. I couldn't believe how fast it was all happening. We wouldn't be able to even contact them again, ever. It was like a death.

My mother and I and the kids were driven home by the marshals. When we got home there were marshals inside the house and out. They had four cars. They had shotguns and rifles. I had to pack enough stuff for two or three weeks or until they could move us into another place. My father and sisters were waiting at the house. They all helped me pack. We were all packing and crying. When they were not looking I whispered to my mother that she should give us some time. We'd get in touch. My father was very good. He held together.

The kids were excited. All they knew was that we were going away. They thought of it all like a vacation. I said that it was more than that. We had to go away so that some people who wanted to hurt us couldn't get to us. I said that they could not call any of their friends and they couldn't go back to school and get their books or sneakers or gym clothes.

The kids had read the papers. They knew about all the people who had been killed. There were stories every week about Jimmy and Paulie. They knew about Stacks and Marty Krugman. They knew Tommy had disappeared. They could see that everything we had was falling apart. Remember, there had been about a year of craziness between Lufthansa and their father's arrest.

I made up a long list of things for my mother to do. There was still stuff at the dry cleaner's. I had bills to pay. My mother cleaned out the refrigerator. There were pictures of a party we'd had. When my mother called about the pictures, the word was out that Henry had turned, and the photographer, who was a friend of Raymond Montemurro's, didn't want to give her the pictures. She said if he didn't give her the pictures she'd send over the marshals. He said okay, but when she went to pick them up he threw them at her. He wouldn't even take the money.

We had packed up everything in large black garbage bags. The kids and I were driven by marshals. There were four or five marshal cars all around us. They took us to a motel in Riverhead. It was a very nice, clean place. They moved us every couple of days. They always had the reservations made and we went right to our rooms. The marshal just gave us the keys, but they always stayed outside the door. They stood around with walkie-talkies and rifles in slings under their raincoats.

We'd stay as far away as Connecticut or Montauk. In the morning they would drive us all to the FBI headquarters in Queens or to McDonald's Strike Force offices in Brooklyn. I would sit around doing needlepoint, and the kids would play or read, and Henry would sit inside talking to the investigators.

We were just hanging around while the Marshal Service recreated us as different people. The paperwork took time. They asked us if we had any choices for our new names. They had shredded everything about our past. It was an amazing moment, sitting there in one of the Strike Force corridors with the kids, trying to dream up new names.

We got new Social Security numbers, and the kids got new identifications for school. The marshals explained that the kids would keep their grade records but that the transcripts submitted to the new school under our new name would be blank where the previous school was asked for. Also, when the girls registered in their new school, a marshal would go to the principal and explain that they were part of a family involved with government security. They would make it sound like their daddy was a government master spy or something very important.

The marshals were very nice. They were very good with the kids. They talked to them and played cards with them and kidded around with Ruth. They treated everyone with great respect. They were always gentlemen. The way they did it helped enormously.

After a couple of weeks I went back to the house in Rockville Centre. There were marshals all over the place. They had arranged for movers. There were trucks waiting and so were my parents. I still didn't feel as though I was leaving them behind forever.

But my family, and mostly my mother, had always been telling me what to do. All my life her nudging had driven me crazy. She was one of those smothering people. She did it out of love, but she smothered you anyway. My mother is one of those people who has got to be in control of everything twenty-four hours a day. I had this little notion in the back of my mind that maybe if we had a new life and new names and new everything it wouldn't be too bad. I would be really independent for the first time in my life. If Henry and I were to go away and get new names and new identities, I'd be able to breathe and take over my own life.

I thought a lot of things might change. There'd be no more Jimmys and no more drugs and no more Robins. Our lives would have to be different. Henry would live normally for the first time in his life. He'd be home at night. We would have regular friends. It could be like wiping everything clean.

On May 27, 1980, Henry Hill signed an agreement with the United States Department of Justice Organized Crime Strike Force (Eastern District of New York) that read:

This will serve to confirm the agreement reached between Henry Hill and the Organized Crime Strike Force for the Eastern District of New York.

This office is conducting an investigation of possible illegal activities on the part of James Burke, Angelo Sepe and others in connection with the theft of several million dollars in cash and jewelry from the Lufthansa Cargo Building at John F. Kennedy Airport. You have agreed to inform officials of the Department of Justice of everything you know concerning the above-mentioned crimes and any other criminal activity in which James Burke and Angelo Sepe have participated. In addition, you have agreed to testify, if called, before all federal grand and petit juries hearing these matters.

It is understood that no information or testimony given by you (both before and after the making of this agreement), or evidence derived from information or testimony given by you will be used against you in any criminal proceeding other than as indicated below. As you know, at the present time, you are under investigation for your involvement in the robbery at the Lufthansa Cargo Building. It is understood that this office will forgo any prosecution of you which could arise out of this matter in light of your cooperation in these matters. In the event that any other law enforcement authorities contemplate prosecuting you in connection with your involvement in the Lufthansa robbery we will recommend they not do so.

In addition, it is understood that this office will forgo any federal prosecution of you which could arise out of a narcotics investigation presently being conducted by the Nassau County District Attorney's Office and in connection with which you were arrested.

It is understood that in the event that you are prosecuted by any other law enforcement authorities in connection with any violation of the law, this office will bring to the attention of the prosecuting authorities the cooperation which you furnished in connection with this agreement.

It is further understood that this office will seek to place you in the Federal Witness Protection Program along with your wife and children and any other associates who become in need of protection as a result of your cooperation with this office.

This understanding is predicated upon your complete cooperation with the Government including the immediate, full and truthful disclosure of all information in your possession which is relevant to these matters. This agreement will not prevent the Government from prosecuting you for perjury should it be discovered that you have given false testimony in connection with these matters. In addition, in the event that you do not fully comply with all the other terms of this understanding (immediate, full and truthful disclosure, testimony, etc.), this agreement will be nullified. Should this occur, the Government will be free to prosecute you with regard to any and all violations of the federal criminal law in which you may have participated, and to use against you any and all statements made by you and testimony you have given prior and subsequent to the date of agreement.

HENRY: The hardest thing for me was leaving the life I was running away from. Even at the end, with all the threats I was getting and all the time I was facing behind the wall, I still loved the life.

We walked in a room and the place stopped. Everyone knew who we were, and we were treated like movie stars with muscle. We had it all and it was all free. Truckloads of swag. Fur coats, televisions, clothes—all for the asking. We used Jimmy's hijack drops like department stores. Our wives, mothers, kids, everybody rode along. I had paper bags filled with jewelry stashed in the kitchen and a sugar bowl full of coke next to the bed. Anything I wanted was only a phone call away. Free rented cars under phony names and the keys to a dozen hideout apartments we shared. I would bet thirty and forty grand over a weekend and then either blow the winnings in a week or go to the sharks to pay back the bookies. It didn't matter. When I was broke I just went out and robbed some more.

We ran everything. We paid the lawyers. We paid the cops. Everybody had their hands out. We walked out laughing. We had the best of everything. In Vegas and Atlantic City somebody always knew someone. People would come over and offer us shows, dinners, suites.

And now all that is over, and that's the hardest part. Today everything is very different. No more action. I have to wait around like everyone else. I'm an average nobody. I get to live the rest of my life like a schnook.

Epilogue

When Henry Hill joined the Federal Witness Program he became one of forty-four hundred other accused criminals who chose to testify against their former associates and disappear rather than stand trial. As far as Henry Hill was concerned, entering the Justice Department's $25-million-a-year program was the only option he had.

Ed McDonald soon realized that Henry Hill had casually committed so many crimes himself that he sometimes failed to recognize that he had even done so. One day, for example, while being asked about the Lufthansa robbery, Henry said he had been in Boston. It was the third or fourth time he had mentioned Boston, so McDonald finally asked what Henry was doing there. Henry answered matter-of-factly that he had been bribing Boston College basketball players in a point-shaving scheme at the time and had had to keep everyone in line. "I played for the Boston College freshman team," said McDonald. "I had been to a few of the games Henry had fixed. It was my school. I almost went across the table at him, but then I realized that to guys like Hill it was just a part of doing business. To Henry shaving points on college basketball wasn't even illegal. He had never even thought to mention it. I came to realize Henry didn't have too much school spirit. He had never rooted for anything outside of a point spread in his life."

It is safe to say that the Federal Witness Program got its money's worth out of Henry Hill. He took the stand and testified with such detached authenticity—he barely looked at the defendants against whom he appeared—that juries came back with one conviction after another. His testimony helped get Paul Mazzei seven years on drug charges, and his testimony in the basketball point-shaving case, which McDonald insisted upon prosecuting himself, got the twenty-six-year-old Rick Kuhn ten years, the stiffest sentence ever received by a college player convicted of fixing basketball scores. Hill's co-fixer, Tony Perla, was sentenced to ten years and Perla's brother Rocco to four. Rich Perry, one of the mob bookies known as "the fixer," pleaded guilty to a gambling conspiracy when he realized Henry would testify against him, and got away with a one-year sentence. Henry helped federal marshals track down and recapture Bill Arico, the suspected international hit man. Philip Basile, the Long Island disco owner, was sentenced to five years' probation and a $250,000 fine for arranging the no-show job Hill used to get early parole.

Henry even went on tour. Surrounded by marshals and accompanied by Jerry D. Bernstein, the Strike Force prosecutor who got the Basile conviction, he went to testify in Phoenix, Arizona, in connection with the alleged organized-crime links of a major liquor wholesaler that had been about to become the largest wine and liquor distributor in the state. On the eve of Henry's taking the stand, however, the company withdrew its application for licensing and agreed to withdraw from doing further business in the state.

On February 6, 1984, Henry took the stand against Paul Vario. Vario was being tried for having assisted Henry to gain early release from Allenwood by helping him get his no-show job. After a three-day trial, Paul Vario was found guilty of conspiring to commit fraud. On April 3, 1984, he was sentenced to four years and fined ten thousand dollars. After his appeals were exhausted, Vario entered a federal prison in Springfield, Missouri.

Later that year Henry took the stand against Jimmy Burke in connection with the murder of Richie Eaton. Henry testified that Jimmy had told him he killed Eaton over a $250,000 cocaine deal. When pressed on the matter by Burke's attorney, Henry stared directly at Jimmy and said that when he had asked Jimmy about Eaton, Jimmy said, "Don't worry about him anymore, I whacked the fucking swindler out." On February 19, 1985, Jimmy Burke was sentenced to spend the rest of his life in prison for the murder of Richie Eaton.

Henry was never able to help McDonald crack Lufthansa—the case that essentially had gotten Henry into the witness program in the first place. By the time McDonald had Henry as a witness on Lufthansa, the people who could trace the robbery back to Jimmy were all dead. Except for Henry and Jimmy, there was no one left. Stacks Edwards, Marty Krugman, Richie Eaton, Tommy DeSimone, Terry Ferrara, Joe Manri, Frenchy McMahon, Paolo LiCastri, Louie and Joanna Cafora, Anthony Stabile, and even Angelo Sepe and his new girlfriend, nineteen-year-old Joanne Lombardo. And during Henry's first year in the program, Germaine's twenty-year-old son, Robert junior, was shot and killed on a Queens rooftop.

Henry's confrontations with his old pals on the witness stand left him unmoved. Neither Jimmy Burke's threatening glares nor the sight of the seventy-year-old Paul Vario seemed to disturb him. Vario, Burke, Mazzei, Basile, the basketball players—everyone Henry had committed crimes with became bargaining chips he used to buy his own freedom. He initiated the investigation into the mob's "stranglehold" on Kennedy Airport's cargo business, along with Strike Force prosecutor Douglas Behm, that resulted in yet another indictment of Paul Vario, as well as indictments of Frank "Frankie the Wop" Manzo and other Lucchese family powers. He gave McDonald and his men as many cases as he could, and he sent away his old pals. It was effortless. He ate a mushroom-and-sausage pizza and drank Tab before taking the stand against Vario, and he negotiated a ten-thousand-dollar magazine article with *Sports Illustrated* before testifying about the Boston College point-shaving scheme that got twenty-six-year-old Rich Kuhn ten years in a federal prison. When Jimmy Burke was convicted of murder, Henry was almost gleeful. In the final showdown with Jimmy, Henry had survived, and he had used the government to pull the trigger.

Of course, no matter how Henry tried to rationalize what he had done, his survival depended upon his capacity for betrayal. He willingly turned on the world he knew and the men with whom he had been raised with the same nonchalance he had used in setting up a bookie joint or slipping a tail. For Henry Hill giving up the life was hard, but giving up his friends was easy.

In the end there were no pyrotechnics, no fiery blasts of Cagney gangster glory. Henry was not going out through a hole in the top of the world. He was going to survive any way he could. In fact, out of the entire crew Henry alone managed to survive.

Today Henry Hill and his wife live somewhere in America. As of this writing he has a successful business and lives in a $150,000 two-story neocolonial house in an area with such a low crime rate that garden-shed burglaries get headlines in the weekly press. His children go to private schools. He and Karen have their own cars, and she has embarked on a small business of her own. He has a Keogh plan. One of his few complaints is that he cannot get good Italian food in the area where he has been assigned to live by the witness program. A few days after his arrival there he went to a local "Italian-style" restaurant and found the marinara sauce without garlic, the linguini replaced by egg noodles, and slices of packaged white bread in plastic baskets on the tables.

But because of his continuing work with Ed McDonald and the Strike Force prosecutors, Henry gets fifteen hundred dollars a month as a government employee, travels to New York eight or nine times a year with all expenses paid, and has food from Little Italy sent in to him at the courts where he testifies and the hotels where he stays.

He is always accompanied to New York by armed marshals to make sure he doesn't get murdered or mugged. In fact, Henry is so carefully guarded and his new identity is so vigorously protected by the U.S. Marshal Service that even the Internal Revenue had to whistle when they tried to dun the old Henry Hill for his back taxes. Thanks to the government for which he works, Henry Hill has turned out to be the ultimate wiseguy.

Afterword

Prosecutors say the most dangerous time for witnesses is the period during which they are being debriefed and testifying. Since Henry Hill's testimony lasted over five years and resulted in at least fifty convictions, there was lots of time and there were lots of defendants who wanted Henry Hill dead.

"Some of them thought I was staying in touch with my old girlfriends," Hill said. "They had private investigators check the girls' phone numbers. They've got connections to people in the phone company and credit card companies. They can find anybody. Their lawyers bribed court clerks to tell them when and where I was testifying. The feds knew all this and drove me in different cars every day with a different driver, tinted windows, vans, a car in front and a car behind just so nobody could get between us."

It is still incredible to many of the prosecutors and agents who worked on the Henry Hill case that today, thirty years after he decided to flip, and twenty-five years after this book's publication, Henry Hill turns out to be the last wiseguy in his crew still standing. His mentor, James "Jimmy the Gent" Burke, who failed to kill Hill on the ruse trip to Florida, was ultimately convicted of a murder on Hill's testimony and died in prison in 1996 at sixty-five. Hill's surrogate father and Lucchese crime family capo, Paul Vario, was convicted on Hill's testimony and died in a federal prison in Texas in 1988 at seventy-four. Other members of the gang, whose freedom depended upon their getting rid of Henry, wound up either in prison, convicted on Hill's testimony, or killed in routine occupational hazards that had nothing to do with Henry Hill.

For instance, in 1985, Anthony Stabile, forty-four, the lethal Burke hit man, who the federal marshals were particularly concerned about, wound up getting killed in an unrelated drug dispute. Stabile was shot twice in the head, stuffed in the trunk of his new Cadillac Coupe de Ville and set on fire in Ozone Park, Queens. Angelo Sepe, forty-three, another member of the Vario crew looking to get Hill, wound up getting shot and killed himself on July 18, 1984. Sepe was killed in the basement of his apartment in Bath Beach, Brooklyn, after threatening to kill a member of Sammy "The Bull" Gravano's crew. The hitmen, using silencers, first killed Sepe in the entryway of his apartment and then killed his girlfriend, Joanna Lombardo, who was asleep in the bedroom, to erase even the possibility of a witness.

Since 1980, when Henry Hill, Karen, and their two children entered the witness-protection program, the threats have been serious enough for the government to move them at least a dozen times. One night, the Hills had to leave their house so quickly that when Hill's son's girlfriend came to pick him up for school in the morning, she found an empty house and no forwarding address. The feds warned Hill's son about not contacting the girl under any circumstances.

While in the witness-protection program, Hill was addicted to alcohol, speed, and cocaine. He was arrested on drug related charges several times. When temporarily in jail he used his assumed names until the feds got him out. The local cops who arrested him usually had no idea who he was. In 1989, Hill and Karen divorced after twenty-five years of marriage, with Karen receiving custody of the children. Hill was finally removed from the witness program in 1996 upon the death of Jimmy Burke. He continued to have problems with the law (for drunk driving arrests) until 2006, when the actor Ray Liotta, who played Henry Hill in *Goodfellas*, convinced him to enter a serious rehabilitation program. After many earlier attempts, Hill says, it worked.

"After thirty years on the lam," Hill says, "now I feel safe enough to travel under my own name, appear on radio and television shows promoting my books, and go to restaurants and malls with my kids and grandchildren. I'm just like everybody else, almost."

—Nicholas Pileggi
May 2011

Index

About the Author

NICHOLAS PILEGGI is the bestselling author of *Wiseguy, Casino,* and *Blye: Private Eye*. He lives in New York.